Little Canuck

Michel at age 6.

Little Canuck

✦

The Adventures of an Immigrant Boy from Québec

Michel A Blanchette

iUniverse, Inc.
New York Lincoln Shanghai

Little Canuck
The Adventures of an Immigrant Boy from Québec

iUniverse books may be ordered through booksellers or by contacting:

iUniverse
2021 Pine Lake Road, Suite 100
Lincoln, NE 68512
www.iuniverse.com
1-800-Authors (1-800-288-4677)

Illustration by Nicole Blanchette
www.nicoleblanchette.com

ISBN-13: 978-0-595-34820-6 (pbk)
ISBN-13: 978-0-595-79551-2 (ebk)
ISBN-10: 0-595-34820-3 (pbk)
ISBN-10: 0-595-79551-X (ebk)

Printed in the United States of America

Contents

Acknowledgments

I couldn't have written this book without tapping into the long-term memories of my brothers and sisters. For more than a year, I managed to dampen family gatherings with probing questions, then faithfully recorded the replies in my little notebook. I'm grateful for the patient and eager contributions they have made to this memoir.

I also wish to thank my wife, Anita, and our daughters, Nicole and Katherine, for their support throughout this long and time-consuming project. Anita spent untold days and evenings alone as I sought to document these silly childhood escapades.

Above all else, I wish to express appreciation to my mother, Laurette Côté, who enthusiastically shared her life in vivid detail. Even though I am over fifty, she still considers me her baby; she'll forever be my devoted nurturer and good friend.

Preface

I started writing this book in my head back in 1998. My father had just died, and I was spending much of my time alone in San Jose, California, working three thousand miles away from my home and family. The initial inspiration came from friends. Whenever I recounted a memory from my early years, they often responded with hearty laughter and heartfelt sympathy. I began to wonder, *Could these personal stories be worth retelling?*

I grew up on a small dairy farm in Québec; it was an isolated place steeped in fun, drama, hard work, religious fervor, and momentous lessons. Like countless families before us, we eventually left Canada to flee a downtrodden economy, migrating to the United States in 1963. But I never forgot my childhood in Québec.

This is not an autobiography, as I had no desire to write a long-winded narration about my adult years. In fact, this book represents a narrow slice of my existence: most of the story takes place during my childhood and early adolescent years. Why this limited time span? I chose it because we learn our best and most painful lessons when we are young. Also, the endearing innocence of kids can result in the most amusing tales.

I strove to make my stories as truthful as fragile memories will permit. But I know that children's perceptions often exceed adult reality, magnified by filters attuned to their sensitive nature. These are the perceptions of a child.

I have changed names here and there to avoid being haunted from the grave by persons who may have played an embarrassing role in my youthful tales.

1

Demise of a Patriarch

Luck is for people with money. At least, that's what I believed as a boy. I spent my childhood in a little farming community where good luck was notably absent. But my father changed all that one Friday evening during my adolescent years.

I was standing barefoot on stage in the church basement, wearing a hooded tunic over my underwear, sporting a ridiculous beard, and holding a wooden staff in one hand. I was playing the part of Joseph, the gentle husband of Mary, in a Nativity scene. My parents had attended the Christmas party to witness my wordless performance.

The cast had just returned onstage for the curtain call, standing proud as Sister Rachel reached for the microphone. She thanked the attendees, the cast, the singers, the accordion player, the caterers, the helpers, the parish priest, and God Almighty.

Earlier in the evening, the accordion-playing nun had serenaded us with an impressive medley of waltzes and polkas. Sister Thérèse was a short but energetic musician with an extravagant bosom and a humongous accordion. I marveled at the way the top-heavy nun managed to play without toppling over onto her face.

"And now, it's my pleasure to announce the winner of the door prize," Sister Rachel said. "This evening, we're raffling off something special: a lovely stereo." The audience emitted reserved *oohs* and *ahs*, followed by a generous round of applause.

Wow, a real stereo. It included a radio, a plastic turntable, and little plastic speakers. The components were adorned with stick-on decals that simulated wood grain.

I was impressed, but held out no hope for myself. After all, we never won anything. Well, I do remember winning an apple at school. It was handed out as a consolation prize—a poignant reminder that I'd failed to win any of the good stuff. To make matters worse, the apple was a short-lived gift that came with a sense of responsibility. You couldn't just eat the prize in front of your peers without looking like a selfish little snot; you had to be Christian-like and split it among friends. So, the apple was more a burden than a prize.

"I would ask you all to pull out your admission tickets," Sister Rachel said. "Michel, will you come forward to do the honors?" She beckoned me toward the cardboard box containing the tangle of tickets. She raised the box above my eye level, and I reached deep inside to extricate the winning ticket.

Sister Rachel read out the number slowly and then looked up at the audience of several hundred people, expecting to see the lucky winner rushing the stage. People craned their necks to look at all sides, but nobody came.

I became curious.

"I'll read it again," the nice sister said. Still, nobody approached.

I sensed a glimmer of hope.

"Maybe our winner is in the bathroom," she joked. The crowd laughed. For some reason, it was always funny to hear a clergy member acknowledge toilet duties.

I had a sudden flash of intuition. My own ticket was lodged backstage, inside my trouser pocket. *Could I have won the stereo?* I could barely control my excitement.

"We'll wait fifteen minutes and then draw another ticket," Sister Rachel announced before thanking the audience one last time.

The cast of the Nativity scene ambled offstage at a crawl, as the members chatted and laughed over details of their performance. I felt like shoving aside the shepherd, running past Mary Mother of God, kicking the boy donkey, elbowing the angel, and knocking down the three magi to reach my pants. Instead, I walked with the flow.

I fetched my trousers and swiftly pulled the ticket from one of the pockets. Time stood still as I compared my number with the one I had memorized onstage; they didn't match. "We *never* win anything," I muttered to myself. It was even more troubling to realize that I'd missed winning the plastic stereo by only a few numbers. Then it hit me.

Urgency quickly won over modesty, so I didn't bother walking to the bathroom to change; I yanked up my pants in full view of the female cast members and rushed out.

The shortest path to my parents was back over the stage. I clambered down the stairs and ran out to find my father, as the room garbled with unintelligible voices.

I found my parents engaged in pleasant conversation with strangers; I courteously waited for a break in the discussion before nudging my father.

"Papa, did you check your ticket?"

"*What* ticket?"

"Your admission ticket, the one you got at the door."

"Yeah, I think so."

"You *think* so? Can I see your ticket? You were right behind me."

He tightened his lips, as though mildly annoyed at my request. "I don't know if I still have it. I may have thrown it out already."

"Oh, please don't tell me you threw it away." I was a ball of raw nerves.

"I don't know. Let me see…"

My father began searching one pocket at a time. It seemed as though he was conducting the search in slow motion as I fidgeted by his side, his calmness driving me insane. He felt inside his shirt pocket—nothing. He reached into the side pockets of his trousers—no luck. He looked in the folds of his wallet—not there. He checked his rear pockets—they were empty. Then he started frisking his sports jacket. He searched the two side pockets and pulled out irrelevant receipts and scraps, which he took precious time to inspect with curiosity. My hope had started fading by the time he reached into an inside pocket of his sports jacket and pulled out the ticket. I quickly pried the ticket from his stubby fingers.

"You won!" There was no doubt about it: this was the number I had memorized.

"Good Lord, Hervé. You just won the little stereo!" my mother exclaimed.

"Oh, yeah?" he uttered with barely a hint of excitement.

"You have to go find Sister Rachel right away! Oh God, I hope she didn't give it away," I said. She hadn't called out another number yet, but given our poor track record, I feared that the pleasant nun may have already committed the prize to a more deserving recipient, like the exuberant accordion player with the big bust and nun's habit.

My mother and I were both biting our nails when my father began the insufferable trek to the stage. We watched him saunter toward the front of the church hall with laggard steps. His sluggish pace was maddening; I felt like pushing him from behind with force, like a football player shoving hard against a training sled.

I followed his every step with my gaze, seeing him stop to address people along the way, and watched him approach Sister Rachel. They chatted, she nodded, and he smiled. Moments later, he was walking back our way carrying a cardboard box.

By the time Papa reached our table, my mother was giddy with excitement and my eyes were brimming with tears. Maman congratulated her smiling husband on his prize, but I was unable to speak without risking sobs. *After all these years, we've finally won something.* It wasn't the little plastic stereo that drew out such strong emotions; it was the belief that Papa and I had collaborated in breaking our luckless cycle once and for all.

In the intensity of the moment, I had a sudden urge to hug my father. But I knew that was impossible. We had never hugged before; I would never learn how.

Our most memorable lessons often arrive with a swift kick in the pants. Not always the physical kind, but the emotional type that leaves you teetering on your tiptoes. Sometimes, the offending foot is turned sideways to moderate the blow, and at other times it hits you straight up wearing an angry cowboy boot with a steel tip.

Life was good. I was splitting my time between two coasts, approaching the pinnacle of a rewarding career, traveling the world for business and pleasure. I had long shunned the image of the poor farm boy from Québec, my professional identity helping to mask the modest origins of my large Catholic family.

I received the kick in July of 1998. It was a Monday evening.

"You need to come to the hospital *now*," my sister said during the long-distance call from Québec City. She sounded nervous and frightened; her voice quivered as she spoke.

"How long does he have?" I asked.

"The doctors say only a few days."

The news wasn't a total surprise, but that didn't stop my heart from going into freefall, sliding down to my knees, weakening my stomach as it made its rapid descent. My father was dying. I had known it intuitively for months but never dared admit it, fearing that the acknowledgement might lock in his fate.

"I'll drive up early tomorrow morning," I managed to say, my voice dampened by the swirling cloud of emotions. A mixture of fear, sadness, and guilt churned in my gut.

This was the second time we'd been called to his bedside. A month earlier, his kidneys had failed, starting a precipitous chain of organ failures that doctors were helpless to stop.

As he lay on his deathbed in Thetford-Mines on that June day, he reminisced nostalgically about his life with the clarity and wisdom of a Buddhist monk. He sang high praises to his wife, children, automobile, and new bicycle. By the time he'd finished his elocution, there wasn't a dry eye in the hospital room.

He'd resigned himself to dying but was fighting it with every ounce of his reserve. Moments after delivering his heart-wrenching goodbye speech, a surgeon wearing a white jacket approached his bed.

"There's nothing more we can do here, but there is a risky procedure we can perform in Québec City. It would mean transporting you to the Hôtel-Dieu Hospital in Lévis."

"So, what am I still doing *here?*" my father retorted. He wanted to live.

Minutes later, he was on a fast-moving gurney heading for the awaiting ambulance. My mother and sisters gathered in the hallway and kissed his pale forehead one last time, feeling pessimistic about his chances and finding it impossible to hold back their tears. The surgeon had been clear on the risks. Given his condition, the operation could well accelerate his death rather than extend his life.

"Good luck, Papa," my sisters said, trying to sound hopeful but failing badly.

They would insert draining tubes and plugs in his kidneys in a last-ditch attempt to unblock the failing organs. My eldest sister, Doris, would be the only one accompanying him on the two-hour trip to Lévis. My mother and the rest of us would wait for his return in Thetford-Mines. If he survived, he'd be transported back later that same evening.

I arrived in Thetford-Mines minutes after the ambulance had pulled away. The next hours were charged with intense emotion. We grieved at the prospect of losing him one minute, and laughed in fits the next. We didn't think he had the stamina to survive the intrusive procedure, but we nevertheless marveled at his stubborn refusal to loosen his grip. His fingernails were dug deep into the doorjamb of life.

"He's a tough old man," I admitted in a weak effort to lighten the mood.

Despite the odds, he did survive that first episode. Much to the surprise of the hospital staff, the medical procedure worked and my father was back in Thetford-Mines by evening. The next day, he wept openly—and we all shamelessly joined in—as the doctor told him that his kidneys were functioning again.

That evening, several of us toasted his tenacity with a glass of wine at the St-Hubert restaurant in Thetford-Mines. But the celebration was short lived. We knew that only a symptom of his illness had been abated. The disease still raged inside his body.

Within two weeks, he was well enough to return home. We were relieved that my sister Doris had agreed to move in with my parents to help care for my ailing father. Doris was living in Winnipeg, Manitoba, at the time but had decided to forgo her religious obligations (as a Catholic nun) to be by his side. Two of my sisters and countless relatives lived nearby, but nothing could beat the round-the-clock care that Doris would provide. She was experienced in social work, psychology, and spiritual matters, all of which qualified her for the nurturing role. We breathed a collective sigh of relief.

My parents lived in a spotless four-room apartment in Disraeli, fifteen miles south of Thetford-Mines. Disraeli is a tiny town, situated on rustic Lake Aylmer. My father more or less settled back into his normal daily routine, and my mother resumed her zealous attacks against dirt. My mother can locate dust balls with the accuracy of an Indian tracker. She's always been this way. It's as if her God-given mission in life is to stamp out dirt everywhere. I know this tendency from first-hand experience. The near-fanatical urge to cleanse is an unfortunate genetic inheritance she's passed down to me, and it is the source of discernible nervous tics among my own family members.

The best defense against these pestering problems is to keep a rag and a mop always at the ready. A white rag loaded with furniture polish and a sturdy broom are effective weapons of destruction in the hands of those gifted with the knack for spotting dirt.

My mother is the type who cleans her house whether it needs it or not. She knows better than to wait for dirt to make its hideous appearance. And in keeping with the rituals of our ancestors, she still washes her apartment from top to bottom every spring. Ceilings, walls, rugs, dishes, furniture, and closets—nothing escapes the rag.

Nobody has the nerve to tell her that the spring-cleaning ritual was started centuries ago, when houses were heated with woodstoves that coughed up soot, when men spat black tobacco juice into spittoons and usually missed, and when the swatted entrails of rural insects added vibrant colors to the walls during pesky summers. Spring cleaning is ingrained into her way of life, much like Sunday Mass.

Despite an outward appearance of normalcy, my father was never the same again. He'd survived the June ordeal, but his sense of humor and lightheartedness had died back in Thetford-Mines. He was more serious, often pensive, and prone to tears. He'd sit in the corner of the living room for hours without saying a word.

"What are you thinking?" my mother would ask.

"Nothing," he lied.

He'd been thrown a life preserver that would never be reeled in. He'd trail behind the ship for a while, bobbing in its wake, but still perish at sea. He knew this but never let on. Until the June scare, my father had no idea that his life had been in danger. The doctors tended to speak in vagaries and parables, and that was just fine with him—he didn't want to know. They discussed symptoms but stayed clear of labeling his disease.

"Your bladder is filled with blood clots," the doctor would say. But he'd never venture to explain the underlying cause of those blood clots. It had started as prostate cancer, the untreated condition gradually spreading to his vital organs.

But that close call had changed everything. He knew now that his condition was fatal. He had temporarily escaped the cold hands of the grim reaper, but he was thrashing around with an awakened sense of mortality. My father could never openly admit to dying. He knew that such an admission would cause my mother unbearable distress, given her especially sensitive and nervous character. And he feared that a public acknowledgement would shatter his last vestige of hope for recovery. My father was an optimist. He wanted desperately to recover and, at times, believed it possible.

Even in the last few months of life, he didn't look seriously ill. He still dressed sharply, spoke with the same mental agility, and moved about freely without limp or complaint. He didn't look his age either. He was eighty-six going on sixty. A small man with a long and curved nose, he sported a full head of hair, most of it still its original color. And he refused to go where "old people" congregated—*he* wasn't old.

"Do you have any pain?" I asked him soon after he returned from the hospital.

"No, I just feel a slight pressure," he replied, pointing at his abdomen.

His normal appearance fooled friends and relatives. He looked fine during the day, but my mother and sister dreaded the nights. His health problems would surface in the early hours like demons with pitchforks. He'd awaken from his sleep in a pool of blood, confused and distraught to see the vibrant flow emanating from his body. His bladder and kidneys were deteriorating fast.

In early July, I drove my teenage daughters up to see their grandfather one weekend, sensing that his time was near. He cried inconsolably during and after our departure, aware that this might be the last time he saw his granddaughters. He was right.

And so it was that my brother Jacques and I found ourselves driving north from New Hampshire to Lévis on July 21, 1998. As we drove Route 55 toward Québec City, we could still see the ravage left behind by the infamous ice storm of January 1998. The trees abutting the highway bowed down to earth as though prematurely mourning the loss of our patriarch. We stared at the trees like ancient Romans reading the inauspicious entrails of a sacrificed animal.

We were surprised at my father's condition once we arrived at the hospital. Instead of finding a man lying on a deathbed and attached to beeping medical equipment, Jacques and I found him sitting up in bed, looking his usual self.

They'd just started administering morphine intravenously, so he no longer felt pain.

The moment we stepped into his hospice room, he looked up and grimaced. It's not that he was unhappy to see us, but he knew full well what our unexpected visit signified. Despite our words of comfort, it was impossible to hide the fact that we'd both left jobs and families behind to rush to his bedside—not a good sign.

"I wonder when they'll send me home," he said, gazing into my eyes. This was a trick question. He wasn't looking for an answer; he was asking it to watch my reaction. My father had never been told that he was dying; he was groping around in the dark, feeling the wall for the light switch that might make the living nightmare disappear.

"Focus on getting better and then they'll send you home," I replied, conscious that his piercing eyes were searching for optimism. I felt like a liar and a hypocrite.

Later that afternoon, my brother Jacques and I went scouting for a nearby motel. Judging from my father's condition, it was clear that we'd have to spend several nights in Lévis. We found a modest motel about a mile from the hospital.

"We'll take one double room," I said to the French attendant.

"For how many people?" he asked.

"Eight," I replied, in spite of my embarrassment.

"We can rent you an extra cot," he offered. We walked out of the office with keys to a room holding two full-size beds and a cot. Of course, it was ridiculous to confine eight adults to one room like a band of Angolan refugees. But we had reasons.

The truth is that none of us wanted to leave my mother's side; we wanted to be there to console her when the inevitable moment arrived. Besides, no more than five people would occupy the room at the same time. Jacques and Doris had organized teams to keep a steady vigil over my father. We were assigned five-hour shifts, with three siblings covering the hospital room at every hour of the night.

The quietude of those long nights at the hospital afforded ample time for nostalgia; remembrances of comical family episodes served to relieve the gloomy tension in the air. On his deathbed, my father was managing to nudge his family closer together than ever.

We remained at my father's bedside from morning till night, eating meals in shifts. For days, we ate breakfast, lunch, and dinner in the hospital cafeteria amidst an ocean of blue and white medical uniforms, scrubs, and lab coats.

The morning after Jacques and I arrived, Papa informed my mother and my sister Lucette that he'd just met the funeral director. The imaginary visit had spooked him senseless, and his eyes looked wild as his drugged brain struggled to cope with mortality.

"The undertaker came to measure me for my coffin last night. He's out in the hallway right now, waiting for me to die," he said. Despite repeated attempts to convince him otherwise, he went on believing that the ominous visit had been real.

"It was just a dream, Papa," my mother said.

"No, I saw him with my own two eyes. He was here."

"What would you like for breakfast this morning?"

"Dead men don't eat," he replied.

By Thursday, the morphine was taking its ugly course; my father was rapidly sinking into a sleepy state, growing less responsive to our voices. As I watched the strength wane from his body, I found myself wondering whether it was the disease or the morphine that was killing our patriarch. The poison had already stripped him of consciousness.

The role of morphine in his final days was all the more troubling because my father had at first resisted the numbing medication. I wondered if the world of socialized medicine enforced its use as a cost-saving measure to terminate the life of elderly patients with dim prospects for recovery. If so, did that make me an accomplice?

"The morphine will accelerate his peaceful passing," the friendly hospice nurse said in response to my probing questions. "It usually attacks the weaker organs first. He might die a little faster, but the medicine makes it possible to do so without pain," she added. I felt better, although not much.

Earlier in the week, we were assigned a grief counselor. Our only counseling session with the sympathetic female nurse was held on Thursday in a vacant hospice room down the hall, its attending bed no doubt a regular witness to terminal pain and suffering. In a soothing tone, the nurse had encouraged us to share memories of my father and his life, skillfully steering the discussion toward happier times.

I found the counseling session very difficult. Not only did those memories prompt a flood of unmanly tears, it also made me painfully aware that I hardly knew my father. Guilt seeped into my brain as I concluded that I'd wasted the opportunity to get closer to him. Career had been my priority since college, and now I was paying the price.

Who was Hervé Blanchette? How has he influenced my life? These questions arose often in the quiet of night. The answers arrived in fragments, never adding up to a composite picture of the man. I knew about his physical traits, his unique odor, and his bad habits—these were exposed for everyone to see. But the public persona was only the veneer on the cabinet; I'd have to scratch beneath its surface to find the essence of the man.

The retrospective journey would send me back to my childhood, when we lived on the paternal farm, attended French schools, and dreamed of fanciful futures elsewhere. I would relive my boyhood mischief once more, re-experiencing the drama alongside a sensitive boy whose culture, language, and innocence had been forsaken long ago.

2

Return to the Homestead

St-Gérard was a rest stop on the way to Québec. It was named after St. Gerard Magella, the patron saint of expectant mothers. The town sits on Route 112, the road that runs between Sherbrooke and Thetford-Mines. It was a tiny community of six hundred residents, with a single religion (Roman Catholic) and one industry (farming)—the kind of place where everybody knows everybody else's deeds, mistakes, and habits.

St-Gérard center. Circa 1960.

Like most Québec towns at the time, it was dominated by the Catholic priest. This tradition had been established way back in the seventeenth century, when the French settlers first arrived on the shores of the St. Lawrence River with the Jesuit missionaries. The parish priest was a powerful figure with a serious responsibility: he was accountable for keeping the wicked flock in check, armed only with superstitious admonitions.

The jurisdiction of the parish priest had no boundaries. He made it his business to criticize the way you dressed, inquire about your fertility, and issue edicts that governed the way you raised your Catholic children. For decades, priests had banned all forms of dancing, viewing it as corrupt and seductive behavior. They'd pay well-timed visits to wedding receptions and holiday celebrations just to catch hapless violators. The moment the figure in black made an appearance, the guilt-ridden attendees could be seen jumping out back doors and windows to escape his glare and the ensuing castigation.

But the sacred rules preached on the pulpit were not always practiced by the priests themselves. It had long been rumored that Father Arsenault had fathered an illegitimate child with a mistress. Then, one day, he announced that he was adopting an orphaned twelve-year-old girl and that she'd live at the rectory under his care. Even a fool could see that the mysterious child was a spitting image of the pastor himself, having inherited the same eyes and his unmistakable flat nose.

The Sunday homily at Mass presented the priest with a once-a-week opportunity to influence the entire congregation. His harangues often included graphic reminders of the many aberrant paths that would lead straight to eternal damnation.

The weekly homily may have been effective at delivering poignant lessons on spirituality, but it was the much-dreaded confessional that was used to reproach veering individuals. All good Catholics were expected to attend confession at least once a month, where they'd admit their sins to the intimidating black figure while sitting in a wooden box.

My parents on a date. Circa 1936.

In those days, the confessional was a daunting place, the kind that makes your palms sweat and your head throb with nervous agitation. Nothing good ever happened there. You went to confession to atone for your mistakes, rarely an uplifting experience for the fidgety sinner spilling his guts a breath away from the stern religious figure.

The priest would ask probing questions about their sex life, criticize their child-rearing abilities, or reprimand them for their manner of dress. When a married couple failed to produce an offspring per year, their lack of success had to be justified in the narrow confines of the confessional—preventing conception was a grave Church violation.

"Are you breast-feeding your child?" the priest asked my mother.

"No, I can't," she replied sheepishly.

"Then you're a bad mother!" the pastor declared without allowing an explanation. Laurette would often leave the confession box with tears in her eyes. She'd been taught to fear authority figures at a young age; her father made sure of that.

Grandpapa Côté was an imposing man. I always thought he would have made a great funeral director. Most photos capture him with an unexpressive face, his eyes framed with dark-rimmed glasses that reflect back an austere gaze. He stood as straight as an arrow, his head held high, as if exuding manly pride and determination. His belly was round, causing his waist to settle at chest level, and his trousers were held up by suspenders that seemed to forever pull his crotch far above the comfort zone.

I knew him as a serious yet pleasant person, but my mother had a different childhood image of the man who'd been her father. As often happens, his character had softened with age, becoming gentler after retirement. But she knew him as an impetuous man with a vile temper who spewed venomous rebukes at his daughters. She respected her father as the *paterfamilias*, but despised his hurtful and abusive words. It seems that the man I viewed as a pillar of strength had been a tower of insults in his younger years.

Like his ancestors, my grandfather upheld the same values that had landed with Jean Costé in 1634, when the French patriarch stepped off the sailing vessel, *le St-Jean*. They included an ingrained fear of God, a love of the land, and a strong preference for sons over daughters. These values were shamelessly intertwined.

The domineering Catholic Church demanded that all married couples procreate without hindrance, and the result of this biblical decree was large families. In order to feed their growing brood, most took to toiling the land, planting crops, and raising their own animals for food. By the age of ten, all boys contributed to the operation of the farm.

So, farmers had good reason to discriminate: a daughter was just another mouth to feed, whereas a son provided free labor. The only expectation they had of their daughters was that they marry into respectable families. This goal was enforced with fist-pounding zeal, not so much to secure happiness for the child, but more to prevent a soiling of the family reputation in the eyes of a narrow-minded community.

My grandparents, Eugène and Diana Côté.

"I never wanted girls in the first place!" my grandfather declared in an angry display that involved bared teeth, red face, and clenched fist. He had no qualms about sharing this demeaning perspective in the presence of his daughters. Girls neither contributed to the workforce nor passed on the proud family name. Like most men of his generation, he believed that women had been put on earth for two reasons: bearing children—preferably male heirs—and doing household chores. They were relegated to diaper changing, nurturing, cleaning, cooking, and sex on demand.

"I'd give money to my sons but never to my daughters," Grandpapa declared within earshot of his children. Of all the inflaming statements he would make, none expressed his bias more clearly than this pronouncement. True to his word, he would chastise his wife whenever she "wasted" money on clothing for her girls.

Despite his blatant flaws as a father, Eugène was highly respected by town leaders. And at work, he was known as an equitable and likable man who treated his employees well. He seemed to save all his fury for home, where he was away from the discerning eyes of those who could injure his social standing. His eldest daughters took the brunt of the relentless insults, which eroded the thin fabric of their self-esteem. His aggression was rarely physical, but the stinging words left deep gouges in their hearts.

"You'll never amount to anything," he'd say. Daughters Laurette and Juliette listened impassively to his tirades, aware that any reply would only fuel his anger. In his mind, his boys could do no harm while his girls never did any good. "If one of my daughters ever gets pregnant, I'll kill her," he threatened. Intimately acquainted with his coarse temperament, my mother believed it possible.

In contrast to her husband, Grandmaman Côté was a peach, her physical appearance exhibiting traits often associated with American Indians. Her face revealed a wide nose, generous lips, and small eyes. But despite the persistent rumors and repeated assertions from Grandpapa, nobody could find tangible proof of her Indian ancestry.

My grandmother had always been a generous woman, unquestionably loyal to her husband and selflessly dedicated to her family. Consistent with her generation, she was subservient to her husband above all else, even if that meant compromising her children. Her abject obedience to Eugène was an ongoing source of frustration for the older daughters, who suffered constant verbal abuse at the hands of their father.

"Why doesn't she defend us?" the girls grumbled in the tearful aftermath of such tirades. But Grandmaman would never dare circumvent her husband's authority, remaining silent even when she empathized with the helpless victim. And she could never apologize for his actions either; that would be admitting some wrongdoing on his part.

My grandfather wasn't a bad man, but he was hopelessly mired in seventeenth-century values. The girls loved their mother despite her ineffectiveness at deflecting his verbal aggression, but the incessant ranting would leave emotional scars, infusing their personalities with lasting insecurity.

By the age of thirty-two, my mother had dutifully upheld the Catholic tenets, delivering seven babies and three miscarriages in the span of twelve years. Her third and last miscarriage happened when I was five years old. All of us were born at home in the same bed where we'd been conceived some nine months earlier.

This was long before the age of Lamaze. The doctor used ether to anesthetize the woman and forceps to rip the baby out of the womb as soon as its head crowned. Nobody but the doctor attended the birth; the fidgety husbands were encouraged to stay out of the house to prevent dramatic scenes in the event of medical complications.

L-R: Pierre, Lucette, Denise, Doris, Jacques, Réal. Circa 1951.

There were three girls and four boys in our family. Réal was the firstborn, a scrawny and sickly baby who became a skinny kid with a nervous demeanor. My recollection of my eldest brother is that of a grumpy teenager who at times turned playful like a kitten. Réal left school at fourteen. My mother had been suffering from stomach ailments and depression, so my parents decided that Réal was needed at home. He never went back.

Next, there was my brother Jacques, a hefty blond baby who shed liberal tears until the age of seven or eight. In old family photographs, Jacques is a handsome boy bearing no resemblance to the rest of us. He was outgoing and competitive, with an entrepreneurial spirit that surfaced during his teenage years. Jacques left school after ninth grade. By the age of eighteen, he was working full time outside the farm.

The third born was Doris, a quiet and gentle girl who rarely laughed. At the age of two, she began showing signs of epilepsy, but the mysterious fits later vanished without medical explanation. Doris became an easygoing child with a benevolent attitude.

Denise, another quiet girl, came next. As she approached her teenage years, we often heard her grumbling, as she had a tendency to be moody. Denise was a homemaker from an early age, always there to help my mother with cooking and household chores. She left school at fifteen, after my parents begrudgingly agreed to pull her out.

My recollection of Denise is that of a pleasant and mild-mannered girl, except for the time she wanted to kill me. It was a warm Saturday in July, and we'd stopped for lunch at a roadside burger stand in the small town of East Angus. We were on our way to see relatives for the weekend. Denise was already working by then and had splurged by buying a white ensemble involving an angel-white blouse, bright white shorts, and white sneakers.

I was standing outside the car trying to smother my hamburger with ketchup when the unfortunate accident happened. The plastic squeeze bottle was being obstinate, refusing to respond to my squeezing. Like in a bad scene from an old Abbott and Costello movie, I decided to hold the plastic bottle on a horizontal plane and press harder to stimulate the flow. The brainless move ended up producing more angst than ketchup.

Relieved to feel the plastic bottle finally give way under pressure, I looked up just in time to trace the trajectory of its vivid contents. *Oh shit.* The seasoned red sauce had painted the front of Denise's outfit with violent zigzagging strokes, leaving a red mark of Zorro all over her chest and down her white shorts. The consequences of ruining the favorite garments of a proud teenage girl must be high on the stress meter, because at that regrettable moment I starting fearing for my life.

"Damn little brat!" she kept repeating over and over, the rage preventing her startled brain from conjuring up more creative appellations. "Look at this!" she yelled, looking down at my handiwork while imploring justice from parents and siblings who seemed to be struggling to conceal their rising smirks. But I wasn't laughing.

Denise continued grumbling unflattering epithets as she struggled to wipe the ketchup globs with paper napkins. But her attempts to clean the pure white garments were futile; they were now hopelessly tinted with red smears, and she'd have to face our relatives with stains on her clothing. *Uh oh.* I felt the blood drain from my face and head, as it was suddenly redistributed to my limbs in preparation for flight.

The chase began in earnest, with Denise in angry pursuit and me running for my life like a spineless matador desperate to escape a raging bull. This was the first time in my life that Denise had become a physical threat to my wellbeing.

"It wasn't my fault!" I said in a deliberate tone meant to invoke heartfelt sympathy as my little legs ran frenzied circles around the car to escape my sister's reach. "I really didn't do it on purpose…it was an accident!" I yelled back at the snorting bull, which was closing in for the kill. "Maman, stop her!" I pleaded, praying that parental intervention might arrive in time to save my endangered hide. Every time Denise got dangerously close, I'd suddenly shift direction with a sharp turn.

Eventually, my mother's stern warnings ended the threat of violence. But Denise remained steaming mad for hours. When it came time to get back in the car, Maman ordered me into the backseat and Denise into the front. (I had been sitting in front previously.) That decision may have spared my life, because I was convinced that Denise might try a deadly neck twist or choke hold to avenge the damage to her clothes. That's the day I learned the lesson: *Don't mess around with a teenage girl's clothes.*

The fifth child was Lucette, a tomboy whose height and strength rivaled those of my older brothers. Lucette eventually became the moral overseer of the family. She was never appointed to this lofty position; she just assumed it because she felt it necessary to do so. Her rules were strict and inviolate, so I rarely felt safe around her. Her judgments were harsh and her punishments swift. In the absence of my mother, she took it upon herself to carry out sentences, like a deputy armed with a signed proxy.

"Are you going to let him get away with that?" Lucette would ask Maman in an admonishing tone of voice. This question would surface whenever she felt I had violated one of her unwritten family laws. I feared Lucette more than I did my mother. I once broke her finger with a broomstick while trying to repel her advance. That finger never did heal properly; it remained a crooked and permanent symbol of sibling warfare.

Pierre was next. He was a soft-spoken boy with large, protruding ears that Lucette called his "barn doors." As the child closest to me in age, I often competed with Pierre for attention, our sibling rivalry manifesting as petty jealousies and treasonous tattling to my mother. Pierre would punish my disloyalty by aiming teeth-rattling kicks at my hind region in copious quantities. In turn, these harsh assaults on my ass were avenged with more tattling, propagating a stupid cycle that's as old as mankind itself.

I once saw Pierre drunk on gasoline fumes. He was about eleven years old and had been playing alone in the garage when he got the bright idea to smell the gas can. Finding the odor pleasant, he continued sniffing until his brain had been pickled by the dangerous toxin.

Michel and Pierre. 1953.

"I'm crazy...I'm crazy!" he kept repeating, his eyes glazed over from the fumes.

I watched him stagger into the kitchen from the garage, talking gibberish. Unfamiliar with the hazard (I was only seven), I laughed myself silly watching his queer conduct, thinking that he must have gone insane. But my mother quickly recognized the dangerous symptoms, panicking at the smell of gasoline on his breath.

Pierre was four years old when I came along. It was about two o'clock in the morning on August 9, 1952, a warm summer day in Québec. My sisters had seen the doctor arrive and were anxiously awaiting word from the top of stairs in the cape-style house that my father had built five years earlier. They heard my first cry and later took turns pampering their new baby brother. There were now seven of us.

My father made the fateful decision the same year I was born: he'd relocate the family to the paternal farm where he grew up. Grandpapa Blanchette had just reached retirement age and the old farm was too big for his care. Although disappointed to leave the comfort of their modern home in town, Maman yielded to my father's will, refusing to interfere with the lifetime goal of her resolved husband; he had always loved the land.

The Blanchette men struck a deal. They'd swap houses, and my father would pay an additional four thousand dollars to take over the farm. That was a lot of money back then, especially since my parents still owed two hundred dollars on their house in town. My father had managed to reduce the family debt by subdividing a large lot and selling off portions to his brothers Gérard, George-Émile, and Roland.

Papa was thrilled with the prospect of farming again. He was responding to the lure of the land, the same siren call that our first French-Canadian ancestor, Pierre Blanchet, had heard back in the seventeenth century. He was hoping to increase the family income by selling milk products while reliving his youth in the serene countryside.

The house swap took place on April 10, 1953, when I was barely eight months old. Maman would soon regret consenting to that move. The old farmhouse had been left a dirty mess, my grandmother being far less meticulous about cleaning than my mother. The wood floors were filthy, the slat ceilings were in bad need of paint, and all the walls had to be resurfaced with either paint or wallpaper. With seven kids in tow, Maman accepted her fate and set out to make the house a more livable place for her family.

The rest of the farm was no better. Intent on keeping a small supply of animals in town, my grandmother had absconded with all the best yielding cows and half the chickens. My father was left with a dozen young cows that were incapable of producing enough milk to cover the farming expenses. The pillaging of cows had made for a rough start; my father was already in debt, with little hope of turning a profit.

The old farm was a throwback to the prior century. For starters, it lacked plumbing, a major amenity we'd been enjoying for years. There was no toilet, bathtub, or shower. In the summer, we used the two-seater outhouse in the backyard for bathroom duty. In the colder months, we used a metal bucket with a wooden lid that my father had installed in the dirt cellar. Papa would empty the stinky contraption on the manure pile along with the chamber pots that lay under our beds for nighttime urgencies. Maman was continually embarrassed to direct our visitors to the outhouse or metal bucket. As for our weekly baths, we took them while standing in a shallow metal tub.

The place also lacked electricity. This was even more disturbing than the absence of a toilet and running water. The wood stove, its round metal grate dominating the kitchen floor in the cellar, was the only source of heat in the poorly insulated farmhouse. In the winter, the kitchen was usually overheated while the upstairs bedrooms remained frigid.

The only source of light came from primitive kerosene lamps, and thus the threat of fire forever loomed over our heads. And without a refrigerator or icebox, all fruit and vegetables had to be stored in the dark root cellar. When available, meat had to be consumed fresh from the butcher, and leftovers were canned for future meals. Canning involved placing the cooked food in sealed glass jars that were then boiled. The tedious task of ironing required heating a heavy metal iron on the woodstove all year round.

In August of that year, my father came down with a severe case of jaundice, his skin and eyes turning yellow. He remained gravely ill for months, as the stubborn liver disorder was left untreated. By this time, my mother was regretting the move to the farm; it had degraded the condition of her family and almost killed her husband.

But things did get better. Eighteen months after the move, electricity reached our farm, the result of a political promise that had been made to my father before the elections and surprisingly upheld afterwards. Plumbing would arrive later, when I was six years old. I still remember watching my father dig the trenches and lay down the heavy pipes in the earth. It became a novelty to flush the toilet just to watch the water swirl out of sight.

Many of my childhood perceptions are linked to the old farmhouse. I can still hear the soothing whish of the clothes washer, its washtub rotating with a gentle hum that ascended to the top of the stairs and seeped inside the bedroom. I slept fitfully amidst the comforting reverberation, which seemed to whisper, "You're safe here."

It took Maman a few years to adapt to the rural environment, but she gradually came to appreciate life in the country. As for the kids, we adjusted immediately, loving the newfound freedom and endless supply of farming adventures. My fondest childhood memories involve this place; it's all I knew until the age of ten. It's here that I would learn my most memorable lessons and suffer my most poignant losses, unaware that we were already engaged in a losing battle that would eventually lead to abandonment.

3

Rural Adventures

The farm was an exciting and fun place to grow up. I have no recollection of boredom, as the operation of the dairy business injected a vibrant energy of its own. The daily chores gave a sense of order and purpose to our lives, and the animals added color.

The seventy-five acres supplied us with a bounty of occasions for adventure and foraging. There were hills to climb, forests to explore, large rocks to scale, and pastures to traverse. The large rock near the old farmhouse still brings back a flood of pleasant memories. Both my father and I played on that rock as young children.

Kids know a fun place when they see one, so we were the envy of cousins who lived in towns and cities. They sought desperately to spend time on our farm, especially during the summer months, when the place abounded with life. It was a safe harbor where kids could play with wild abandon and never exhaust their opportunities for discovery.

At the age of seven, I had the unfortunate experience of trading the farm for a summer weekend in "the city." My parents were going with relatives on an overnight visit to Uncle George-Émile, who lived several hours away from St-Gérard.

"You can stay here or with Aunt Juliette," Maman said.

The decision seemed easy. Aunt Juliette's kids were some of my favorite cousins. The thought of spending a glorious weekend in the center of town, where the roads were paved, was too hard to resist.

"I want to stay with Aunt Juliette," I said, blurting out the words before Maman could rescind the offer. The idea of frolicking in town had sparked my imagination.

My parents dropped me off in town on Saturday morning. My boy cousins decided to take advantage of the fact that the farm was unsupervised and walked up to our house to spend the day with my siblings. So I was left in town with

Sylvie—who was two years my junior—and her mother. In a few hours, I would deeply regret my decision.

After lunch, my aunt insisted on putting us both down for a nap. *She must be kidding.* I hated naps. My mother knew this, having put an end to the useless ritual long ago. Naps were a total waste of time, wasting the better part of the day and leaving me dazed for hours as my brain slowly readjusted to its wakeful state.

"But I don't take naps at home," I tried to convince her.

"Well, we all take them here," she countered. "It's only a few hours." The disappointment settled in my gut. I was doomed.

Not only did she enforce the nap, she even warned me not to get up until she did. So I lay down on my back in bed, fully dressed, staring at the ceiling, blanketed in boredom, and thinking about my cousins, who were engaging in fun adventures on our farm. The rest of the afternoon was no better. Sylvie and I were ordered to stay in the backyard, which seemed to be about the size of our chicken coop. I was bored out of my mind.

My parents picked me up on Sunday afternoon. We were barely out of the car when my sister Lucette and my brother Pierre encircled my parents and began recounting their weekend adventures with buoyant enthusiasm.

"We built a buggy with Guy and Christian yesterday," Lucette said, a proud smile lighting up her animated face. "You should see it. We can steer it with a stick. We took the wheels off an old wagon, used old boards from the back of the garage, and cut old pieces of sheet metal to make the hood. Then we used baling wire to tie the axle to the steering handle. We found an old brass lantern in the attic over the chicken coop and hung it over the wooden windshield to make a headlight."

My heart sank.

"We named it Ketchup," Pierre interjected with his own brand of exuberance. "We baptized it with an old ketchup bottle that we filled with water. Lucette even wrote a song about the buggy. Then we all took turns riding and pushing it," he added.

I felt like running down the hill to the barn and crying my eyes out in private. I envied them and felt sorry for myself at the same time. All this had happened over the weekend, while I had suffered a pointless and mind-dulling fate in St-Gérard.

"I'll never stay with Aunt Juliette again," I said to Maman. My words drew quite a chuckle; they sounded rather forceful coming from a seven-year-old. But I meant it; the miserable weekend had taught me the following lesson: *Elsewhere is not necessarily better.*

Our cousins from the city sometimes arrived dressed up in their Sunday best. I took pity on kids whose parents warned them not to get dirty. I never understood the concept of taking kids out to the countryside and then banning outdoor adventures. This was a delightfully messy playground: the large trees, grassy fields, dusty hay, and mountainous manure pile were there to entertain us.

My Uncle George-Émile and his family lived about eighty miles away, and they made infrequent visits to the farm. But when they did visit, their children were always dressed immaculately. They wore shiny shoes, with the girls in pretty dresses and the boys in white shirts and sports coats. But this never stopped us from parading them through the barn, cow stable, and chicken coop. They'd stand irresolute at the entrance to the stable watching our proud demonstrations, pinching their untrained noses to block out the smell. Réjean, the cousin closest to me in age, would often go home with dirty trousers and shoes, having climbed trees and scaled rocks in wanton violation of his mother's laws.

The dirt road on our rural route was shaped like the letter T, with the southern end leading to Route 1. The Moreau farm sat at the leftmost edge, ours was situated on the rightmost end, and my grandparents lived at the intersection. In reality, the line crossing the T extended far beyond the limits of automobiles.

Remnants of a turn-of-the-century road meandered past our farm and the Moreau property. Although covered by a grass cloak, the road still clung tenaciously to its original shape, like a dry riverbed. This was the road to adventure. Its thick foliage, sporadic building ruins, clean brook, wild animals, and abundant fruit provided endless opportunities for summer discovery. But you never ventured here alone.

The place was filled with unsettling quietude, supernatural powers, and bears that would eat your wimpy ass for a snack. You cleared out of there at the slightest hint of dusk; you'd never survive the night. The ghosts of past travelers would terrorize your brain until it turned to mush and you became a sniveling and drooling cretin ready for the straightjacket. And if the ghosts didn't get you first, the ruthless denizens of the night would come out in flocks to drag your body into the hopeless depths of the forest, to consume your flesh in a ritual animal festivity resembling Christmas dinner.

My parents strictly forbade us to roam the wooded regions in the fall. In November, the hunters would descend on the forests in droves to stalk Bambi. We'd often hear the sound of gunshots resounding in the crisp autumn air. We were as terrified of drunken hunters as we were of ghosts and goblins. They were mean, dangerous, unpredictable, and incapable of distinguishing between animal and human forms.

At the age of eleven, my sister Lucette had experienced a close encounter with drunken hunters that was still held up as a lesson for the rest of us to heed. While playing with Pierre and my cousin Christian near the wooded boundary of our property, she was startled to encounter men in bright orange hunting jackets. They were holding liquor bottles, staggering on their feet, and cackling like hens.

Always the responsible one, she instinctively grabbed her young playmates and headed for cover behind the old rock wall made of field stones. But it was too late; the hunters had already spotted them and were intent on making sport of their fear. They could hear boisterous laughter and slurred speech as bullets starting zinging above their heads, hitting the branches in nearby trees. Seconds later, shots ricocheted against the rocks that hid their small, defenseless bodies. They were scared shitless.

My nine-year-old brother, Pierre, was bawling his eyes out—as I'm told he often did regardless of the circumstances—when Lucette grabbed his hand and made a mad dash for the safety of our farm. They ran all the way home screaming like banshees.

The uninhabited area past the Moreau farm was called "Lanize" after the family who'd once occupied the property. We never knew this mysterious family, who had left behind dilapidated buildings and brick foundations that forever teased our avid imaginations. We ventured out in these parts mainly in the summer, when thick foliage covered the land with a green blanket that heightened our nervous agitation. Once, while walking the narrow road through a tunnel of hovering trees, a black bear lazily crossed our path, reminding us that wildlife—not humans—ruled the land. We ran all the way home.

A narrow brook ran through the countryside, its water so clear that we could see crayfish crawling on its rocky bottom. We fished there in the summer. All it took was a suggestion and we'd run off to the woods to break off a branch to use for a fishing pole.

We'd dig up worms, raid the old tackle box in the garage for line, hook, and sinker, and head for the stream with a baloney sandwich in hand. We'd settle on a large rock, take off our shoes, and sit there in silence to avoid alerting the fish, enjoying the soothing gurgle emitted by the brook. If we were lucky, we'd pull up a trout or two. But even when we returned empty handed, it had always been a fun day.

We certainly didn't fish to put food on the table; we did it for the challenge of the catch. The only person who seemed to appreciate fish in our household was my father, the same person who ate disgusting sardines out of flat tin cans with rollup covers.

Eating fish was a serious ordeal, but since we were Catholic, my mother occasionally served up some disgusting catch for Friday dinner in compliance with the no-meat rule. That was never a good thing. I loved Maman's cooking, but fish was not her specialty; she had no idea what to do with the damn things. Her only recipe involved butter and a hot frying pan that threw up horrid white smoke, stinking up the whole house. The stench was usually bad enough for me to pinch my nose in disgust.

"Micheeeeeel!" my mother would yell in a rising pitch whenever she caught me holding my nose to block out the putrid odor. I was being ungrateful. Maman hated to cook fish as much as we hated eating it, and the experience made her irritable.

She expected us to eat fish as though we enjoyed it. After all, kids were starving in underprivileged parts of the world, we were reminded. I was always skeptical about the legitimacy of these claims, figuring it was an adult scam to manipulate kids into eating stuff they hated. *Who are these Chinese kids, anyway?*

"Well, they can have my portion," was a brave but foolish statement to make. You'd find yourself staring at four walls for the rest of the evening.

Fish disgusted me. The foreboding smell was punishment enough, I thought, but to be forced to eat the acrid flesh should at least take off some purgatory time, like Catholic "indulgences." (Indulgences were small acts of sacrifice or repetitive prayers that mysteriously atoned for your minor sins, the equivalent of time off for good behavior in the penal system.)

The fish was usually lake trout, strong tasting and riddled with pointy bones. Not surprisingly, my father adored the taste of fresh trout. The dreadful thing was never filleted; bones were apparently part of the religious sacrifice.

"Maman, there are bones in here," I said to delay the inevitable.

"Take them out."

"What if I miss one?"

"Chew your food slowly so as not to swallow them."

It's hard to look fortuitous when your eyes are frantically searching for the bones that will kill you. I knew the horror stories and was convinced that eating fish was downright dangerous. The bones would puncture your intestines, causing you to roll into a fetal position while you screamed at the stabbing pain in your gut. You'd die slowly and mercilessly, cursing all fish and all Fridays. I never met a victim of fish manslaughter, but I sensed this lesson to be true: *Friday fish dinners can kill you.*

I loved the four seasons. Each brought its own sort of excitement. Naturally, summer was the crème de la crème of seasons. We were free to roam the country-side like convicts escaped from school, while our acres bloomed with trees, fruit, and wildflowers.

The land abounded with maple, spruce, pine, birch, and oak trees that were scattered around the countryside in clumps. The maple trees provided sap to make syrup in the spring and generous shade in the heat of the summer. In the breeze, the motion of the leaves created a swaying silver sheen that could be downright intoxicating.

The fields were colored with clusters of yellow, purple, white, orange, and pink flowers that added a pleasant fragrance to the air and provided endless pick-ing opportunities for kids. (Maman was the frequent recipient of our well-inten-tioned bouquets.) Wildflowers included ground ivy, black-eyed Susans, pink and white clovers, day lilies, black mustard, Canada thistle, orange hawkweed, and wild roses.

The trees and flowers were pleasant enough, but the fruit was my favorite. The orchard near our house featured pears, green apples, and red apples. During apple season, fresh fruit became a staple of our diet. We regularly ignored my mother's warning about eating the green apples, sometimes at the expense of our aching tummies.

Nature also supplied an abundance of seasonal fruit without our help. Our complement of wild fruit included strawberries, dwarf raspberries, black raspber-ries, dewberries, blueberries, cherries, and crabapples. These same varieties had been gratefully consumed by our immigrant ancestors some 350 years earlier.

Blueberries were my mother's favorite fruit, so blueberry picking became a serious family activity. She'd travel miles to reach a virgin blueberry patch. The kids would accompany her on the forage, little beggars equipped with plastic buckets.

On occasion, families would band together to participate in a more ambitious blueberry-picking expedition. Once, Grandpapa Côté organized a trip to Garthby, a town north of St-Gérard. My mother and Aunt Juliette eagerly enlisted their families. We were to travel deep into the woods to reach timber clearings. These virgin clearings were shielded from civilization and allegedly held blueberries the size of crabapples.

On the designated morning, families gathered at my grandfather's farm with picnic lunches. We were under strict orders to leave the dogs at home to avoid attracting bears. We were then driven to the nearby town of Garthby, on a hay wagon pulled by a tractor, and dropped off at the entrance to the woods. My grandfather knew these parts—presumably from his logging years—and would serve as our experienced guide.

We entered the forest on a narrow path, the kids intoxicated by a sense of adventure and the adults jovial with anticipation. The woods were serene, heightening our cheerful and carefree mood. The day was warm and muggy, inviting the mosquitoes to descend on us in droves while we swatted at the relentless buzzing sound.

Within an hour, my grandfather had guided us to the first timber clearing, which contained the most sumptuous berries we had ever seen. The fruit was large and bountiful. At noon, we blissfully ate our sandwiches while sitting on old tree stumps. By mid-afternoon, our buckets were filled to capacity and the time had come to retrace our steps to the tractor.

After walking around in circles, it became readily apparent that we were lost. We'd traveled off the beaten path hours ago to reach another timber clearing and had lost our bearings in the process. My grandfather was busy gauging our current location from the position of the sun, trying to calculate new headings.

"Stop making that ruckus and stick together," one of the mothers barked. Adult nerves were starting to unravel; they were getting impatient with our silly antics.

It was getting late. Once darkness fell, we'd lose our compass in the sky and it would become impossible to navigate the woods. We were surrounded by millions of blueberries, so it wasn't the lack of food that worried me.

"What happens if we don't find a way out before dark?" I asked, the disturbing thought launching a wave of butterflies down my innards.

"We'll just have to sleep in the woods. It could be fun," my cousin Christian replied.

"But there are bears out here."

"Grandpapa has a pocket knife. He can use it to protect us," another kid said.

Grandpapa had overheard the banter and turned to address us. "If we're not back by suppertime, they'll send out a search party," he said in a calm voice. His words made me feel better, even prompting a temporary surge of bravado.

After walking awhile and stopping to check the position of the sun a zillion times, my grandfather finally succeeded in getting us back on track. But the kids were disappointed; we wouldn't experience a night in the wilderness after all.

My favorite summer desserts were the fruit cobblers. We ate strawberry cobblers in June, raspberry cobblers in July, and blueberry cobblers in August. Maman would bake them right before dinner and serve them piping hot from the oven. The fruity aroma drove me nuts with anticipation—their sweet taste was a benefaction straight from heaven.

Our farm was far from idyllic. We lived in an old farmhouse that was sided with asphalt shingles textured with green pebbles. The farm buildings were unpainted and weathered from years of exposure. And the dirt road coughed up incessant dust into the summer air. But we did live amidst the generous bounty of nature.

Our house stood on the crest of a hill overlooking green pastures where the cattle grazed in the warmer months. About a mile down from the house, our property ended on the shores of Lake Aylmer, a large lake that extended across several townships.

On a hot summer day, we'd occasionally walk down to the lake to bathe. My mother, who was petrified of drowning accidents, would remind the older siblings of the safety rules—the younger ones would be their solemn responsibility. We were ordered to wash and return home swiftly. The serious occasion was never for entertainment.

Armed with bathing suit, towel, and bar of soap, we'd march through the pasture, careful not to step on the abundant cow flops that littered our path to the big lake.

Reaching the lake was never as easy as it seemed. We had to traverse marshy bogs, hedgerows, and slippery stumps that had been left over from the days of commercial logging. We'd then find a suitable tree to change into our bathing suits and tread gingerly into the water as sharp rocks jabbed the soles of our feet with every step.

My siblings playing on our property near Lake Aylmer.

Cries of "eee...yeow...ouch!" resounded above the calm waters of Lake Aylmer.

While we stood in barely two feet of water, the facecloths would dutifully appear as we passed around the communal bar of soap as though it were some precious artifact. The lake would suddenly burst into bubbles as we scrubbed our skin and rinsed our hair in the waters of Lake Aylmer—probably to the dismay of the fish who would have to inhale the soap bubbles.

The ill-behaved kids who ventured out for a careless swim would be admonished by the sibling in charge. As for me, I viewed the lake as nothing more than a gigantic bathtub. I'd been taught to fear large bodies of water and didn't know how to swim.

Upon reaching school age, I joined the lofty ranks of once-a-week bathers. Our bath was always taken before dinner on Saturday afternoon. On occasion, my mother would decree an extra bath when she found evidence of dirt on my skin. But from around the age of seven, my regularly scheduled bath was only once a week. Of course, Maman always reserved the right to inspect my ears and neck after each bath.

The old farmhouse never did have a bathtub. In the summer, we'd take our bath in a shallow round metal tub that was placed in the old dusty garage connected to the house. This allowed us to bathe without my mother fretting over water spillage. In colder weather, the same metal tub was moved to the dirt cellar near the wood furnace.

Maman worked much of the afternoon to supply the water for our baths. She'd heat the water on the stove and call out our names in age order, from eldest to youngest. Two kids always shared the same water; this conserved the well and reduced labor. I always bathed after Pierre, standing in his soap scum and hair residue.

The heavy wooden garage door slid on metal wheels. At bath time, we kept it partly open to let in the sunlight while preserving a modicum of privacy. As the last kid in line, my bath had no time constraint, so I'd stand naked in the metal tub with my eyes riveted on the outdoors, captivated by the scenery. Stripped of my clothing, I became part of nature, like the birds, swaying trees, grazing cows, gentle wind, and puffy clouds.

My bath was also a time of song. Soothed by the water and ensnared by the beauty of nature, I'd sing my favorite songs, swaying my hips back and forth to the rhythm.

I discovered serious music at the age of eight. Before then, my musical repertoire was made up of traditional folk songs, such as "Partons, la Mer Est Belle," and nasal-sounding country songs that were often the target of our childish ridicule. My parents rarely listened to music, but when they did, it was old-time country radio. Their favorite country music artists included Marcel Martel, Paul Brunelle, and Willie Lamothe.

These musicians may have been popular with the elders, but they seemed to suffer from overgrown adenoids that caused them to emit hilarious nasal sounds. Some also rolled their R's incessantly, and their rumbling lyrics irritated my ears. We'd often run around the house pinching our noses to mimic their sound amidst fits of giggles.

My sister Lucette was the family clown, mocking everything with flair. She could reproduce animal sounds, chronic lisps, and country singers with nasal perfection. She could also imitate the goofy-looking politician who proudly wore a white beret and stuttered in paid political announcements on television, much to our amusement.

The publicity pictures of these country singers didn't do them justice either. Their props often included an exaggerated cowboy hat and a horse standing in the background. Their hats were cocked back on their heads in a go-ahead-and-slap-it-off sort of look, making them look more like slow-witted hillbillies than professional musicians.

But in 1960, my music repertoire expanded with a jolt. My sister Denise was working in Sherbrooke and had become fond of a contemporary radio station. At the time, our only radio consisted of a finicky old unit stored on the kitchen counter.

While my sister listened to her favorite Sherbrooke station one day, I overheard a song that literally brought tears to my eyes. It was a sentimental ballad sung by a female artist whose name I didn't know. The music floated in the air like the sweet fragrance from a rose, its lyrics pricking my heart like a thorn. I instinctively ran toward the radio to listen more closely, as the static noise impaired the song's clarity. By the time the song was over, my eyes were brimming with tears.

"Your eyes are all red. Do they hurt?" my mother said.

"No, I just rubbed them," I lied to conceal my wimpy response to the music.

The romantic music had lifted my soul to a place I'd never been, the sensation leaving me speechless. I had to have more, but that would prove harder than it seemed. The Sherbrooke radio station seemed bent on more talk than music.

Between the weather, news, and politics, there was hardly any time for music. I'd dawdle around the kitchen just to catch a good tune on the radio, counting my blessings if I heard one good song every hour. This made listening to radio a tedious affair.

There was Lucille Dumont singing romantic ballads; Édith Piaf singing a heart-rending "Non, Je Ne Regrette Rien"; and Michele Richard, the young daughter of a popular fiddler with a TV show on CHLT-TV in Sherbrooke. Michele was only five years older than me and already a singing sensation. She had the voice of an angel, a smile that could melt ice cubes, and a face that even an eight-year-old could adore. And there was Luis Mariano, the Italian opera singer, who sang "Maman, la Plus Belle du Monde," a fitting song about a little boy who finds his mother beautiful.

So, it was songs like "Maman, la Plus Belle du Monde" that I'd belt out while standing in a tub of lukewarm water, with my eyes fixated on the great outdoors.

The fall and spring seasons seemed short to me, barely spanning two months. That's because I measured the seasons by changes in temperature rather than the calendar. The first snowstorm signaled the beginning of winter. And when the outdoor temperature topped sixty degrees, it was summer again as far as I was concerned.

The fall season was overshadowed by the return to school. This was a serene time of year, when school became the central part of our daily routine once again. And the spring was a time of hope and excitement; we were restless calves eager to run out to pasture.

Winter was a long, drawn-out affair in Québec. Snow started falling in November and stopped in April. Despite the long winters, I always looked forward to the snow; it made it possible to engage in fun activities like sliding, skating, and snowshoeing. In addition, the clear winter skies offered the best nighttime viewing, sprouting billions of stars.

Most years, the dirt road leading to our house was closed to traffic during the snow months. A large metal roller occasionally came by to flatten the landscape, making the surface passable on foot and horse-pulled sleighs. The road became a bright white veil that stretched across the land, adding to our cozy sense of isolation.

We often walked to school in freshly-fallen snow, my eldest siblings laying down a path for the smaller kids. At times, it was so deep that we struggled to climb over drifts. At other times, icy rain laid down a thick crust that made walking fun and easy. The ice crust allowed us to walk over the snow-covered fields like Jesus had walked on water.

My father kept a workhorse on the farm. One horse was named Dick. For years, Dick was our only means of transportation throughout the winter. I remember going to midnight Mass in the family sleigh with snowbells ringing in the crisp air, while we sat under a horsehair blanket to escape the icy wind. But I found nothing romantic about those sleigh rides. My eyes were usually riveted on the horse's tail, which sometimes lifted to discharge stinky farts and at other times ejected droppings the girth of my leg.

One of the highlights of the winter months was sliding. On a clear Sunday afternoon, we'd cross the Moreau farm to reach the best sliding hill in town. It was less than half a mile from our house and usually packed with kids from the village. The place was a veritable zoo, filled with a throng of crazy kids with daredevil attitudes.

There was no limit to the variety of sliding apparatus. We were tame by comparison, sliding down the hill on the family toboggan, which my parents had given us one Christmas. But without the means to afford a more respectable sliding contraption, town kids improvised with the ingenuity of brave knuckleheads.

Anything could be made slippery with a generous application of polishing wax. Even cardboard boxes were sometimes loaded with kids and launched down the hill. Wood pallets with greased skids were used as well. You could even see car doors and hoods with giggling kids astride, their hard metal parts polished to a dangerous sheen.

Standing on the hill was never a prudent move. One loud thump and your padded body would be doing an ungraceful cartwheel through the air, just as a shiny car part hurled past you at imbecile speed. Limbs were sometimes broken.

Despite the risk, sliding was a thrill. Our sled would be loaded down with four or five kids, as we shot through a blinding mist of snow that impaired both visibility and steering. If we were lucky, we'd slide gracefully to the bottom without incident, eager to repeat the experience all over again. When not so lucky, we'd bounce off a bump, lose control, and flip the toboggan partway down the hill. Or worse, we'd fly down the hill past the tree clearance and hit a stump at whiplash velocity.

One of my favorite memories of winter fun took place when I was nine. It was a Friday evening, and an icy rain had been pelting the area. Suddenly, the lights went out everywhere as the power lines broke under the weight of ice. The sky soon cleared, revealing a bright and full moon that reflected off the surface as though it were shiny crystal.

Someone suggested that we go skating even though it was close to bedtime. My parents relented in the face of the serendipitous circumstances. Giggling with childish anticipation, we were off to fetch our old skates from the hand-me-down pile.

The Moreau family had moved away by then and the Gagné family had taken over their farm. This was a big improvement, in my opinion, because the Gagné clan had kids of every age. And the whole family seemed to be fun loving, finding most things humorous. There were finally kids our age living within walking distance.

One of the Gagné kids, Jean-Marie, became a good friend. He was two years younger, but that was close enough for me. We were often together, peer soldiers armed with stick rifles fighting a faceless enemy in the nearby woods, or playfully wrestling on the ground in a boyish test of strength.

On this surreal winter evening, we headed off to fetch the Gagné kids, wearing skates that were in the approximate range of our shoe size. The Gagné boys soon came out wearing their old skates, and we all proceeded to slide with childish abandon over surfaces created by nature and lit by the radiant moon. We had a blast, and we were disappointed to see electricity restored, wishing we could skate the whole night away.

One of the most enchanting aspects of the winter season involved the Holiday festivities. Our large families would take turns congregating in each other's homes over the Christmas season. Huge meals were planned, with delicacies like meat pies and ragouts reserved exclusively for this time of year. We usually attended at least five of these family get-togethers per season.

The largest room in the house was the kitchen. Long makeshift tables made of wood planks were set down, spanning the length of the room. Boots were removed at the door, resulting in a colossal pile of rubber near the entrance. Coats were placed in layers on the beds, as forty or fifty people showed up in the span of thirty minutes.

These times were joyous beyond description. They were long and drawn-out affairs providing uninterrupted access to cousins. And we had lots of cousins. The jovial atmosphere was further magnified by the inebriated uncles, serious men who suddenly turned soft as kittens. Shots of whiskey and gin were distributed and chased with ample bottles of beer. The beer was always served at room temperature for practical reasons: the volume made it almost impossible to refrigerate. In contrast, the women rarely drank alcohol at these gatherings. Booze was a man's potion.

The kids took advantage of the chaos, running around like reckless nymphs and taking advantage of their parents, who were preoccupied with the meal or engaged in conversation with other festive adults. We'd tromp tirelessly through the first floor, up to the second floor, and down to the basement to make sure we missed none of the excitement.

The festivities were not restricted to dinner time either. One meal was held early Christmas morning, after midnight Mass. It began around one-thirty in the morning and ended in the wee hours. There we were, eating turkey, meat pies, and mashed potatoes swimming in ragout in the early hours of Christmas Day.

Aunt Juliette customarily served the early Christmas morning meal. As if that wasn't enough, my mother would follow with a second meal in the afternoon, when the festive atmosphere would resume with a fierce intensity.

And then there was New Year's Eve with my Côté grandparents, who lived a short walk from our farm. It would start in the evening and last till one or two o'clock in the morning.

The New Year's Eve party tended to be more boisterous than the others because my Côté uncles drank more heavily than those on the Blanchette side. Here, too, shots of hard liquor were downed and chased with beer. Grandpapa Côté never drank alcohol, but his sons more than made up for his sobriety.

At times, the festive atmosphere would even lure kids into sampling the alcohol. While celebrating at the home of my Côté grandparents one year, Rénald, one of the naughty cousins my age, found a flask of gin in one of the coats strewn on the bed.

"Do you want to try it?" he said after taking a couple of good swigs.

"Maybe," I replied, not really interested but more eager to show him that I had balls. His ears were bright red as he flashed a daring smile.

I reached for the pint and raised it to my lips. One sip later, and I was coughing like an old Rambler in bad need of a tune-up. My throat was burning, and my ears felt hot.

"How can they drink this crap?" I exclaimed in a hoarse whisper.

"It's not so bad," Rénald replied without showing remorse. But that was the end of my drinking. The stuff smelled like the torturous Mercurochrome my mother poured on our open wounds. It baffled me that adults willingly drank that putrid liquid.

Our family gatherings also featured traditional folk music. Several uncles played musical instruments—some quite well—that they pulled out of protective cases only for the holidays. My Uncle Roland played the button accordion with the dexterity of a touch-typist, tapping his feet in rhythm as his fingers moved effortlessly across the keys. So did my Uncle George-Émile, although distance prevented his regular attendance.

The adults would clap their hands to the music and dance the quadrille in groups. Kids added to the frenzied pace by clacking kitchen spoons against their thighs. The thumping action of dancers got so loud that the floor often reverberated under our feet.

Uncle Théodore played the fiddle well, but only after tuning the instrument for an excruciating period of time, trying the patience of his listeners. Zing, zing, zing. He'd tune the violin for about thirty minutes before playing his first piece. Then he'd stop abruptly and resume tuning the instrument as though disgusted with the sound. Ding, ding, ding. The adults sighed with disappointment while the kids joked. Eventually, he'd resume the piece, accelerating the tempo like a horse slowly shifting into a gallop.

There was also singing. Most songs involved audience participation. These were called "*chansons à répondre*," which means "songs to answer." An uncle would usually stand up and belt out each verse, while the audience responded with the familiar refrain. Everyone, including the kids, knew the words to these old familiar songs.

We sang Christmas songs, such as "Petit Papa Noël," old sailor songs, drinking songs, such as "Boire un Petit Coup C'est Agréable," romantic songs, and silly songs. Later in the evening, the mothers would escort their kids out of earshot—so they thought—while the men delved into their repertoire of dirty songs, which they called "*chansons cochonnes.*"

The kids often gathered at the top of the stairs, within perfect hearing range; the staircase created a tunnel effect that carried the sound upwards. I'd hear the words, but the *double entendres* often escaped my comprehension. Despite our banishment, we'd usually manage to sneak back downstairs to watch the goings-on.

Uncle Théodore was a legend among kids. It wasn't just the content of his dirty songs that we found rip-roaringly funny, it was his delivery. Red faced from the liquor, he'd sing songs while waving both hands up and down in a vertical sweep, like the pope giving the holy blessing. This motion began even before his mouth had assaulted the first verse, while his alcohol-impaired brain struggled to elicit the lyrics. The audience suffered through long musical interludes as he fumbled with each verse. Miraculously, the relentless gesturing never faltered during these unfortunate pauses.

"*Dans vos culottes, madame*" ("In your breeches, madam"), he sang, as the kids, hidden in the wings, bent over in fits of uncontrolled laughter. "I see something black and furry," he continued. My uncle had taught me a valuable lesson: *Liquor makes you silly.*

Christmas dinner at Aunt Juliette's. Circa 1954.

The only drawback to the festivities was the meal tradition: kids always ate last. Despite the sizable tables, there was never enough room for both adults and children. So, the adults ate first and the kids were served at a second sitting. If there were empty chairs at the adult sitting, a select few of the older kids might get lucky and be allowed to fill the empty spots. But this never happened to me, because I was too young.

The second sitting lacked some of the better food items. The meat pies and ragouts were often gone by the time the kids ate. And the turkey was sometimes all dark meat. But despite these minor setbacks, we never lacked food. After the main course, the table was cleared and restocked with yummy desserts decorated with Christmas colors.

The Christmas morn and New Year's Eve meals were tiresome though. By the time the adults were finished eating, it was usually the wee hours of the morning. The little kids were more sleepy than hungry, our heads lurching involuntarily toward our chests. Despite our sleepiness, we had to approach the table at the insistence of our guilt-ridden mothers, who seemed uncomfortable having kept their children hungry.

I loved farm animals; they were part of our extended family. Every animal, with the exception of the chickens, was assigned an individual name. The dogs, cats, pigs, horse, and cows all had unique names. Not brilliant names, mind you, but names nevertheless. My brother Jacques took charge of naming our pets, settling on dazzling and ingenious labels like Fido, Princess, and Puppé. Yeah, these names were clever all right.

There was Bobineau and Bobinette, the pair of male and female pigs that would later reward our family with generous ham dinners. There was Dick, the work horse that was eventually traded in for a Massey-Ferguson tractor. And there were Brunette, Blondine, Caillette, and la Grande Blanche, a few of the faithful cows in our dairy service.

Once in a while, we'd take in an unusual pet. My brother Jacques had adopted a baby raccoon that he named Teddé. It was domesticated, friendly, and cute as heck. The little thing would sit on our shoulder, cooing and bouncing up and down to our stride. Teddé would climb ropes upside down and even ride on the back of our dog Fido. The unusual sight of the little raccoon straddling the dog, with his head bobbing up and down like a cowboy on horseback, was hilarious every time.

The kids loved Teddé, but my parents didn't share our enthusiasm. The little raccoon was inherently mischievous and constantly on the lookout for foraging opportunities. It had figured out how to pry open the screen door to raid the kitchen. This upset my mother greatly, as she was forced to discard every food package Teddé opened.

It was quite an attention getter. Well, at least it got the attention of our bread man. He'd just made a delivery one day when we saw him running back to our door, breathless.

"Do you have rifle?" he asked my mother, his eyes wild with panic. "There's a raccoon in the back of my van!"

My father, Lucette, and I were standing in the kitchen when we heard the frantic plea of the bread man. Papa quickly reached for the porch door.

"I'll take care of it," he said, passing the bread man at the threshold. The poor man looked stupefied as he watched my father climb into the rear of his van. Teddé was domesticated most of the time, but not when he was eating. At feeding time, he'd hiss and bare his teeth at the approach of any person or animal.

Mere seconds after Papa reached the van, we observed a ball of black and brown fur arch through the air and then fall hard onto the dirt road behind the truck. My father had grabbed Teddé by the tail and flung him with all his might. The raccoon rolled onto the gravel surface and guiltily scurried away in the opposite direction.

We thought the bread man would mess his pants as he watched in horror. My mother had to pay for the damaged bread, but we got a good laugh at the poor man's expense.

There was also the case of the pet chicken. My sister Lucette could deliver a flawless chicken imitation. Unless you happened to be staring at her mouth during the performance, you couldn't tell the difference between real clucking and her talented mimicking. Her tone, pitch, and inflections were stunning. I tried hard to duplicate the sound, but my counterfeits all sounded asinine.

Lucette used that astonishing talent to rally chickens to her side. One particular chicken fell for it; apparently she was not one of the smarter members of the poultry family. She named it Bédit. Lucette would walk into the chicken coop, summon Bédit by name, and walk out carrying the domesticated fowl under her arm. Bédit would sit comfortably in the crook of her arm as Lucette proceeded to pet it like a feline.

One day, my mother announced that Bédit had stopped producing eggs. This automatically placed her on death row, in line for Sunday dinner. Needless to say, Lucette didn't take well to the idea of losing her precious—if not gullible—pet.

"It costs money to feed an old chicken," Maman told Lucette.

"But she's my pet," Lucette pleaded with tears in her eyes.

My mother eventually gave in to her tearful pleas, reluctantly granting Bédit a special reprieve. From that day forward, Lucette entertained a very lucky chicken.

I always thought that the cows were attractive animals, with their big eyes, long eyelashes, and moist noses. They were usually friendly, too, which added to their appeal. I fancied grooming them, petting their faces, and hand-feeding them grain as the caress of their sandy tongues tickled my skin.

But on occasion, my siblings would take advantage of our docile cows. I was often a witness to their crimes, although not brave enough to initiate them. The most daring exploits inevitably involved my cousin Christian, the son of Aunt Juliette and one of my favorite boy cousins. Christian was often on the farm, dreaming up mischievous ways to play with the animals.

My brother Pierre was usually a quiet kid, but Christian acted as a catalyst to stir up his dormant insolence. Wherever Pierre and Christian went, there was trouble. It started when they were little. By the time the boys were three or four years old, my mother had already caught them playing a dangerous game in the basement. Christian was sitting on the blade of my father's table saw, just as Pierre was reaching for the electric socket with the plug in hand. They were curious as to how Christian would look sawed down the middle.

I often tagged along so I could report them to parental authorities when all hell broke loose. It stands to reason that my undercover role made me rather unpopular with Pierre, causing him to administer repeated blows to my lower back regions.

At times, their mischief took the form of innocuous pranks. I once participated in dressing up a cow. The benign exploit was instigated by none other than Christian. The two boys began by fetching a cow from the pasture and bringing it back to the stable. We assembled a lovely Indian headdress from cardboard, beautified it with chicken feathers, and fastened it to the head of the cow with a string under its chin. Next, we fetched four old boots from the attic, fitted them over the hooves, and secured them around the ankles with laces, giving the unlucky cow a dunce-like appearance.

Once we had finished admiring our handiwork, we put the cow out to pasture. We found its attire hilarious. Its work boots clomped loudly against the cement floor as it trudged out of the stable, the chicken feathers flapping in the gentle afternoon breeze.

But later in the day, we were disappointed to see the cow return without attire, as we had hoped to see it pull up in full garb. We never found a trace of the headdress and boots either; even the family cows seemed to hide evidence of our scatterbrain schemes.

On another occasion, Pierre and Christian wanted to ride the cows. This was a spin on the rodeo, without the horse or bull. They'd nudge a cow up against the wood fence and one would hold it in place while the other climbed on its back. Once the boy was astride, the cow would usually make a beeline for the lowest tree limb in a desperate attempt to knock off the little ruffian from its back.

"Stop that! You're hurting the cow," I yelled several times. But they ignored me.

I resolved to put an end to their abuse. Since they snubbed my threats, I had no choice but to march into the kitchen and snitch everything to my mother. My tailbone would eventually recover from Pierre's angry kicks. At least the cows were safe.

My closest animal friend was Puppé, a medium-sized dog that appeared to be part Collie but mostly mutt. My brother Jacques assigned Puppé his sage name, which means...dog. We always had dogs on the farm, but this little guy was the best. Some of our other dogs barely exhibited enough wits to chase their own tails, but Puppé was full of life; he was playful, loved kids, and showed spunk. And he was also my best friend.

On schooldays, Puppé was always the first to greet me back home. He'd run a mile ahead to greet my arrival, barking the entire distance and bouncing at my face as if jumping on a dog trampoline. He was a frenzy of huffs, licks, and fur.

It never occurred to me that these rural adventures might end abruptly. Both sides of my family had been farming for centuries, so I naturally assumed the tradition would continue on down the line. I too would someday toil the fields and milk the cows, just like my ancestors. The clock was ticking, but the farm still had lessons to impart.

4

Unforgettable Lessons

Living with farm animals tends to make you humble. Seeing animals come and go is a poignant reminder that the cycle of life applies to every living thing. The constant sight and smell of manure too has a way of keeping vainglorious tendencies in check. In fact, there's shit just about everywhere, outside in the fields and inside farm buildings. You constantly see it, smell it, step in it, and scoop it up by the shovelful.

We were often witness to the birth, life, and death of our animals. Cows delivered their calves in the spring, sometimes with great difficulty. My father would spend hours in the stable assisting with difficult births. If the placenta came out before the calf, or if the hooves of the calf pointed upward, we knew this meant trouble. Papa would tie a rope around the feet of the calf and pull hard to speed up problem deliveries. At times, both the cow and calf perished from the complications of birth.

My father never allowed his younger children to witness the births. He would order us to leave the stable as soon as labor became advanced, worrying that the sight of blood and the wailing of cows would be too much for his children to bear.

The food chain also dictated that animals be taken to slaughter. My father never killed his own animals, so we were thankfully spared the butchering demonstrations. Instead, he transported our cows and pigs to a slaughterhouse.

Chickens were a different matter, though. By default, my mother was the designated killer of poultry; my father had always shunned that responsibility. She'd sound a verbal warning long before the slaughter, giving us plenty of time to cower away from the scene of the murder. Although she preferred us not to watch, we always stayed.

There were two ways to kill a chicken. The first involved inserting a sharp knife in its mouth to cut a major artery. The chicken hung by its legs on a hook outside the garage, bleeding to death. This slow method allegedly yielded more

43

tender meat, but it looked cruel. The chicken died slowly, flapping its wings, eyes glaring at its executioner.

The second method involved chopping off its head with an axe. This was messy but quick. The dumb chicken never knew what hit it. My mother preferred the axe, but Grandmaman Blanchette was a staunch believer in the slow knife.

I'd stand about fifty feet from the garage, close enough to watch the actions of the executioner and observe the morbid effects on the helpless victim. I was a rubbernecker, curious about the unfolding tragedy but always left pale with discomfort.

"Is it dead yet?" I'd ask Maman, repulsed by the sight of the unlucky bird hanging upside down on the hook, its life fluid seeping into the reddening earth below. When I thought it was dead, it would inevitably twitch a wing or open its beak in silence as if to launch a denunciation at its tormentor.

Once it was over, my mother would often ask the kids to strip its feathers. This was a revolting chore. Maman would pour boiling water on the cadaver to soften the skin, and the boiled feathers would emit a pungent odor. Then we'd yank the feathers from their roots with our hands, a loud ripping sound permeating the air with every pull.

At times, the threat was to the life of a family pet, serving to emphasize the fragility of the animal kingdom. One such pet was Princess. Princess was a small black and white dog that we adored; it was about the size of a large cat. It had no discernible breed, no doubt a mongrel, like the rest of our pets.

Our second neighbor, the Moreau family, had a female dog about the size of a German shepherd. Mrs. Moreau was visiting my mother one summer day when we were startled by a noisy commotion outside. Alarmed by the growls, I ran to the living room window just in time to see Spotté, the harebrained Moreau dog, shaking its head violently.

"What's in its mouth?" my mother asked in a panicky tone.

"Oh no, it's Princess!" Lucette screamed out.

Princess's face and neck were locked in the deadly jaws of the jealous Spotté, who swung its head left and right in a furious attempt to murder our favorite pet. Everyone ran outside in a mad dash to halt the brutal attack, but it was too late. Our little pet lay on the gravel road in a pool of blood. It had a hole in its head, a punctured eye, and a mangled neck. And it was making pathetic whining sounds that ripped our hearts out.

L-R: Lucette, Denise, and Doris with our dog, Princess.

We moved Princess to the cow stable, where it lay on a burlap bag struggling for its life. It would try desperately to lift its head but was paralyzed from its injuries, squealing high-pitched moans that sent shivers up my spine. There wasn't a dry eye in the stable. By the time I got up the next morning, Princess was dead.

"I'll kill Spotté myself," Lucette said, baring her teeth in anger.

We all wanted revenge. Our hate for Spotté had never been so great. We could taste blood. We longed to see its furry head poised on the tip of a lance, left to be devoured by the crows. It only seemed fair that Spotté be destroyed. After all, that's what they did when a dog mauled a child, and this mutt had murdered our family pet in cold blood.

But nothing happened to Spotté; the Moreau family downplayed the gross injustice to protect their murderous dog. My sister Lucette pleaded with my parents to take action, but they knew that no good could possibly come out of intimidating close neighbors, so nothing was done. Spotté would continue brutalizing our neighborhood for years.

A few years later, our dog Puppé would also have a close call with destiny. It was July, and I was eight years old. My father was driving the Massey-Ferguson tractor, cutting hay in one of the fields that adjoined the apple orchard. I was standing on the tractor behind his seat, leaning against the inside fender in my usual place.

Puppé loved to watch us working in the fields. The sound of the farming machinery drove him to a frenzied pace. He'd run in large circles at top speed, eyes wild with excitement, ears flapping back against his head, and barking merrily with approval. This time was no exception; he sprang in tight circles around the tractor at lightning speed.

The hum of the sickle mower was suddenly interrupted by the unmistakable sound of pain-filled dog yelping. My father heard it too. He immediately stopped the tractor and shut down the engine, and then he tried to trace the origin of the sound. Puppé had run into the sharp blades of the mower, leaving a trail of blood in his wake. But he was nowhere to be found.

"Go check the barn. I'll check the garage," my father said. The barn and garage were his customary resting places, but we could find no trace of Puppé there.

My father finally found the injured animal hiding behind the chicken coop, licking his serious wounds. He was scared and unfriendly, baring his teeth at my father when he tried to approach. One of his hind legs had nearly been amputated; it was hanging by a thread.

I had the ominous feeling that Puppé would die that night, suffering a fate similar to Princess. Not sure what to do, my father decided to wrap his damaged leg with cloth, hoping this would keep out the infection and absorb the blood flow. Then we left. Calling a veterinarian was not an option; it would have been a frivolous expenditure that we couldn't afford. Heck, we rarely went to the doctor ourselves.

"We have to leave him alone now," Papa said.

We hadn't seen Puppé for days. I suspected that he'd gone off somewhere to die and braced myself to face the loss of my favorite family pet.

"Do you think Puppé is dead?" I asked Maman.

"I don't know. He was scared. Maybe he's hiding till his wounds heal."

I was outside a few days later when I spotted Puppé galloping in my direction. I was moved to tears. His rear leg lay useless, hanging in midair like some shrunken appendage, but he was still able to run like hell on just three legs. He ran around me in wide circles at high speed, as if boasting of his miraculous recovery. Puppé was back.

We were poor, but I didn't know it. I had always linked poverty with starvation. Since we were well fed, I had no reason to believe that we were poor. After all, we were no different than the neighbors and the majority of our relatives.

My older siblings had taken full-time jobs to supplement the family income, while they continued to labor on the farm mornings, evenings, and weekends. I'd seen them turn over their weekly pay to my father; that's what all farmers did in those days.

But I knew that my Aunt Lina, my mother's younger sister, had a tougher life than the rest of us. I'd seen the evidence with my own eyes. Her son Rénald was in my class at school; it was impossible not to notice his shabby clothes and the gaping holes in his shoes that exposed feet without socks. And my beady eyes hadn't missed the startling fact that his little sister often lacked underpants beneath her tattered dress.

One day, Rénald was sent home from school for having inadequate shoes. I felt sorry for my cousin; poverty was certainly not his fault. The rain was pouring down in buckets, and he had no galoshes over his shoes, a blatant violation of the school dress code. Not only did he lack galoshes, but the sole on one of his drenched shoes was almost torn off, making a loud slapping noise against the polished floor tiles. Rénald was gone for an hour and returned with black electrical tape around the tip of the offending shoe, causing the kids to laugh even harder at his plight.

I got along well with Rénald, but my naughty deeds paled in comparison to his. My cousin had the personality of a used-car salesman, often making boastful, exaggerated claims. This is the same kid who taught me silly lyrics to the tune of "Le Sauvage du Nord":

> *Ton portrait que tu m'as donné,*
> *Je l'ai jeté dans le potte.*
> *Et toutes les fois que je vais pisser,*
> *Ton portrait gigote.*

> Your photo that you gave me,
> I threw away in the crapper.
> Now every time I take a pee,
> I see your face flutter.

"Come to my house for lunch tomorrow," Rénald said one day at recess. My mother always prepared a bagged lunch for me, but the kids in town could eat lunch at home.

Enticed by his generosity, I accepted the offer. The next day, we playfully trotted across town to his house at noon. But I regretted the mistake almost as soon as we crossed the threshold into the kitchen. My Aunt Lina was surprised to see me; my cousin had never told her about the invitation. I was an unexpected guest.

After she had scoured the kitchen cabinets in search of food, she bashfully admitted that she had nothing to feed us except leftover bread. So, our lunch consisted of a slice of bread with a sprinkle of sugar on top. And since there were no chairs in the house, she invited me to sit on the kitchen table while I munched on my bread.

"You didn't ask your mother, did you?" I said as we walked back to school.

"She must have forgotten," he replied. But I knew better. The incident had further lowered my confidence in his words, and I never accepted his invitations again.

Almost everyone in the little farming community of St-Gérard was more or less poor. Economic times were tough, jobs were scarce, and families struggled to feed their own. I had no idea that we were constantly pushing our credit limit at the grocery store. My father tried to make regular payments against our growing debt, leaving little else in the coffer. I'd sometimes find Maman crying over a letter. I didn't realize then that her tears were due to creditors threatening to repossess our meager assets.

"What's the matter, Maman?" I'd ask.

"Oh it's nothing—just a letter from Caza." Caza was the name of the clothing vendor who sold my parents their better clothing. His merchandise was of better quality and higher priced, the kind of clothes reserved for Sunday Mass, weddings, and funerals.

Some of the less respectable store owners in town occasionally took advantage of the farmers. When the family debt was too far in arrears, the store owner would threaten legal action. The outcome was predictable; the family would donate the only worthwhile asset at their disposal: a parcel of land. This had happened to Grandpapa Côté.

In a bad year, these unscrupulous men accumulated significant amounts of land. They'd hold on to the property until market conditions improved, and then sell it off at a hefty profit. This practice approached thievery, but farmers had no choice but to cooperate. The merchants had the power to shatter credit ratings, further endangering the family.

We never lacked for food, though—my parents made sure of that. We ate simple yet satisfying meals. Most meals included some kind of meat and boiled potatoes. Potatoes were the main staple of our diet, playing the same role as sticky rice in Japan. My mother usually prepared dark gravy to give the bland potatoes flavor.

We had little clothing, but that never bothered me; I didn't know any better. My school clothing consisted of one pair of pants and two shirts. Another pair of pants was reserved for Sunday Mass and special occasions, while a single pair of shoes serviced both school and church. Most of my clothes were hand-me-downs.

Our families may have been poor, but the kids lacked for nothing. Nature furnished numerous "toys" at no charge, and if those weren't enough, we made our own.

Kite flying was a popular summertime game. We built our own kites, making the frames from small sticks held together with coarse twine. The sail was made of brown paper bags that we glued to the stick frame. And the tail consisted of knotted rag strips. These contraptions flew passably well, but were highly susceptible to tearing.

From time to time, we'd assemble a huge version of this kite—still made of paper—and attempt manned flight off the roof of the chicken coop. Every effort was rewarded with a precipitous nosedive back to earth. Undeterred, we'd climb back up on the chicken coop and repeat the experiment amidst a chorus of clucking sounds.

I once thought we had won a little red fire engine, the kind with pedals and a silver bell with a pull rope. Since I was the only kid in our household small enough to use it, this would have become *my* personal toy. The Brunelle family store was raffling off this dream toy to attract customers, and my parents had filled out an application.

On raffle day, the winning number traveled over telephone lines at dazzling speed. My mother was standing in the kitchen comparing the winning number to her ticket stub, as I stood at her side watching with great anticipation.

"We've got it!" she exclaimed, as bodies rushed to her side.

I gasped at our amazing luck: *we won the beautiful fire engine!* Without waiting another minute, I rushed through the screen door onto the porch and ran down the steps to share the good news with my brother Pierre. There were tears in my eyes as I imagined myself sitting behind the little steering wheel, the envy of the kids in town.

Unaffected by my startling news, Pierre headed for the kitchen to verify the accuracy of the lofty claim. He returned moments later with no hint of a smile.

"It's the wrong number," he said. *What?* "Maman read it wrong."

I ran back inside the house just to make sure he wasn't lying; he unfortunately wasn't. Calm had been restored in the kitchen, but for me, the afternoon was ruined beyond repair: I had lost the only thing I had ever won.

Santa didn't bring much either. We rarely received individual presents; there was usually a single present under the tree for the whole family. Santa once brought us a family toboggan. Another time, he brought us a badminton set. We had to wait the torturous months till spring before we could enjoy this unseasonable present.

My early memories of Christmas are not of opening presents; unwrapping gifts was not an important family ritual. More so, they involve family gatherings and the giddy atmosphere that engulfed our spirits throughout the festive Holiday season.

My first personal Christmas present arrived when I was six years old. I had expressed an interest in stuffed animals, never expecting my wish to be fulfilled. My parents bought me a black and white teddy bear. It had perky ears, a rubbery nose, and a gaping mouth shaped in a pleasant half-smile.

Following the tradition established by my brother Jacques, I named the stuffed animal Teddé. From that day forward, Teddé accompanied me everywhere. Whenever his white fur got too dirty, my mother would take him away for a week, empty out the stuffing, wash it, and hang it out to dry. But he never came back quite the same; the redistribution of stuffing always changed his shape and appearance ever so slightly.

One day, I caught my brother Pierre defacing Teddé. I couldn't imagine anything more rotten than bringing harm to my precious stuffed friend. Not surprisingly, Pierre was assisted by my cousin Christian. They were busy smearing red lipstick on his rubber face and lips when I saw them. And they were snickering even as I entered the room.

"*Maudit fou!*" ("Damn fool") I screamed. The two boys just laughed.

My mother's lipstick had permanently stained the rubber on Teddé's face, serving as a constant reminder of my brother's devilish wrongdoings.

The stress of raising a large family in unsettling times put a severe strain on Maman. She fretted constantly over the bills, panicking at every threatening letter. My father, on the other hand, rarely worried about debt. Unlike his insecure wife, he exuded a reckless confidence that seemed to say, "No problem." But my mother worried enough for both of them.

Maman was hospitalized on several occasions. One day, when I was about five, my father abruptly ordered me to go upstairs. I sat on the top landing and listened while my mother sobbed uncontrollably and Papa addressed her in a calm and monotone voice. Days later, he drove her to the hospital in Sherbrooke, where she remained for weeks.

"What's wrong with Maman?" I asked my father.

"It's her nerves," he replied vaguely.

"How long will she stay?"

"Until she's better," is all he said.

I never went to see her in the hospital. I missed her terribly and worried about her health even as a five-year-old. But kids weren't allowed contact with hospital patients, and so it was futile for me to accompany my father on his visits to Sherbrooke.

When I was six, Maman was hospitalized yet again. I briefly stayed with my Uncle Adrien and Aunt Muguette, who lived on a farm in the town of Disraeli. I loved those playful and good-natured cousins; several were close to my age.

It was Sunday when my aunt announced they were planning to visit my mother at the hospital that afternoon. They would travel the fifty miles to Sherbrooke in their old Chevrolet pickup truck with rounded fenders. It could seat three people comfortably.

"Would you like to come?" my aunt said with a sympathetic look. I nodded, thrilled at the prospect of seeing Maman again. "You can't come inside, but you'll see her at the window." That wasn't exactly what I had hoped for, but at least I'd get to see her again.

I rode the distance in their old truck, squeezed between my aunt and her eldest son. Once we reached the hospital, my aunt and uncle went inside, leaving us boys alone in the truck with a bottle of cola and strict orders not to budge.

My uncle soon returned, moving his truck to a better vantage point in the parking lot. We all stepped outside. He lifted me onto the hood of the pickup and then pointed to a third-floor window just as Maman made an appearance. She looked like the Blessed Virgin, dressed in a blue bathrobe and wearing an angelic smile. She waved.

I waved back to the fragile figure in the window. My eyes brimmed with tears and my lower lip quavered uncontrollably. She looked like the most beautiful woman in the world. I struggled to keep my composure, trying hard not to make sobbing noises.

My uncle was usually a nice person, but he had zero tolerance for tears. I'd seen him beat his own kids—once with a belt—after catching them crying without good reason. His generation subscribed to the philosophy that parents had to toughen their kids with discipline. Since tears were a blatant admission of weakness, he'd respond to them with a severe reprimand and the occasional beating. So I kept the tears to myself.

Maman stood at the window waving for a few minutes and then disappeared again. Sadness enveloped me as I wondered how long it would be before she came home.

My cousin made the mistake of arousing his father's temper as we were leaving Sherbrooke. He was still sipping his cola bottle through a straw, making slurping noises. Without a word, my uncle rolled down his window, ripped the bottle from his son's hands, and flung it out of the truck with all his might. My eyes followed the trajectory of the ill-fated bottle as it hit the paved sidewalk and struck the foundation of a brick home, smashing into pieces.

The ride home was silent and somber, as none of us were willing to risk another demonstration of adult petulance. I longed for Maman more than ever.

I witnessed affluence for the first time in 1960. I had just turned eight. Denise was fifteen, working as a live-in nanny for a well-to-do family in Sherbrooke. She'd gotten the job with help from my Uncle Paul-Émile, who apparently knew the family.

The Blouin family owned the old Hotel Normandie in the center of Sherbrooke, along with an adjacent restaurant. Given his lifelong reputation as a lady's man, it's likely that my uncle had met the owners during one of his many adulterous trips to the city.

Denise was responsible for babysitting, washing clothes, cleaning house, and feeding the four Blouin children. Charles was a precocious twelve-year-old, Suzanne was nine, Richard was six, and Lynn was around five. Charles acted like a wise guy in front of us younger kids, but all the other Blouin children were pleasant enough.

Over the summer of 1960, Denise brought Suzanne, Richard, and Lynn to our farm for overnight visits, alternating between the three. My sister always came home one day a week. She'd arrive by train on Sunday morning and head back to Sherbrooke the next day.

Suzanne was a pretty girl with long blond hair and a light complexion. She was always dressed to perfection, and her wardrobe struck me as excessive. She was the first to visit our farm and seemed unimpressed with the sights and smells of the country.

The next kid to visit was Richard. He was a soft-spoken boy dressed in white shorts and sandals—not exactly ideal clothing for romping around the farm. The smell of dust and manure often caused him to pinch his nostrils shut. Nevertheless, Richard had an adventurous spirit and we got along pretty well.

"Maybe you can come visit *our* house next time," he said while we played.

"I'd like that, but I don't know if my parents will let me."

"I'm sure *my* parents wouldn't mind," he added. I was suddenly enthralled with the prospect of spending the weekend in Sherbrooke. I'd never slept in a strange home before, and the description given by Denise made this place sound like a castle.

It felt like forever, but the visit did finally materialize in November. My parents agreed to drive me to Sherbrooke. Denise would give us all a tour of the house, and then I'd stay behind until Sunday, when we'd both take the train back to St-Gérard.

It was a Saturday morning when my father drove us to Sherbrooke. I was so excited that I could barely contain myself. Not only would I get to spend a night in the big city of Sherbrooke, but I would also ride a passenger train for the first time in my life.

The Blouin family lived in a modern house in the north end of town. It sat on a corner lot in a plush residential neighborhood, across the street from a golf course. As we pulled up to the house, my eyes were darting side to side, soaking up the marvelous sights. I'd never seen a street so beautiful in my life. It was entirely paved, and it even had sidewalks.

Denise greeted us at the door. Kisses were exchanged as if it had been years since our last contact, the unfamiliar setting encouraging family intimacy. The Blouin parents were not home, so Denise had no qualms about showing us around the house.

I found the place amazing. By today's standards, the two-story home would probably rank as an upper middle-class home. But compared with our old farmhouse, this place was a veritable chateau. It had an attached garage, an in-ground swimming pool in the backyard, and a finished basement—something I'd never seen before.

The sunken living room was a beautiful space with bouncy wall-to-wall carpeting and a redbrick fireplace in the center. Denise told us that kids were not allowed in that formal room; it was strictly used to entertain business and special guests.

"You mean nobody uses this room?" I asked. The idea of a fabulous room kept locked and off-limits to most people was a foreign concept to me.

The house also had a formal dining room, something else I'd never seen. Here again, the room was reserved for special occasions, the family taking its meals in the kitchen.

The flooring in the house alternated between thick carpeting and shiny hard-wood. Compared with the old linoleums in our farmhouse, these floors were dazzling. I spent the weekend walking around in my stocking feet to avoid dirtying them.

The house had a bathroom on the first floor and another full bath on the second floor where the bedrooms were located. The upstairs bathroom even had a bathtub with a showerhead, luxuries that we'd never experience on the farm.

Each of the Blouin kids had their own bedroom too. Richard's room had vertical bunk beds, something I'd seen only on television. I spent the night sleeping in the lower bunk in Richard's room, down the hall from the fancy bathroom.

And their basement was nothing like our old dirt cellar; it was finished, like the rest of the house. That lower space included a large family room complete with television set, a bar stocked with liquor, and a dedicated laundry room.

The lower level also held a locked freezer that lay on its side like some mysterious sarcophagus. Denise had the key; she opened it just to show us that it was stocked with every imaginable frozen delicacy a kid could want. It contained various flavors of popsicles, ice cream cups, ice cream sandwiches, and other frozen consumables I'd never seen before. Denise had permission to unlock the freezer every afternoon, long enough for each child to pluck a frozen item from its generous belly.

My parents and siblings finally left as Denise embarked on her Saturday housecleaning chores, and I was eager to start my own private adventure. Charles vacuumed the floor, while the rest of us hovered around Denise offering to lend a hand.

Suzanne later escorted me out for a walk around the neighborhood. As we strolled, she supplied an enthusiastic narration about the surroundings. I was astonished at how pristine and clean the place looked compared to our messy farm grounds.

"This is our pool," Suzanne said as we circled the backyard. "I dive off the board," she added while I stared in amazement at the scary diving board. The pool was already winterized, its blue innards hidden by a large tarp that stretched across the surface.

A sudden feeling of inadequacy settled in my gut. Here I was, afraid of water like a big baby, while Suzanne and her siblings boasted about diving off the board and swimming like salmon in the large pool buried deep in their backyard.

I saw Mr. Blouin for the first and only time on Saturday evening. He came home after supper, introduced himself with a compassionate smile, and almost immediately ran off downstairs toward the lower family room and bar.

"Let's go play with my father," Richard said.

I was shy with strangers, so I cowered behind the Blouin kids as we made our way down the stairs. When we entered the family room, Mr. Blouin was slouching back on the couch, sipping from a highball glass and lazily watching a football game on television.

The three kids rushed up to their father, climbed on the couch, and started tickling him, giggles instantly emanating from their mouths. The father responded by tickling each child in return, their gleeful screams and laughs penetrating the air.

"You can come and play too," the father said, stopping momentarily to look in my direction. I was sitting quietly on a chair some ten feet away. They soon resumed their play, the four of them rolling on the carpet in a fit of giggles.

But I was unable to approach. After all, this was not my father; I had no right to share their intimacy. I actually felt sorry for myself. My father had never played with me like that—not even once. Papa was an aloof man who did little with his kids.

As I watched the Blouin kids engage in carefree play, I realized that there was a huge chasm between this home and ours in St-Gérard. The difference had less to do with the beautiful furniture and carpeting, and much more to do with family values. My father clung to the traditional role of his ancestors—kids were the mother's responsibility.

I finally met Mrs. Blouin early Sunday morning. She casually announced to Denise that she was heading out to check on the hotel and was bringing Richard and me to their restaurant for breakfast. *Wow.* We never went to restaurants at home. The only food establishment in town was a hamburger stand opened in the summer. On rare occasions, we'd stop there to sample the yummy French fries sprinkled with salt and vinegar.

She drove to the hotel and walked us into the diner-style restaurant next door. Before rushing out, Mrs. Blouin lifted Richard and me onto the round swivel benches at the counter, instructing the short-order chef to make us whatever we wanted.

The cook had known Richard forever and seemed to predict what the boy would want for breakfast. Richard agreed to an egg, some bacon, and a slice of toast. But I had no idea what I wanted or what they served in these places. Breakfast at home always consisted of toast with a sweet topping. On the rare occasions that we had overnight visitors, Maman would make sunny-side-up eggs and bacon, but that was about once a year.

"You want some eggs, little boy?" the cook asked. I sheepishly nodded yes.

"One or two?" he continued.

"Two."

"How about bacon?" he inquired. I nodded.

"How many toast?"

"Four," I replied in a soft voice.

I loved toast. I may have weighed about fifty pounds, but I could eat a boatload of toast. I usually had two or three for breakfast, but I had eaten as many as seven in a single sitting. The heavyset cook gave out a hearty belly laugh, which I took as an indication that my answer exceeded expectations for an eight-year-old.

The yummy smell of the grill filled my head even before our portions arrived. My plate was heaping with eggs, bacon, and pan-fried potatoes. The conspicuous mountain of toast sat in a side plate on the counter. I ate everything. Since my order had provoked laughter, I made a point of proving my appetite to the cook.

Mrs. Blouin drove my sister and me to the train station around noon, and I said goodbye to the Blouin kids. It turns out I would never see them again. Denise would permanently leave their service not long after my memorable visit.

We boarded the train, and Denise let me sit at the window. The train ride was a dream. The unfamiliar sensation of riding on rails, the sporadic sound of the horn, and the blurry passage of landscape kept me busy for the duration.

I was disappointed to see it all end. As we pulled into St-Gérard, my parents were standing on the platform. My sojourn had been brief but long enough to tease me with the sweet taste of affluence. Our old farm was no longer the best place on earth to live.

5

A Passing Cloud

My father was like a passing cloud, a white mass floating in tranquil passivity. We took his presence for granted until the rain came. And then you knew he was there.

Papa was a small man, measuring 5'5" and weighing just under 120 pounds most of his life. His nose was long and pointy and curved slightly downward, like those I'd seen on distinguished ancient Romans in textbook images. He had a wide and thin mouth, a characteristic he would pass down to succeeding generations, and sported a full head of hair, parted on one side. His hair was dark brown—much like his bespectacled eyes—and laced with silver in later years.

He walked with a slight stoop, his head held high like a German pointer giving chase, the curvature of his spine emphasizing the pointy butt that dragged behind him like a little caboose. I had inherited that same posterior, causing a little tent to form near the back flap of my jackets. My father had moved through life at one consistent speed: slow. His calm and confident demeanor could have diffused a riot scene.

I knew my father as a quiet and docile man with a droning voice, and he rarely showed emotion. But when he did, you were in deep shit. My mother was the disciplinarian in our family; my father was a pushover with a gentle heart. I felt blessed on those rare occasions when my mother threatened us with "wait till your father gets home." As I don't recall a single beating at the hands of Papa, her warning was a sort of reprieve.

Given his sturdy emotional makeup, raising my father's fury was a regrettable accomplishment. I know because I managed to do it several times, with consequences I still remember in vivid detail. It's not that his treatment was harsh—it rarely involved corporal punishment—but seeing him lose his composure was like watching a saint suddenly sprout horns; he'd transform into a stranger.

My mother and I were sitting side by side at the kitchen table one weekday evening; she was helping me with my arithmetic homework. I was eight years old, frustrated by seemingly unsolvable problems and the spiteful teacher who had assigned them.

"What's the answer to this question?" she asked, pointing at my homework paper.

"I don't know."

"Well, you have to try," she said, traces of exasperation showing in her voice.

"I can't figure it out."

"I can help you, but you have to do the work."

"I don't feel like it," I whined in a most uncooperative tone of voice. I'd lost my patience with arithmetic, having grown ornery as darkness descended on the farm. My father was sitting nearby in the wooden rocking chair, silent and aloof as always.

I never even saw him coming. I felt his presence behind my chair just as he reached down for my waist and extracted me from the seat in a tempest. He then carried me off under his arm like a Frenchman carrying a crusty baguette.

I glanced back at Maman from my unnatural stance as terror settled in my brain. I saw the corners of her mouth turn up ever so slightly, and I knew my fate was sealed; she wouldn't be coming to my rescue after all. That facial gesture told me that although she didn't approve of my father's angry display, she wouldn't intervene on my behalf. It was my fault that I'd pushed past the limits of parental tolerance; I had it coming.

I knew exactly where we were going: he was taking me to bed. We reached the steep wooden staircase and he started climbing the steps with a determined gait. I didn't make a sound, aware that anything I said would only aggravate my already precarious state.

Once we reached the top of the stairs, he dropped me in a sitting position on the landing with my feet hovering above the top step. That sudden drop felt more like a fall, my ass cheeks banging hard against the linoleum flooring. Kneeling on one knee, he reached for my left sneaker with the intention of undoing my shoelace. As his stubby fingers yanked hard on the loop, his progress was halted by a knot in the lace.

Wasting no time, he reached into the back pocket of his trousers and pulled out the multi-purpose pocket knife he'd been carrying on his person for as long as I could remember. The hair on the back of my neck rose as I watched him unfurl the shiny metal blade with a brisk motion that was uncharacteristic of the man I knew.

I usually trusted my father, but in that fleeting moment, I really wondered if the anger had turned him into a murderous lunatic. *What is he doing with that blade?* I had heard of fathers going stark mad, sometimes even killing their families in a fit of rage. Would I be like Isaac in the Bible story, the young son of Abraham who was to be sacrificed like a lamb? Except this time, would my father finish the job once and for all?

The answer came moments later when he slipped the cutting edge of the blade over the tongue of my shoe, severing all turns in the lace with one upward thrust. He then repeated the show of force against the second sneaker without checking for knots.

He flung my limp sneakers and damp stockings on the landing adjacent to my bed. Pulling me to my feet with rough hands, he then stripped off my trousers and shirt in a blur of rapid hand movements, throwing the clothing on the floor near the banister.

I found myself standing on the landing in my white cotton underpants, scared to budge an inch without a directive. He carried me to the bed, whipped off the top covers with one arm, and dropped me down on the mattress with a bounce. I lay on my back as he pulled the blankets back over my supine form and receded back down the stairs to the kitchen and my mother. Not a word had been spoken throughout the ordeal.

By this time, my heart was beating in a frenzy of knocks and my breath was shallow from fright. He had never struck me, but the experience felt every bit as intense as a beating. Silent tears flowed as I lay motionless, already regretting my crankiness. The white puffy cloud had momentarily turned dark to hurl a bolt of lightning.

On occasion, the sound of blasphemy would portend Papa's rising anger like lava fountains before the big volcanic eruption. My father seldom swore in the presence of his children, so I always reacted to his vulgar cues with the agility of a panicky deer, heading for the nearest exit in search of the great outdoors.

"*Mon p'tit criss!*" he'd mutter. On the surface, this expression translates to a benign "my little Christ." But in our colloquial French, these few words were hardly a compliment—they were reserved for angry moments and usually preceded parental consequences. They struck terror in the heart of every naughty child, especially when the word Christ was made to sound more like *Crrrrissss*, the letter R rolled and the S hissed with irate emphasis.

The most flaming French-Canadian blasphemes were always religious in nature. Unlike the popular American swears, with their strong sexual overtones, French Canadians prefer abusing religion to relieve their nervous tension. Québec had been a staunch French Catholic colony from the beginning; I suspect that our immigrants from France had once launched these same curses against the domineering Jesuits.

No religious figure or object was immune from blasphemy. In addition to *criss* (Christ), popular swear words included *viarge* (virgin), *calvère* (calvary), *calice* (chalice), *baptême* (baptism), *tabarnak* (tabernacle), *ostie* (host), *ciboire* (ciborium), and *sacrément* (sacrament). Since *calice* sounded too tame when delivered in its normal intonation, it was always pronounced *kawlice*, its first syllable stretched as needed to suit the nature of the offense. *Kawlice* signaled mild frustration, but *kawwwwlice* conveyed total outrage. And for dramatic effect, the profanity was often spoken with inflections that resembled yodeled cries. All swears had the same effect on my young brain: they sent me the unambiguous message, "Flee the scene—now."

When the seriousness of the provocation called for a more ardent response, blasphemes could be linked together, sometimes in long chains. Uttering a loud *viarge* might be adequate for coping with a stubbed toe, but it would have been wimpy in the face of malfunctioning farm equipment. Here, the circumstances would call for something like "*maudit calvère de criss de viarge,*" the preposition *de* serving to link the swear words into an uninterrupted religious litany.

In addition, all good swears could be prefixed with *maudit* (as in *maudit calvère*) or with *saint* (as in *saint sacrément*). These adornments would automatically double the offending power of any spoken profanity, sort of like a double-win payout in a game of Blackjack. So, whenever my father uttered, "*Mon p'tit criss de kawlice,*" I knew he meant business, stimulating my swift exodus to escape the alarming threat.

There were also softer versions of these swears for milder occasions and more gentle personalities. These milder cusses were often spoken by women, who didn't dare venture out into the blasphemous world of men. But the words still managed to convey an earthy sense of frustration. They included *mautadit, cibole, tabarouate, tabarnouch, calvette,* and *véreux,* words still phonetically linked to their more offensive cousins.

I'm convinced that French is the best swearing language. The harsh sound of French consonants vaulting off the front palate makes Quebecois French quite effective for delivering profanity. Intonations like "*maudit criss de kawlice*" can resonate through the air with the impact of shattering glass. That sound still gives me goose bumps.

Despite the occasional flare-up, my father was not an impetuous man. On the contrary, his speech, body language, and gait exuded a soothing calmness that made me feel secure to be under his care. He seemed to float through life at an undaunted pace, giving the impression that he stood largely unaffected by life's little vicissitudes. My mother, on the other hand, was a nervous soul stripped early of her self-confidence, her soul wounded by the ruthless behavior of insensitive men.

It's not too surprising that my grandfather's emotional tirades would inspire his older sons to make their own decrepit contributions. Teenagers Théodore and Henri, both older than my mother, were habitual offenders. With more than a dozen people congregating at the table for meals, it became a family custom for the men to lob insults at the girls. The older daughters became the butt of their jokes, enduring constant mockery.

The traditional breakfast fare at the Côté house was crepes. These were served every morning except for Sunday, when the family was rewarded with beans and homemade bread after walking home from Church. Being the eldest daughters, my mother and her sister Juliette were assigned to breakfast detail every day, sitting alone at the kitchen table long after the rest of the family had satisfied their appetites.

Some mornings, Théodore and Henri took great pains to prolong the work of their sisters, each ordering up to fifteen crepes in deliberate acts of harassment. By the time the two sisters sat down at breakfast, there was often nothing left to eat, the teenage boys having exhausted the supply of crepes, their success celebrated with donkey laughs.

When he worked at all, Théodore labored as a log driver five months out of the year. The rest of the time, he stayed home doing practically nothing, served three square meals a day by the very sisters he enjoyed badgering. He was the splitting image of his father, mirroring both his physical appearance and his biases.

The girls might have discounted the verbal abuse from their older brothers if the boys had demonstrated an ounce of moral fiber. But they exhibited glaring character defects that made the relentless taunts even more insulting. My grandfather did nothing to interfere with their boyhood fun, as if training his lion cubs to attack their prey.

Théodore indulged in binge drinking, consuming alcohol until he passed out from toxemia. The habit almost killed him, as he once spent a cold night lying facedown in the street, the resulting pneumonia threatening his life. But that harmful habit was not inherited from his father; my grandfather never drank, even as a young man.

For his part, Henri played the role of dimwitted sidekick, his cackling laugh piercing the air at mealtime. He was a cowardly boy whose main ambition was to escape work itself. Henri had also inherited the worst physical traits from all sides of the family: a short and stumpy frame, a bulbous red nose, beady eyes, large lips, a high forehead reaching back to the crest of his skull, and a raspy voice that expectorated blasphemes along with throat-clearing noises. To top it off, he was also an avid spitter, no doubt reacting to the cigarette smoke he'd been inhaling since the age of ten, rolling the tobacco in plain brown paper when cigarette paper was out of reach.

But it seems that Uncle Henri was not in the least hampered by his plain looks. For reasons that befuddled the envious men who tracked his romantic interludes, he always managed to attract beautiful women to his side. He'd been engaged on three separate occasions, aborting the relationships at the last minute as if wanting to sample all the fruits of matrimony without succumbing to its onerous commitments.

Rumors about the source of his romantic appeal abounded, with many settling on the theory that his better endowments lay south of the bellybutton. The credibility of this rumor was fueled by his crotch grabbing antics. All his life, my uncle unabashedly adjusted his "package" in public just about every ten minutes, like a baseball pitcher preparing to throw a game-ending curveball. It was as if he wore boxer shorts three sizes too large, prompting him to frequently rearrange the angle of his generous form.

Both boys spent much of their teenage years living a sedentary life on the farm, protected by a doting father who turned a blind eye to the shortcomings of his progeny. Driven by the irresistible pull of testosterone, they regularly traveled together like Mutt and Jeff in search of immoral deeds. Every November, they'd leave the farm for weekends of hunting, equipped with food, rifles, and...freshly-pressed suits.

"Why the suit?" their siblings would ask.

"It's for Sunday Mass," the boys would answer. Everyone except my grandparents knew that hunting was a front for their weekend frolics with loose women.

From the age of fourteen, my mother and her sister Juliette were assigned the humiliating chore of washing and grooming the two brothers who taunted them. The routine was carried out at the kitchen counter every night after supper. The old farmhouse lacked both electricity and running water, so the girls had to pump water from the well, heat it in a kettle on the woodstove, and pour the hot water into the metal basin on the kitchen counter. The esteemed male adults would strip down to their waist, as the girls proceeded to wash their hair, face, underarms, and torso. Yet, the ingrate sons continued mocking and teasing even as they were being groomed by their sisters.

As soon as my mother announced her wedding engagement, the men in her family sought to escalate the ridicule and insults, many of which were directed at her fiancé. "With those big feet, you'll fall flat on your face in the church aisle," her father taunted, as his boys joined in with their maniacal laughter. It wasn't enough that they had destroyed her self-esteem; they were determined to pummel it to the very end.

My father's calm demeanor reminded me of a story Uncle Gérard, my father's brother, once told us. I never knew whether the account was real or fictional. It involved a man who lived in Garthby, a town situated about six miles from our farm. The man received a phone call from the police chief one tragic day while home for lunch.

"I'm sorry to inform you that your wife has been killed in a car accident," the chief said with regret in his voice. Having broken the devastating news, the chief then asked him if it would be possible to come identify the body.

"Well, I'll be down just as soon as I finish my lunch," the man replied.

Now, you can't be much calmer than that. Although my father would certainly have reacted differently under such terrible circumstances, the story nevertheless exemplified a breed of individual with nerves of steel. I considered my father in that category.

I admired my father's assuredness from an early age, since it was an attribute I lacked. My central nervous system had been wired more like my mother's, causing me to live in fidgety anticipation of trouble. My feelings were easily hurt by minor actions and words, quiet tears forming in my eyes in response to the smallest provocation.

In my family, Papa was the one to deal with the more stressful decisions and events. Before reaching the age of ten, I recall only one visit to the dentist and one visit to the doctor in Disraeli. In both cases, it was my father who escorted me for medical treatment, his soothing tone helping to lessen my paralyzing dread of doctors.

I was a six-year-old with an infected tooth. I'd never been to a dentist in my life; preventive care was a luxury we couldn't afford. At the time, it was customary to simply pull out the bad teeth when you reached the teenage years, replacing them with either a dental bridge or a full set of dentures, depending on the extent of the damage.

As he drove me to the dentist's office in Disraeli, my father dispensed a few monotone assurances. "It'll be fast and painless," he said. But I had a bad feeling when they escorted me into the stark room with the intimidating dentist chair, the threatening metal instruments glimmering behind the glass cabinet doors. The barber-like chair, the pure white garments, the stainless-steel instruments, and the blinding spotlight in my face made this place about as inviting as Frankenstein's laboratory.

The smiling nurse placed a padded board across the arms of the big chair and lifted my trembling body into a sitting position in preparation for the dreadful deed. The old dentist attempted to distract me with a little humor, but I found absolutely nothing worthy of laughter, my eyes locked onto the fancy pliers already poised in his large hand. One tug later and he was waving the offending tooth before my eyes as if it were some prized possession.

I tasted blood in my mouth moments before the face on the smiling nurse began fading into the background. Moments later, my vision was abruptly restored by an acrid stench invading my nostrils—the dentist was waving smelling salts at my nose.

My father had been in the room throughout my dental misadventure, an amused witness to my near-fainting incident. Although the circumstances were rather unfortunate, I nevertheless relished the unusual attention he was bestowing upon me. I rode home biting down on cotton swabs and bathing in the warmth of Papa's benevolence.

My visit to the doctor's office was somewhat less traumatic, possibly because the disease had already numbed my sense of reality. Once again, I was six years old, this time with a severe case of chickenpox. My body was covered with large blisters that oozed a cloudy liquid every time I scratched them. My mother was worried about the severity of the symptoms, so my father had taken me to the doctor in Disraeli.

"Do you go to school?" the friendly doctor asked me.

"Yes, I'm in first grade," I replied in a low voice, chronically bashful of strangers.

"Are you at the head or the tail of your class?" he asked to distract me from the hypodermic needle. I didn't understand that expression, so I guessed at the answer.

"The tail," I said, causing both the good doctor and Papa to chuckle.

The doctor then administered a shot in my butt to relieve the symptoms, as I lay facedown on the examination table with my trousers at half-mast.

On the way home, my father pulled into a small grocery store and plodded inside, returning a few minutes later with a box of animal crackers. We shared the crackers on the drive home while I enjoyed his uncharacteristic attention.

I was seven years old when a chimney fire threatened to engulf our old farmhouse. Creosote deposits had built up inside the chimney from burning wood through the long winter months. I still remember the rumble noise of the fire and the stifling stench of the gray smoke that permeated the clouded air inside the house.

"Take the kids to your father's house," Papa said calmly to my mother. It was around nine o'clock in the evening, and we were evacuating the house in case the chimney fire spread to the century-old building. There was no fire department in St-Gérard, so dealing with such emergencies fell to the owner, good neighbors, and nearby relatives.

We could see the scary flame and smoke rising out of the chimney as we walked the short distance to Grandpapa's house. Once there, my mother spent her time at the kitchen window, peering in the direction of our house while biting her nails with vigor.

It took several hours, but my father eventually came back to fetch us that night, telling us that it was safe to return to the house. I was in awe of his emotional steadiness, proud to be the son of a man who could remain unflappable during a harrowing ordeal. But I never told him this. My father was not the kind of man to show affection for his children, so we never expressed our mushy feelings. He was my protector, the person who made my world secure. It was my mother who dispensed the affection. My father was the rational left brain, while my mother played the part of the emotional right brain.

My father was remarkably calm. When I was thirteen, I suffered second- and third-degree burns in a scalding accident. It was lunchtime on a Saturday. I negligently bumped into my mother as she walked from the stove to the table carrying a large kettle of boiling water for tea. The kettle struck my right shoulder, leaving a second-degree burn in its wake, and then dropped to the floor as it spilled boiling water on my feet and right leg, resulting in third-degree burns. The skin on my leg was glued to the inside of my trousers like cheese on the inside cover of a pizza box, blood pouring out of the exposed flesh.

My mother reacted to the accident with remorseful tears, apologizing for the mistake that had been more mine than hers. While I ripped off my trousers to abate the pain, my mother kneeled on the floor to clean up the watery mess, the only response she could muster in her distressed state. Her self-esteem had been dealt yet another blow.

"Don't cry, Maman, it doesn't hurt much," I lied in a lame attempt to console her. But the pain was unbearable. It felt like my leg was on fire as the air bit into the raw flesh like acid, my eyes watery from the intensity of the discomfort.

Predictably, it was Papa who took charge of the panic-drenched situation. He fetched some white cloth to cover my wounds, and helped me hop on one leg to the car that would take me to the hospital. His pace was unruffled, as always, as if he saw the accident as little more than a minor inconvenience. "You'll be fine; it's no big deal," his confident bearing seemed to convey. He was our Rock of Gibraltar.

My father never played with his children; it was the same for all farmers. They worked from dawn to dusk just to feed their families and left childrearing to the mothers. That's how it was, and we expected nothing more. In the world of shared parenting, it seems strange to admit that I never played with my father, but it's true. The men of his generation had no time to befriend kids; life was too serious to indulge in wanton play.

Maman encouraged my father to be more active with his boys, at times suggesting that he take us to town on his weekend errands. But it rarely happened.

"What if I have a car accident?" he'd counter, suggesting that the hazard of taking his boys along might outweigh the benefits of the bonding experience. I suspect he didn't know what to do with us, and so masked the awkwardness in aloofness.

Maman was not only our nurturer and disciplinarian; she also served as an interpreter for her boys. As approaching my father directly would have been a brazen act, it was my mother who would relay the message if I needed something from Papa. It was as though Papa spoke Swahili while his sons understood only French.

I'd gone sliding on a pleasant winter day, lying flat on my belly in a little wooden sled with steel runners. After leaping over some hard bumps down the snow-covered hills, I made my way back to the house to use the bathroom. While standing over the toilet bowl, I immediately detected blood in my urine. It wasn't much, but it was enough to initiate a panic sequence in my brain. I ran out of the bathroom looking for Maman.

"I'm bleeding down there," I said to my mother, pointing my finger toward my fly. The ride down the slippery dips on my belly had apparently burst some blood vessels.

"I'll have your father look at it right away," she said before turning on her heels. She returned a few minutes later to tell me that she'd made the request; he should arrive momentarily to check on my…lower parts. (These regions were nameless.) I anxiously stood near the bathroom for about thirty minutes awaiting his arrival.

"I haven't seen Papa yet," I told my mother. She exhaled a puzzled "hmmm" and went off to find her husband, returning once more with a promise that he'd be there soon.

But he never came, the silent rejection leaving me confused. *Was he embarrassed to see my body?* I couldn't understand how modesty could overpower his concern for my health. I concluded that maybe he just didn't care enough to rise above the prudery.

"Has he come to see you yet?" Maman asked me about an hour later. She sounded annoyed with my answer. "Do you want me to go ask him again?" she said. I declined her offer, knowing that a third request would be just as futile as the first two. She offered to check me herself, but it was unnecessary; the bleeding had already stopped.

I threatened his modesty one last time as I approached puberty. Tiny blotches had appeared on the underside of my penis, and I was petrified that something was wrong. I'd heard vagaries from school chums about diseases that afflicted your weenie, and I wondered if I had caught one of these, as I was ignorant of their causes.

"I have some spots down below," I told Maman in private, pointing my index finger in the general direction of my crotch.

"I'll ask your father to check," she said. But just like the last time, Papa never even acknowledged my concern. I have no memory of my father seeing me naked. Nudity violated his immovable sense of modesty, which remained steadfast even when our health was at stake.

Papa was a devoted family man, the type who views his work as a job rather than a career. His occupation was merely a means to an end, an unpleasant necessity that took him away from his family and farm eight hours at a time. Given this mindset, he was not much of a professional role model for me. Nor did he pressure me to pursue a college education. If I had decided to settle down as a janitor after high school, he would have probably accepted my decision without argument. After all, a job was just a job.

"Do what you want," he often said.

Although my father was aloof with his children, he was the opposite with his wife. My parents were inseparable, apart only when absolutely necessary. Papa was the type of man who depended on the companionship of a woman. Had my mother died first, I suspect that he might have been counted among the men who perish a few months later, after abandoning all desire to live without a lifelong partner.

On rare occasions when my mother did leave his side for a day or two to visit a distant relative or attend a religious retreat (which she did as a young woman), my father would mope around the house aimlessly, lost without his devoted partner. Left alone, he was helpless, even skipping meals, as though it was frivolous to nourish a lonely body.

My parents were soul mates; their closeness was indeed impressive. I remember seeing them exchange signs of affection even as a young child. I must have been around five years old when the three of us were standing in the kitchen on a blustery winter day. My father had stayed home from work due to the harsh winter conditions.

Maman was standing at the kitchen window looking out at the storm while leaning back against my father, who had his arms coiled affectionately around her waist. They were talking softly and smiling at each other, the storm helping to foster a cozy intimacy. I hated seeing Papa ooze affection; this was *my* mother he was holding. So I tugged at Maman's legs in vain attempts to separate them. They laughed.

"What will you do when we're both gone?" my father teased, still clinging to my mother's waist. He asked this question more than once, eliciting the same answer from me each time: a loud, desperate sob. I knew that it would be impossible to survive without the care of Maman and the strength of Papa. My tearful replies made them giggle, adding insult to my injury—so I cried even harder.

My father's calm stature compensated well for my mother's nervous disposition. And her sensitivity softened his serious demeanor. They complemented each other like oil and vinegar, separate entities that mixed well to deliver a balanced relationship. They coexisted as a team without overpowering each other's differences.

Even close couples have their occasional spats. For my parents, the source of most altercations involved bills and cars. Raising a family of seven children on a low-income farm necessitated living off credit. We accumulated unpaid bills to buy groceries, clothing, and farm accessories.

My father seemed content to live on borrowed money, happy as a pig in mud. To Papa, accumulating interest was not a big deal, credit being a heavenly instrument. But my mother hated bills, unnerved by all financial obligations that hung over our heads. Papa exhibited little urgency to pay off debt, but Maman sought to eradicate it in a hurry. This major difference of opinion caused predictable clashes.

Papa at times chose to be discrete about new debt: he simply didn't tell her. This was always a bad idea, as some statement or overdue notice would inevitably come along to reveal the creditor, stirring her excitable nature and resulting in a tearful display.

Another source of annual disagreement between my parents involved automobiles. To my father, a car was a polished work of art. He'd been enamored with mechanical things since his teenage years, exuding an unbounded passion for cars most of his life. Papa gazed at a Dodge as though admiring a Cézanne painting; a Chevrolet might as well have been a fine Renoir; a Buick was like a precious Rembrandt; and, a Cadillac—the ultimate luxury car—was the equivalent of a Michelangelo fresco.

My father at age 18, with his first bicycle.

Admiring the cars was not so much the problem; it was the fact that he traded ours in every spring that spelled trouble. My mother fought and usually lost the battle of wits that preceded each swap. My father was like a calf released from the stable, exuberant with a sense of springtime freedom. The annual ritual drove my mother crazy.

My father was always armed with clever logic to justify trading in the family car. The excuses were kept vague so that no brave soul could ever deny or verify his claims. He'd say that the engine was running rough, as if total engine failure might occur at any time. Or perhaps the valves needed replacement—he'd discerned that from the engine noise. Or maybe the transmission was going—he could feel the gears slipping.

As a child, I learned to dismiss his trading excuses; we knew that he spewed them only when he was possessed by car demons. He was determined to rationalize his actions, but none of us took him seriously, even mocking his dubious declarations in private.

Papa's car-trading procedure involved orchestrated steps that gradually wore down my mother's resolve. When it came to automobiles, my father was a highly persistent man. If there had been such a thing, he could have won an Oscar for Best Actor in an Automotive Drama.

He'd begin the annual ritual by making subtle statements that expressed concern about the state of his automobile. Thus, the seed of doubt was planted. These concerns would be repeated as often as necessary to lay down the foundation for the next step.

The second step involved an innocent Sunday drive with my mother that just happened to traverse a used-car lot. By pure coincidence, this would be the same car lot that my father had visited alone on prior occasions. The fact that this very place held the latest object of his automotive fascination, the perfect cure for our current auto woes, would be a sheer stroke of luck. If my mother's mood allowed, he might even take her for a ride in his dream car, counting on the exhilarating experience to make an emotional appeal on his behalf.

With steps one and two out of the way, he was now at liberty to bring up the option of trading the family automobile, eager for the slightest sign of agreement from Maman. At this stage, she had to be very careful with her words and body language; he could take a barely discernible utter or nod as explicit approval to proceed.

If my mother gave her approval (which she rarely did), the trade was consummated before sundown, like a shotgun wedding. If she refused, Papa would revert to sulking, taking on the pathetic air that he reserved for these occasions. He suddenly lost his appetite and put on a downtrodden face, playing the part of a wretch.

Having failed to convince his wife, Papa would then seek to choreograph his children into the act. From the time I was a teenager, I'd have to listen to propaganda every time my mother turned down his offer to replace the family vehicle.

Every time he'd invite me to accompany him on an evening stroll, I suspected the motive for the "chat" even before he had opened his mouth to promote the numerous benefits of the prospective new family vehicle. I hated these proselytizing walks; I was afraid to hurt my father, but usually I steadfastly supported my mother's frugal position.

"The car is acting up again," he might say.

"What's wrong with it?" I'd ask, trying hard to sound neutral.

"I think it's the carburetor."

"Can't you get it fixed?"

"Maybe, but I think there are other problems."

"Like what?"

"The transmission doesn't feel right either."

"Can it be repaired?"

"Transmissions are expensive. It's probably best to get rid of the car."

"You should talk to Maman about that."

"She doesn't understand. I know when a car is on the brink."

When all else failed, Papa would fall back on the principle of "act now and ask forgiveness later." He was well acquainted with this motto, applying it regularly throughout his lifetime. He'd often pull up with the new car in spite of my mother's adamant opposition. She'd then shed some tears and give him the cold shoulder for a few days. But she'd never stay mad for long; his charm would soon restore her affection—he'd won again.

I can't remember all the cars my father owned; there were too many. The brands included the likes of Dodge, Ford, Studebaker, Hilman, Oldsmobile, Plymouth, and Pontiac. He'd alternate between big ones and little ones just for the pleasure of diversity. At times, they were too small to accommodate the whole family, requiring me to stand or sit on the knees of siblings. Over his lifetime, he sampled sedans and station wagons of all shapes, sizes, and colors, cars the family could rarely afford.

As Papa entered his retirement years, my mother tightened her fiscal control over family expenditures, effectively blocking his unjustified trade-ins. Undaunted by her efforts, he simply turned to less costly mechanical and electronic toys. He took to buying bicycles, still cameras, movie cameras, radios, stereos, and even men's jewelry.

At the age of seventy, Papa managed to purchase a sizable motorcycle without telling my mother, somehow escaping her financial radar. He even obtained his motorcycle license without raising her suspicion. He had owned a motorcycle back in his bachelor days, so this was a rekindling of a long-lost passion.

Papa at age 75, on one of his smaller motorcycles.

"Hervé has a nice motorcycle," my Uncle Jean-Paul blurted out one day.

"*What* motorcycle?" Maman retorted, staring my father down with a suspicious look.

"I was going to tell you," he said sheepishly. He had discretely stored the black motorcycle in a rented garage—a place my mother had no reason to visit.

"So, when are you going for a ride?" my uncle teased my mother.

"Never!" she barked. I found it humorous to see my father maneuvering city streets on his black motorcycle, an elderly man wearing a biker helmet. The truth is that I admired him. He was living his dream without fretting over the opinion of others, while most of us suppress our fancies until they fade away.

My father loved cars till the day he died, taking vicarious pride in the automotive conquests of his children when he could no longer pursue his own. Mere days before entering the hospital for the last time, he walked outside his apartment in stocking feet to inspect my sister Lucette's new Toyota Camry—he was beaming with glee.

About a month before succumbing to his illness, Papa made his last major acquisition: he bought an $800 bicycle he'd never get to ride. Even at eighty-six, mechanical things still brought him immense pleasure. As he lay on his deathbed, he spoke longingly of the day he'd ride that new bicycle. But the day would never come.

I often stop to think how lucky my father was to live a long life in mostly good health, married to a woman he adored, pursuing his interests with unrelenting passion until the very end. It seems that Papa had become my role model after all.

6

Risky Pursuits

Life on a farm is full of risk. The mere presence of animals adds danger, even friendly animals posing a threat to children. Nervous cows have been known to deliver kicks that maim and kill. Heck, their weight alone is enough to crush small victims.

Cow horns were a constant hazard. My father would saw off the pointy tips to reduce the risk of impalement, but they could still produce a mean bruise. I was once in the stable standing at the head of a cow, feeding it grain from my hand, when it violently shook its head from side to side to fend off the annoying flies. As it did, one of its horns caught me square in the chest, knocking the wind out of me and causing me to bend over in pain. When I could finally breathe again, I cautiously lifted my shirt to uncover a bleeding flesh wound and a large purple bruise near the nipple. It hurt like hell too.

Farm animals also attract wild game. Foxes, raccoons, and bears all paid visits to our farm. The chicken coop was eminently vulnerable to nighttime attacks, the marauding animals hankering after the delicacy of domestic fowl for their evening snack.

A face-to-face encounter with a rabid raccoon that's baring its sharp teeth at your crotch can definitely ruin a good day. My father kept an old shotgun and a .22 caliber rifle in the closet to deal with these emergencies. The only problem was the bullets; my mother kept them well hidden in another room, out of reach of her children. By the time Papa had scrambled for bullets, only the slower animals remained to face their fate.

I hated snakes; they gave me the creeps. I found those scaly, limbless reptiles with forked tongues and elastic mouths nearly as intimidating as bears. Their surreptitious motion always made their slithering appearance an unpleasant surprise. The fact that there were few poisonous snakes in our region did little to reduce my apprehension.

Unlike me, my brother Pierre and my cousin Christian had no fear of snakes; they would catch them just for fun. I once watched them trap a field snake and drop it down the oil intake pipe on the running tractor. Boiled by the hot oil, the snake recoiled out the chamber like an arrow launched from a bow. The boys walked over to inspect the charred and wrinkled carcass, smiling with pride at their brave accomplishment.

I was walking down the road near our house one day, having just stepped out of the nearby apple orchard, when I felt something tickling my leg. I reached down to check out the annoying sensation. Much to my horror, there was a snake crawling up my pant leg, heading for the warmth of my crotch.

I jumped like a bucking bronco, trying vigorously to shake it loose, but nothing seemed to work. The stupid thing was coiled tightly around my thigh. I was envisioning its grooved fangs biting my groin when I abruptly yanked down my pants and repelled it with my bare hand. The unlucky reptile was flung onto the gravel road, its life soon ended with a large stone.

Wild critters may have been intimidating, but the bull was by far the most imposing beast in our lineup of farm animals. That's why my father relieved him of his breeding responsibility in 1960: he feared for the safety of his kids. But before the bull retired to that big pasture in the sky, he had scared us shitless on numerous occasions.

The bull seemed to live a most contemptible existence. He'd spend most of his time segregated in the bullpen, away from the gentle cows he was so hellishly bent on hurting, feared by his own caretakers. He'd shamelessly stroll around the fields with his hairy privates in plain view, behaving like a creature without a brain. I found it hard to reconcile the sight of the fragile baby bulls we nurtured in the stable with these vagabond animals that stormed the fields with a bad attitude.

Our bull commanded respect. It was both mean and stupid. Without warning, its pupils would dilate in anger and its nostrils would flare into little orbs, while it expelled snorting noises that conveyed a genuine desire to disembowel any living thing.

We avoided the bull at all cost, but Papa shuffled him between pastures and we didn't always pay attention to where he was. Our careless disregard of this detail made for some memorable experiences. As soon as the bull would advance, we'd dash over stone walls and wood fences to escape his territory. We moved like panicky gazelles fleeing a lion, nimbly reaching speeds that pushed the human limit.

But we didn't always succeed. One such occasion arose when my sister Lucette and I were returning from a pasture below the farm, where we'd gone in search of wild blueberries. The hunt for blueberries had been satisfying enough, but our return trip across the field was quickly marred by the alarming sight of the bull. Warning bells rang in our brains.

He was standing directly in our path, staring us down with a killer's gaze, as if to say, "Prepare to die." His front feet were spread apart while his hooves tore up the earth in rage. His head shook violently from side to side, and his muzzle made terrible snorting sounds. He looked a lot like the mad bull I'd seen in a Bugs Bunny episode, except that it was snot—not smoke—that shot out of his nostrils every time he snorted.

We'd been caught off guard but were keenly aware of the danger we faced. Our nemesis was tearing up grass about forty feet from our paralyzed bodies, as we reeled back in fear. We could be victims. The bull would give chase, ram us with his head, gore us with his horns, and then trample us to death. And I hated the sight of blood.

"Don't move," my sister said with a mixture of panic and authority in her voice. This didn't strike me as such a swift idea though. Lucette and I were standing shoulder to shoulder; the bull could have taken us down like a couple of bowling pins.

"Shouldn't we run to the fence?" I asked in a low whisper to make sure that the bull didn't hear my words and intercept our plan—the one in the Bugs Bunny cartoon would have.

"NO!" she barked. "We'll stand here until he gets bored and turns away—wait for my signal before running over to that fence," she said, nodding toward the right.

The bull continued his threatening demonstrations, his horns bobbing up and down in a show of force, his grotesque underbelly parts jiggling with each devilish move.

It's not easy to stand in the path of an enraged bull and act brave. I weighed about fifty pounds, little obstacle for a two-thousand-pound muscular behemoth. No wonder the devil himself is depicted with bull horns on his head; this bull was the devil incarnate.

In a weak moment, I seriously considered leaving my sister behind and running my selfish little ass over to the fence without her. I knew I could make it. I was excellent at running, a self-preservation skill I'd polished long ago to escape my naughty deeds.

But the cowardly action would not have been without damaging conse-
quences. If Lucette survived, I probably wouldn't—she'd beat the crap out of me.
If she didn't make it, I'd have to cope with the Catholic guilt forever. In the end,
I decided to stay.

"Run *now!*" Lucette suddenly yelled. As predicted, the bull had momentarily
lost interest in our trespass and turned away. We ran at lightning speed toward
the fence, bounding over the wooden posts in seconds. We were safe again.

Farm equipment posed another danger to kids living on a farm. We had two tractors, a sickle mower, a hay loader, a hay fork, and in later years a rented hay baler.

Our only tractor accident involved my mother, when she was at the wheel. I
was too young to remember the incident, but the story became a family legend.
Although Maman never had her driver's license, my father had taught her how to
drive the old tractor.

We still lived in town the day Maman took us out to the country for a visit
with her parents. She'd amassed enough courage to drive the tractor on public
roads, after training in the fields. The drive would be easy; these were dirt roads
with light traffic.

Our tractor had a small wooden platform affixed to the back, used for transporting small loads. The support arms on the platform slid into the back of the
tractor and hovered about two feet off the ground. We often sat there while my
father drove us around.

That day, Maman loaded all seven kids onto the little wooden platform,
instructing the older children to care for the younger ones during the short drive
to the country.

My mother saw the oncoming car as we were approaching the area called
Lanize. The small dirt road wasn't wide enough to accommodate both the tractor
and the car, so she panicked. Lacking experience in two-way traffic, she steered
the tractor to the shoulder of the road, but she grossly overcompensated. The
wheels on the tractor lifted to one side, like a dog's leg before the downpour. The
sudden shift caused the little wooden platform to detach and flip over, throwing
the litter of kids into the gutter.

Miraculously, the tractor itself managed to stay upright. Stunned by the accident, Maman gathered her kids and walked back to town, refusing to remount
the tractor. Réal, by now a mature ten-year-old, climbed aboard and drove back
to town in her place.

Aside from small bruises and scratches, none of us were hurt. Although we'd
escaped with little physical harm, Maman was left with deep emotional trauma.

Her mind would often replay the accident, horrified by the thought that her kids could have been crushed to death. Had the accident happened a little further up the road, the tractor might have tumbled down the small ravine and into the brook below.

For a woman with a low self-esteem, this had been a significant emotional event. From that day forward, she drove neither the tractor nor the car ever again.

When Lucette was around twelve, she managed to convince my father to let her rake the fields while he was at work. "I know what to do. I'll be careful," she said.

"And I can sit on the rake," I piped up. Operating the hay rake was simple even for an eight-year-old; it involved pushing and pulling a single lever.

The next morning, Lucette mounted the tractor while I climbed up on the big metal rake. This was my first time alone on the contraption, and it was exhilarating to have such responsibility. I was enjoying myself enormously until it started to sprinkle and Lucette aborted our chore. She was terrified of lightning, so she decided to accelerate the pace, hoping to escape the rapidly-approaching thunderstorm. As she rushed back to the barn in panic, she drove down a steep embankment, approaching from an angle.

My heart started pumping furiously the moment I saw the left wheel of the tractor lift off the ground; then I felt the rake do the same. Flipping a tractor was often fatal to the operator. Hardly a year went by without somebody getting crushed by farm equipment. So, feeling the rake lift off the ground activated a panic sequence in my brain.

"Jump!" my sister yelled.

It took great effort to resist the momentum of the rake. I stood up on the raised side, pushed as hard as I could with my feet, and jumped clear of the moving contraption. Lucette thought about jumping off the tractor too but decided to hang on after all.

When I glanced back, the wheels of the tractor and vacant rake had descended back to the ground. Although an accident had been narrowly averted, the incident shook Lucette's confidence as much as it did mine. I never ran the hay rake again.

My father had two tractors: an old International and a new Massey-Ferguson. I had no use for the old tractor, but I fell head over heels for the red and white Massey-Ferguson. It was lower to the ground but much wider and stronger than the International. Its large rear wheels and loud engine exuded raw power like no other. It was an ideal toy.

My brother, Pierre, on the Massey-Ferguson tractor.

I patiently waited till the age of seven before driving the tractor. Although he didn't know it, my father had already taught me everything I needed to know. I had often ridden on the tractor with Papa, either standing behind his seat or sitting between his legs. I had studied his handling of the controls from both positions. It looked easy.

"Can I drive it, Papa?" I'd ask. He'd let me sit on his lap and hold the steering wheel while he manipulated the rest of the controls. But I wanted more.

I knew that it was hopeless to ask my father permission to drive the new tractor, since the fear of accidents was an ever-present concern in the minds of my parents. So I decided to hijack the tractor without their permission. It was the only way.

The opportunity arose one early morning after we had finished milking the cows. We always took the tractor to transport the full milk cans from the cow stable to the garage, where they'd later be picked up by the milk company. The responsibility for fetching and driving the tractor normally rested with Réal and Jacques, the eldest siblings.

On this autumn morning, I made up my mind to beat them to the task. While my brothers were still cleaning the gutters in the stable, I ran up to the house where the tractor was parked and mounted the majestic Massey-Ferguson. My father trusted us to adhere to the family rules, so he always left the key in the ignition.

The controls were simple enough. While pressing down on the clutch and brake pedals, you had pull the choke knob, turn the ignition key to the right, and press the shiny chrome button on the console to fire up the engine. Acceleration was controlled from a chrome lever on the column, and shifting from a stick on the floor. Once the tractor started moving, it would be easy to steer—this beauty had power steering.

Nervous with anticipation, I stood up on the clutch and the brake. I was too short to reach the pedals from a sitting position, so I'd have to stand for the duration of the ride. I released the handbrake, pulled the choke, turned the key, and pressed the starter button. The engine immediately came to life with a roar, putting my hijacking plan in jeopardy.

I jiggled the floor lever into first gear, took my foot off the big brake pedal, and slowly lifted my left foot off the clutch. The tractor bucked like a wild bronco, as the engine choked unmercifully. *Not enough acceleration*, I thought. I repeated the whole cycle once more, this time raising the accelerator arm to give it more gas. The engine died again, the tractor lunging even more violently this time.

I now began to suspect that I was releasing the clutch too quickly. So I repeated the familiar steps another time, releasing the clutch so slowly that it seemed like minutes vanished before it had moved at all. The hair rose on the back of my neck when the tractor finally started rolling. *I did it!*

The steering wheel was as easy to handle as I had hoped. I pointed the tractor in the direction of the gravel path leading down to the cow stable. My mother would have been horrified to see her seven-year-old son standing at the controls of the big tractor, but at that moment, the thrill of the ride was blocking out any fear of retribution.

Once I reached the stable, I'd have to back up the tractor to the door for loading. That could be a tricky maneuver for an inexperienced boy. Feeling proud of my exploit, I swung the big tractor away from the stable door to prepare for my approach.

After shifting the gears into reverse, I popped the clutch again, meaning I would have to restart the tractor within hearing range of my siblings. Beads of nervous sweat started accumulating on my forehead. But there was no sign of my brothers, so I resumed the backup maneuver.

BOOM! My heart did several flips inside its ribcage. The wooden platform attached to the back of the tractor had collided with the stable door. The engine died and I waited in silence to see if anyone would come running out of the stable; nobody came.

I restarted the motor with grave trepidation. This time, I succeeded in stopping at the designated spot near the door. I quickly turned off the engine, disembarked from my metal horse and rushed up to the building to check on the damage. I could see large gouges in the door jam and stable wall, the wood chips on the ground attesting to my mishap.

I decided to say nothing about the accident, hoping that nobody else would notice. The stable was an unpainted old building, so the chance of anyone noticing fresh defects was unlikely, I thought. I entered the cow stable, and everything looked normal. Then I heard my brother Réal say something to Jacques about fetching the tractor.

"I already got the tractor. It's sitting outside," I said, afraid of what Réal would say. A puzzled look passed over his face, but he turned back to his chores without a word.

My parents never found out about my first tractor ride. I would have been punished if they had—I had broken their trust. It wouldn't be the last time that I took the tractor without parental authorization, but it was certainly my most memorable.

We once had a close encounter with dynamite. On occasion, my father had used sticks of dynamite to blast large and stubborn rocks out of his fields. He had then stored the leftover sticks in the dairy room, a place accessible from the summer kitchen just off the garage.

Each spring, my mother spent much of her time eradicating dirt and clutter. On this particular day, she'd been busy cleaning out the old dairy room with impressive speed, having just returned to the kitchen to dispose of her finds.

The old kitchen stove included a large firebox for burning wood. Standing nearby, I noticed Maman holding an old newspaper in one hand and the cast-iron cover to the firebox in the other. She was about to throw in a newspaper but hesitated for a second.

"Hervé, can I throw this out?" she called out to my father, who was sitting nearby.

I'd never seen my father move so quickly in my life. He jumped to his feet as though a bolt of electricity had been shot up his butt.

"No, no, no. Give me that newspaper!" he yelled, alarming the rest of us.

He grabbed the newspaper from my mother's hand and unrolled it carefully to reveal the sticks of dynamite that had been concealed in its folds. Maman responded with a flood of nervous tears, standing at the stove with one hand resting against her heart.

My mother's zeal for cleanliness had almost killed us that day. My parents would have probably perished, along with those of us who were standing near the kitchen.

Papa decided to discard the dynamite that same afternoon. He ordered us to take cover behind the farm buildings while he ignited the sticks that had threatened our lives. The loud bangs rocked the earth, a poignant reminder of our close call with destiny.

Farm animals and equipment did introduce risk, but the earliest hazard I encountered as a child was the wooden staircase in our farmhouse. I regularly traveled down these stairs on my face, on my back, and on my head, ungracefully tumbling backwards and forwards to suit the family occasion. By the age of six, I'd been knocked out more often than a boxer at training camp.

The staircase to reach the second floor was located in the kitchen. One side lacked a guardrail, permitting me to plummet unimpaired onto the kitchen floor, while the other side consisted of a hard wall dividing the main and summer kitchens.

From the second floor, the stairs pointed straight down at a wall that my free-falling head regularly struck with the force of a battering ram. The landing at the base of the stairs made a ninety-degree turn into the kitchen. If my spill veered slightly to the left, my head would engage the metal hulk that served as our refrigerator.

I would periodically make the treacherous journey from second floor to first floor in a speedy blur that was accompanied by loud thumping sounds. *Bang, boom, crash.*

"Maman, Michel fell down the stairs again!" one of my siblings would shout.

I began the fine childhood tradition of tumbling down stairs before I learned to walk. Fearing that these repeated knockouts would transform me into a drooling pinhead, Maman even tried serving the family meals in the summer kitchen for a while, far from the main staircase. But that solution was only temporary.

The staircase called out to me like the Siren of Ulysses. It was intimidating and at the same time challenging, something to revere and conquer, like a towering mountain. And I frequently succeeded in completing the climb. Witnesses tend to remember the disasters, but I do recall many triumphant moments standing at the top of the stairs.

The problem was rarely the ascent; the greater risk was in the return trip to the kitchen floor. The danger of falling was notably heightened by my short legs and the steep stairs. Facing the down staircase required balance and precision—skills I had not yet perfected.

My rapid descents weren't always caused by my own ineptitude either. At times, they were induced by negligent humans. Kids rushing the stairs could distract my fragile balance and concentration, precipitating my plunge onto the kitchen floor.

Even adults were the culprits at times. One memorable tumble plagued my brain for a long time. I was about five years old when it happened. On this Sunday, our farmhouse was brimming with uncles, aunts, cousins, and my Côté grandparents.

I was among the throng of kids who'd climbed the stairs and were playing noisily on the second floor. Grandmaman Côté suddenly made an unexpected appearance at the top of the stairs, shouting for us to relocate our games to the supervised downstairs.

My grandmother quickly encircled the kids while grumbling about the loud noise and making herding gestures to stimulate our rapid exit. Her efforts were rewarded with a stampede, and she closed in behind the fleeing mass with the skill of a trained Collie.

I needed more time and concentration to negotiate the descent, so I was one of the last kids to start down the stairs. I had barely climbed down two steps when my grandmother lifted her knee to step off the top landing. Her kneecap struck me in the middle of the back, and I catapulted down the stairs toward the inviting wall.

"Michel fell down the stairs again!" the cry went out at once.

It was a brutal fall. I hit the landing and then bounced headfirst into the side of the unforgiving refrigerator. My mother was worried to tears, after seeing my eyes roll into my head, my face turn ashen, and the unnatural growth on my head emit a purple glow.

I remained unconscious for several hours. I remember waking up sitting on my mother's lap, with a cold facecloth on my forehead and the house empty of visitors. She was humming a gentle song in my ear as she rocked back and forth in the chair.

I knew that Grandmaman had accidentally caused my fall. After hours of dopy silence, I finally worked up the nerve to reveal my disturbing secret.

"It was Grandmaman who pushed me down the stairs. She hit me with her knee."

"No, I'm sure your grandmother would never do that," Maman said.

"Yes, she was behind me. It was an accident."

"You must have imagined it. She would have told me if she had done that."

Maman never did believe me. She held her mother in such high regard that even an accident was outside the realm of possibility. The case was closed.

Doctors were summoned only when death or childbirth was imminent. Therefore, I'd recover from this fall without medical assistance, just like the other times. The permanent scars branded onto my scalp are the only proof of these misfortunes.

We had few toys, so we made our own. We enjoyed making our own weapons too.

We'd create longbows using pliable branches and assemble crossbows from wood fragments we found in the garage. The strings on the bows were usually made of baling wire, whereas those on the crossbows were thinly cut pieces of old tire tubes that had once serviced a tractor or automobile. The tips on the wooden arrows were covered with bent bottle caps (pounded in place with a hammer), and the tails were decorated with fresh feathers retrieved from the chicken coop for the occasion.

The effectiveness of our bows and crossbows was generally determined by the tautness of the string. An older sibling usually helped me string my bows. Otherwise, my arrows would fly the feeble distance of spittle.

The arrows launched from a well-built crossbow were dangerous; they could puncture skin and pierce eyes. One of mine had broken the skin on a distraught Lucette. She later avenged the minor injury with an innocent prank.

"I have a surprise for you," she said one day as I played in the front yard.

"What is it?"

"It's a candy. Close your eyes and open your mouth."

I was a gullible eight-year-old, so I gladly opened my mouth and closed my eyes in anticipation. She dropped little nuggets on my tongue. The dry texture reminded me of shredded wheat.

It tasted awful. I hurriedly spit the content into my hand, disgusted to be looking down at dry rabbit turds. Lucette was laughing hysterically when I rushed in the house to rid my mouth of the terrible taste. I rinsed my mouth for about fifteen minutes.

We made our own darts too. They were even more dangerous than crossbows, so we used them strictly for target practice. A wooden broomstick made the perfect shaft for our darts. We'd first saw off a six-inch piece of the handle. Then, we'd file off the head of a three-inch construction nail and pound one end of the nail into the dart. A small hole was drilled in the other end, where a chicken feather was inserted for the flight.

The finished dart measured a good nine inches in length, including the pretty feather. A homemade dart deserved respect, with its long and pointy nail sticking out of the top. We never deliberately threw darts at each other, but accidents did happen.

I got along well with my cousin Francine. We were the same age, shared similar interests, and generally walked to the beat of the same drum. She was spending the day at our house when we decided to throw darts one warm Saturday afternoon.

We were standing at the top of the unpainted staircase in the garage, taking turns throwing homemade darts down at the wall near the base of the stairs. The elevation increased the velocity of each throw, causing the darts to snap hard against the wood.

"I have to go to the bathroom. I'll be right back," I said, running down the stairs.

I did my business and soon returned to resume the game with Francine. As I neared the staircase, I could hear her darts hitting the wooden planks at regular intervals.

"Francine, I'm coming up," I yelled toward the top of the stairs.

The thumping sound of the darts momentarily stopped, and I interpreted the ceasefire as an acknowledgement from Francine. Stepping onto the landing at the base of the stairs, I quickly turned and began the climb toward my playmate.

Suddenly, my head was thrown back with a dull thump. The stabbing pain instantly brought tears to my eyes. I could taste blood running down my throat.

It took me a split second to realize that I'd been hit in the face with a dart. It had entered the upper right nostril near the bridge of my nose, a fraction of an inch from my right eye. The construction nail passed right through my hard palate, its pointy end embedding into my mouth. My tongue instinctively reached up to meet the nail, feeling a sharp jab. As my eyes began to swim in an ocean of black dots, I managed to discern the profile of the lovely chicken feather poised astutely above my bleeding nose.

Seconds later, I entered a total state of panic, uncertain about the extent of my injury. *Was I dying? Did the dart pierce my eye? Did it penetrate my brain?* I didn't know the answer to any of these questions. I was scared senseless.

Francine had seen everything. She stood frozen on the top landing, unable to muster the courage to come to the aid of her petrified cousin. I didn't wait for her reaction.

Without uttering a word, I turned back around, reached for the bloody dart sticking out of my nose, and ripped it out forcefully. I then threw the damn thing on the ground and rushed into the house, hoping to stay conscious until I could reach help.

I found my mother in the kitchen. I was mumbling incoherently and pointing frantically at my nose. I felt lightheaded, my limbs were the consistency of rubber, and I was having considerable difficulty convincing my mouth to make sensible sounds.

To Maman, the pimple-size blotch on my nose didn't seem like cause for concern. Amidst my mumbles, she detected the words "dart" and "Francine" and realized the source of my ramblings. The ocean of black dots was rapidly transforming into a dark blanket—I was on the verge of fainting.

I awoke to find myself alone in my parents' bed off the kitchen on the first floor. A cold facecloth—the universal soother—was poised on my snout. I called out to Maman.

"Will I be all right?"

"It's not serious," she said. "The hole in your palate is already closed. But I don't want you to play darts anymore. You came very close to losing an eye. You should talk to Francine too. I think she's feeling really bad about this."

Moments later, my cousin made a bashful appearance at the entrance to the bedroom, forcing a nervous smile. She stood at the threshold, testing my mood.

"I didn't see you coming up the stairs," Francine said in an apologetic tone.

"It was my fault. I called up to you, but I guess you didn't hear me."

I suddenly felt like a spineless weakling. I had overreacted to the trivial injury and was still lying in bed in the middle of the afternoon like a kid with the bubonic plague. I quickly rose out of bed, threw on my clothes, and went out to play.

I was a gullible boy, playing "Monkey See, Monkey Do" to mimic the behavior of my older siblings and cousins. That sometimes got me in trouble.

It was a hot August day in 1960. The summers in Québec were short, but the humidity level could become unbearable at its peak. It was the kind of heat that kept your face flushed and sent a steady trickle of perspiration down your spine.

One day, Aunt Juliette walked up to the farm with her kids to escape the oppressive heat. My father and older brothers were at work. Pierre, Lucette, my cousin Christian and I bantered in the kitchen, as Maman and her sister settled in the small living room.

At some point, Christian and Pierre got the bright idea to cool off with ice cubes. My mother always kept two plastic trays of cubes in the freezer compartment above the refrigerator. The cubes were served with fresh lemonade after hot summer days working in the fields. The cubes were of the large, rectangular-shaped variety.

Naturally, I thought the older boys had hit on a brilliant idea. Christian and Pierre must have been sucking on their third ice cube by the time I decided to join them. They were slurping loudly, exaggerating the sucking sounds just to be funny.

I reached into the freezer and shook my first ice cube from the white plastic tray. That thing seemed so big that it barely fit inside my mouth. Mimicking Christian and Pierre, I too began making slurping noises, sucking on the ice cube with vigor.

I knew I was in trouble as soon as the ice cube slid down my throat. It was lodged beyond finger reach, and I could feel the hard bump near my trachea. I tried to speak, but nothing came out. Nor could I inhale or exhale. The kids standing around the kitchen seemed oblivious to my life-threatening dilemma, so I ran into the living room.

I rushed up to Maman, who was sitting on the couch chatting with her sister. Stopping directly in front of her, I opened my mouth to speak, but could emit only a terrifying gurgle. I grasped my throat between my thumb and index finger in desperation.

"What's the matter, what's the matter?" she shouted with panic in her voice.

Everybody in the room instinctively stood up, as loud and confused voices began speculating about my ailment. I was playing charades for my life.

"He's choking! He's choking!" somebody yelled.

I'm told that my eyes were wide, my face was drained, and my lips were blue. The buzz all around me was slowly fading into a foggy dream. The suffocating feeling was neither painful nor unpleasant; I was losing all sensation in my limbs.

Several anonymous hands started hitting my back forcefully, but the ice cube continued clinging stubbornly inside my throat. I was beginning to weaken, finding it increasingly difficult to stand up on my own two feet. The voices were getting more distant.

"Hold him up by the legs!" somebody suggested amidst the tension.

I was dead weight, a fifty-pound blob of rubber. And the all-too-familiar black dots were again obscuring my vision. *Am I dying?* I didn't care.

I hung upside down like a bat, my head inches above the kitchen linoleum and my rubbery arms drooping down to the floor. *Wham, wham, wham.* They beat me like a dirty carpet, causing my body to sway with every blow. All I could see were shoes.

I distinctly heard the villainous ice cube clinking against the floor. It was expelled swiftly, sliding across the kitchen linoleum. The others heard it too. I gasped for air and my lungs instantly filled to capacity, giving me a head rush. I was deposited on the linoleum floor in a heap, resting on my back as I struggled to regain my senses.

"Breathe! Breathe!" Lucette screamed in my face. I was already breathing, but her nerves were frayed and she was frantically looking for further signs of life.

"Are you all right? Say something!" the voices shouted.

The black dots dissipated, the blood flowed to my limbs again, and the oxygen quickly reinvigorated my brain. That's when the emotions caught up with me. I was still lying on the floor when I broke out in a loud sobbing cry. Pride usually kept my tears at bay, but this time I found it impossible to hold back. I sobbed long and hard.

To bystanders, my noisy demonstration signaled the end of a life-threatening peril, and they heaved big sighs of relief. Through my tears, I could see a wall of pale faces.

"He gave us a good scare," I heard Aunt Juliette say.

I'd scared myself too.

I would never forget my near-fatal encounter with an ice cube.

I viewed my cousin Christian as a sort of pied piper. I admired him because he was smart, funny, and adventurous. He became a role model for me.

Christian was a skinny boy with black glasses, dark hair, and a perpetual smile. He was also mischievous, a relentless spirit forever in search of adventure. But he never stayed in trouble for long, using his copious charm to win over forgiving parents.

This was the same twelve-year-old who had shattered my belief in Santa Claus. Santa was very poor in our part of the world, but he still came around at Christmas.

It was late November. Christian and Pierre were in the front yard while I circled around like a buzzard, hoping to join in their play. It had started to snow.

"I like snow. It means Santa Claus is coming soon," I said.

Christian looked back over his shoulder in my direction and let out a short giggle.

"So you still believe in Santa Claus?" he asked in a mocking tone.

The thought had never really occurred to me, despite my confusion over Père Noël. The nuns had told us that Saint Nicolas was the true Santa Claus, but that skinny old saint sure didn't look like the fat man in the red suit and white beard.

"Of course I believe in Père Noël," I retorted.

"There's no Santa Claus. He's not real," he said with finality.

"Yes he is!"

"No he isn't."

I was devastated. Despite my great admiration for Christian, I wondered if he was just teasing me. I ran inside the house, hoping to invalidate his claim.

"Maman, Christian says there's no Santa Claus," I blurted out.

"Well, Christmas is about baby Jesus," she answered. She was waffling.

Maman had spoken with the forthrightness of a political candidate running for office. Christian had just pulverized my childhood conviction beyond all hope.

I stood in the barn talking with Christian and Pierre on a warm July afternoon in 1960. The barn doors had been left wide open, allowing the summer breeze to play with our hair. Christian was trying hard to convince me to participate in their latest experiment.

Their game plan was to use the hay fork as a human transporter. This three-foot-high contraption looked like a double harpoon. It was made of heavy metal and painted green, with two sharp prongs to secure the load on its journey to the hayloft.

The hay fork was used only in July. That's when hay was collected and stored in the hayloft to feed cattle the remainder of the year. The fork was taken down after hay season and stowed in the utility shed, where it would remain until the next summer.

Our barn was about a hundred feet long, fifty feet wide, and fifty feet high. Reaching the barn doors required walking up a rickety wood ramp that led to the aisle. Large hay stalls occupied the left and right sides of the center aisle. The hayloft—the final destination of Christian's experiment—lay at the far end of the barn structure.

The system for moving hay to the loft involved simple technology. We'd back up the hay wagon into the barn aisle, attach the hay fork to the horse (on a rope and pulley), and lower the fork into the hay wagon. Once the hay had been satisfactorily impaled, we'd pull the trim rope to raise the prongs that secured the load on its transport. The horse would then advance to an endpoint, lifting the hay-stack toward the barn ceiling.

The load would travel the length of the barn on a trolley track. Once it had completed the vertical climb, it then slid across the barn on a rail. The split track near the hayloft allowed the fork operator to direct the hay load left or right. Once it had reached its final destination, the operator would discharge the hay onto the stack using a tether.

Christian was applying his splendid charm to convince me to become the first human cargo ferried on the hay fork. My light weight made me the perfect candidate for the trial run, I was told. The normal steps for transferring hay to the loft would be taken, with two major exceptions. First, Christian and Pierre would furnish the horsepower. Second, the fork would be lowered gently over the hay-loft to permit me to disembark.

"Is it safe?" I asked with skepticism in my voice.

"Of course it is. That fork lifts big piles of hay," Christian answered.

"But what if I fall?"

"We'll go slowly—all you have to do is hang on tight."

Christian spoke in such a relaxed and confident tone of voice that I found him hypnotizing. I trusted him implicitly, even more than I trusted Pierre. It's not that I didn't get along with my brother, but rather that I had given Pierre many axes to grind. I often ratted on him to my mother, which led to parental repri-mands and the occasional spanking. I feared retaliation. *Could this fork ride be payback?*

"Just try it. If you get scared, we'll bring you down right away," Christian said.

These last words managed to ease my nervous agitation, and I begrudgingly agreed to serve as the guinea pig for their little experiment. The harpoon fork was lowered to the aisle floor, and I walked up to the intimidating device with grave trepidation.

"Hold onto the top."

My stomach was filled with butterflies and my palms were clammy—not a good thing given that my survival depended on a firm grip.

"Wait! I'm still not sure I want to do this," I interrupted.

"Listen, you can close your eyes if you want. It'll be a short ride."

I swallowed hard, grasped the top of the hay fork, and gave the verbal cue to proceed. Christian and Pierre pulled on the rope, raising the fork toward the cen-ter beam.

The vertical ride up to the beam was petrifying. I initially kept my eyes shut, but I soon found that the darkness only intensified the fear. So I opened them again. My balls, now shrunken to the size of lentils, had inexplicably scaled up to my throat.

The hay fork reached the support beam, slipped onto the rail, and after a jolt began careening down the track. My legs lurched in midair from the sudden movement. I was floating high above the center aisle, supported only by the grip of my sweaty hands.

The ride on the rail was frightening, but the view was awesome. I could see the entire barn structure as if looking through a wide-angle lens, sailing past beams and planks that hadn't been touched since the barn had been raised. I made the mistake of looking straight down, and my scrotum responded with further tightening.

I soon reached the hayloft, which was piled high with hay. As planned, they lowered the hay fork gently, depositing me on the soft straw mat without a hitch.

I was elated, suddenly feeling a rush of euphoria. By the end of the afternoon, I had ridden the hay fork several more times, as had Christian and Pierre. We were like Tarzan, swinging some thirty feet above the barn floor. Yet, one little slip and I could have splattered onto the wood planking like a grasshopper on a windshield.

The hay fork wasn't the only excitement that we sought in the barn. We'd also walk across the wood beams high above the barn aisle like high-wire trapeze artists, pretending to tap dance on the slippery surface. Furthermore, the hay pile provided scaling adventures. At its peak, the haystack stood forty feet high, with perilous gorges on both sides.

Unproven rumors on the danger of suffocation circulated throughout my childhood. According to these stories, the heat, dust, and lack of oxygen deep in the hay gorges could cause rapid asphyxiation and death. Although we found these stories intimidating, they only served to fuel our sense of adventure; we just had to scale those gorges.

The most dangerous sections of the hayloft—so we believed—were the narrow gullies between the haystack and the planked barn walls. In the summer, these spaces were dark, musty, and hot—perfect fodder for our young imaginations.

Christian, Guy (Christian's older brother), Lucette, Pierre, and I would scale down these tight spaces in the summer. We'd do this by fastening a hemp rope to a girder and dropping it down a promising gully. We'd then take turns descending to the depths below.

These scaling adventures were tests of courage. The braver kids went deeper in the gully than little wimps like me. As soon as we lost our nerve, we'd yell up to the kids, who would then pull on the tether to facilitate our ascent back up the mountain.

The rules of the game were few and simple. We were to climb down the rope as far as possible (or as far as fortitude enabled) but stop as soon as breathing became labored.

"Pull me up!" was the normal edict yelled back to the top.

I was once on a rope and descending a dark gully, having just overstepped my tolerance level. The only light came from high above. The smell of dust and mold irritated my nostrils, as I hung there drenched in sweat. Leaning back against the wall planks, I called up to be raised. But nothing happened. I yelled a little louder, hearing panic in my voice. Again, nothing happened. I now screamed in nervous anger. Still, total silence from above.

After minutes of futile screams, I had to scale back up to the top unassisted. I pulled myself up on the rope, occasionally stopping to rest my back against a protruding girder. When I finally reached the hayloft, my peers were gone. Bored with scaling, they'd abruptly abandoned the game, leaving me to fend for myself in the belly of the barn.

7

Schooling Tribulations

First grade was a culture shock. There were no preschools or kindergartens in St-Gérard. Early education rested solely with the mothers until the age of six. Happily cocooned on the farm, I lacked the usual social skills and confidence needed to interact with strangers. Chronic shyness and oversensitivity were destined to interfere with my assimilation.

I had glorious expectations about school. As my sixth birthday approached, Maman and my sisters had embarked on a campaign to rouse my interest. Aware that my sheltered existence was coming to an abrupt end, they tried softening the blow with inflated tales of school fun. In other words, I was bamboozled.

The attractive brown leather backpack my parents bought me made it official. It held my new wooden pencil case, red rubber eraser, and wooden ruler. I was also excited about my new pair of shoes, the new pants Maman had sewed, and the hand-me-down shirts I had received. I was now prepared to play the part of the schoolboy, a little soldier dressed for boot camp, equipped with only a naïve vision of reality.

My head was filled with grand expectations about kind teachers, friendly kids, and entertaining books. It seems that my siblings had overlooked the parts about strict discipline, corporal punishment, schoolyard bullies, and imposing homework.

The only educational institution that existed in St-Gérard was Mater Domini, a Catholic school run by a religious order called the Sisters of the Cross. The two-story red brick building in the center of town serviced grades one through eleven, with a one-story extension in the back of the structure that doubled the number of classrooms.

The highly publicized first day of school finally arrived. I was nervous but excited as I walked the two miles to town with my siblings like a brave little soldier, wearing my new clothes and stylish leather backpack. But my courage would quickly vaporize.

I got cold feet as soon as we entered the schoolyard. My sister Lucette was standing by my side, the appointed deputy in charge of my surrender to school authorities. The grounds were full of screaming kids, and I found the confusing medley of sounds frightening. I stayed close to Lucette for protection, away from the hoard of obnoxious kids.

My heart was pounding by the time the bell rang. Kids started forming lines near the front and side doors, but I just stood there in a daze.

"Go over there and stand in line," Lucette said, pointing at the group of first-graders who were gathering on the front steps of the main building.

I shook my head, refusing to budge. My feet were firmly planted in the gravel yard, my body frozen with fear. Already, the reality of school seemed to contrast sharply with the idyllic images that had been paraded through my gullible brain over the summer.

Lucette grabbed my right arm at the elbow and tried pulling me toward the line. But I jerked the arm free, determined to stand my ground.

It didn't take long for my sister to realize that her words weren't going to do any good. Anxious to fall in with her class, Lucette quickly moved in behind me, grasped both sides of my handsome backpack, and pushed with all her might. I instinctively leaned back to counter her shove and dug my heels deeper in the dirt. But Lucette was stronger than me, persisting in spite of my resistance. My new shoes plowed two parallel channels into the gravel all the way to the waiting line.

"Stay here," Lucette said in an exasperated tone. "That's your teacher there," she added, pointing to the front of the line. She then left hurriedly, and I was alone.

"Line up by height! Smaller kids in front," the teacher yelled. I moved irresolutely toward the line, dreading every step. "I want total silence," she barked in a strict voice.

I considered exercising my impressive sprinting ability to run away from the oppressive institution before the teacher realized I even existed. But I knew that this unpleasant cycle would just be repeated again the next day. My fate was locked.

Looking like prisoners under escort, the kids climbed up the front stairs and followed the teacher into the daunting brick building. Our class was the first room on the right after crossing over the threshold.

Once in the classroom, the teacher assigned us our seats. The little wooden desks and chairs had been lined up meticulously to form straight aisles and rows.

The shiny hardwood floor exaggerated the sound of our steps. The shorter kids were seated in front.

The teacher's name was Marie-Marthe Brunelle. My mother knew her well, but she was a total stranger to me. She was pretty enough and nicely dressed. She introduced herself, called out our names to take attendance, and then started reciting the rules.

I was crying even before she'd finished with the rules. Not a loud cry, but more of a quiet sob. She heard my sniffles and turned in my direction.

"Is something wrong, Mister Blanchette?" she asked. All heads turned to stare.

But I was unable to answer the question, petrified of this new authority figure and distressed to be among kids I'd never met. I continued crying softly.

"Do you need to go to the bathroom?" she said. I shook my head. "Do you feel sick?" I shook my head once more.

Her devoted attention served only to intensify my crying. She approached my desk, seeming concerned about my emotional state. Her voice dropped its authoritative tone and became more compassionate, almost motherly. She leaned close to my face.

"There's no need to be afraid. I won't hurt you," she said. These words opened up the floodgates and I cried even harder. She held me to her chest and spoke soothing words; I cried louder still. I felt miserable, my emotions thoroughly out of control.

"Everyone stay seated. I'll be right back," she said, walking through the door and into the empty hallway. She returned a few minutes later with my sister Doris in tow. Doris walked over to my desk beaming a warm smile. My savior had arrived.

"Come with me," she said, reaching for my hand. I stopped crying instantly, feeling the comfort of a loving and familiar face as we exited into the hallway.

I spent most of that day sitting in the eight-grade class next to Doris. I'd start crying all over again each time she brought me back to my class, so I ended up spending much of the first week sitting in upper classes with either Doris or Lucette.

My performance over the first school year was hardly stellar. I ended up catching every communicable disease that seemed to pass through town, missing weeks of school. Like a relocated aborigine, I lacked immunity from common germs and viruses. In addition to frequent colds, I was down with the flu, measles, chicken pox, and bronchitis. My introduction to school had been traumatic on both my mind and my body.

The two-mile walk to school became part of my daily ritual. We'd plod our way to town in all kinds of weather. Rain, sleet, and snow often enlivened the march. Québec was hardened to the tough winters, so snow days were rare. I wore a clear plastic protector to stay dry on rainy days and Eskimo-style clothing to keep warm in the cold.

In the winter, I also wore long johns indoors and outdoors to preserve body heat. Our upstairs bedrooms were unheated, so the air got chilly at night. My long johns were of the one-piece variety, with buttons up the chest and a detachable panel at the fanny to minimize skin exposure. These woolen undergarments were a godsend, although they caused my butt and legs to itch incessantly. I'd scratch as though I were stricken with fleas.

It was time consuming to leave the house on a cold winter day. I had to put on two pairs of wool socks, snow pants, a winter parka, heavy boots, a hat with unflattering ear flaps, a hood, a scarf wrapped across my nose and mouth, and two pairs of woolen mittens. Once padded in these layers, I was ready to tackle the frozen tundra. My eyes were the only part of my body that remained exposed to the frozen air.

The snow and howling wind could turn the walk to school into a treacherous venture. We'd climb over windblown dunes, trudging through the waist-high snow in near-zero visibility. My siblings had sent me back home on several occasions, as my short legs were often unable to navigate the steep snowdrifts that obstructed our path. On those days, I'd resume the provisional life of a preschool child, blissfully alone with Maman.

But snow wasn't the only problem. Once, when I was eight years old, a nasty mixture of snow and rain had been pelting the area for days. Lucette, Pierre, and I had just arrived in town on the way to school one morning when we reached an impassible street. The main road was under a foot of water, with slush floating on the surface.

Seeing no alternate route, we resumed walking to school over the flooded pavement with calculated steps, dressed in full winter garb.

As I waded through the dirty water, I unknowingly stepped into an open manhole, precipitating a freefall toward the bottom of the pool. The cover had been pushed off by the force of water, the hidden manhole waiting to swallow an unsuspecting passerby.

I dropped down the manhole like a rock, my leather backpack still strapped on my back. I was instinctively reaching out to stop the fall when my elbows hooked onto the edge of the opening. The cold watery mess rose up to meet my nose.

My body remained lodged in the manhole while I struggled to keep my chin above the floating debris. The freezing water was numbing my limbs, and the heavy winter clothes—now engorged with water—were weighing me down. I panicked, convinced that the force of the water would suck me down into the depths of the manhole.

"Help me!" I yelled.

Lucette heard my desperate plea and quickly moved in my direction. Aghast to see her little brother flailing in what might become a watery grave, she ran to my side, grabbed the straps on my backpack, and pulled hard. I felt myself lift out of the hole slowly; I was shaken but safe. Lucette then took me to a nearby country store to warm me up lest hypothermia set in, while my father was summoned from work. I was driven home in the comfort of an automobile that day.

After the Gagné family became our neighbors in 1960, I often walked back home from school with my friend Jean-Marie. These were pleasant times. Jean-Marie and I would share leftovers from lunch while trooping home over the dirt road.

If we got thirsty, we'd simply bend down and drink from the natural spring that ran alongside the gravel road leading out of St-Gérard.

The trek home from school was calming, as I was heading back to the comfort of familiar surroundings. As I neared the farm, I could always count on Puppé to greet me with welcoming barks and licks. I was safe again.

I gradually fell in love with school. Once I'd subdued my separation anxiety, I quickly learned to make friends and grew rather fond of my first-grade teacher. She usually treated me with kindness, having already experienced my oversensitivity.

I became in awe of school, savoring the musty smell of old books, the odor of polished wood, the texture of rubber erasers, and the slippery surface of wood floors.

My closest school chums were Gérard Poulin and Richard Pruneau—two very different characters. Gérard was a blond boy with an upbringing similar to mine, the youngest member of a large family who lived on a farm outside town. He and I shared similar lifestyles and family circumstances, as we both had lots of older siblings.

But Richard was quite different, which is probably why he attracted my interest. Unlike me, he was outgoing, daring, clever, and funny. His bright eyes sparkled with naughty glitter. His family owned a country store across the street from our school, making him the envy of classmates, as he had access to both toys and candy. Richard was a spoiled "city" boy who'd never sampled the rustic charms of country living.

The daily walk to school took us past several country stores. This recurring exposure would gradually lure me into temptation—I found myself marveling at the store candy. But I had no money, and my parents would never waste theirs on such frivolities.

The solution struck me like a bolt of lightning one day as I stood next to my father at the counter. We were in the little country store owned by Maurice Brière, a place that doubled as the post office. In an extraordinary gesture that intimated paternal tolerance, my father had allowed me to accompany him to town on an errand.

When it came time to pay, I was puzzled by the lack of monetary exchange. The transaction had been sealed when my father uttered the words, "Put it on my account." Now *this* was a startling revelation. My hopes instantly skyrocketed, exalted at the prospect of sampling store candy just like my school friend Richard.

But it all seemed too good to be true; I'd have to make a test run to verify. At first chance, I'd stop by here alone on my way back from school and "buy" something on credit. Candy was cheap, so maybe my parents wouldn't notice. The big unknown was whether the store clerk would allow some kid to charge up the family account.

A few days later, I entered the store warily, my heart knocking like an African drum. This was the first time I'd ventured into a store without my parents; the experiment was risky, but the prospect of a sweet ending made it all worthwhile. I approached the candy stand under the watchful eye of the owner's wife. She smiled, wrinkling her nose.

The candy display was staggering. There were chocolate bars, gum, hard candy, soft candy, peanuts, chips, and an assortment of toy candies. I was befuddled by the variety. I deliberated over the candy rack for about fifteen minutes before deciding on a miniature bag of Planters peanuts. It cost five cents. It took me another five minutes to build up the courage to approach the register, where the store clerk was waiting patiently.

"Can you put this on my father's account?" I asked her in a timid voice. I avoided looking into her eyes, afraid that they'd betray my troubled soul.

"Does your father know?" she asked with a dubious smile.

"Yes," I lied.

"Well, all right then," she said with distrust in her voice.

I thanked her before galloping out of the store, running away from my own thievery. I waited until I was out of town and onto our dirt road before pulling out my little treasure. But my appetite had been supplanted by a huge pang of guilt even before I opened the tiny bag of Planters peanuts. I ate my illicit prize without much gusto, the guilt further compounded by a fear of parental discovery and reprisal.

My experiment had ended in failure, the internal strife too great to bear. I abandoned all further attempts to embezzle candy from the country store.

The painful episode had long been blocked from memory when I overheard my parents. They were in the kitchen, and I was upstairs lying awake in my bed. I could hear them talking in a hushed tone, their queer conduct prompting me to eavesdrop. I pulled back the blankets and tiptoed in my underwear to the top of the stairs.

"He bought a tiny bag of peanuts on credit?" my mother said amidst adult giggles. My father too seemed amused, regurgitating the words I'd spoken to the store clerk. They laughed themselves silly over my little caper, careful not to speak loudly.

I knew nothing about itemized statements, but it was obvious that I'd been busted. Despite her kid-friendly smile, the store clerk had squealed like a pig. My parents might have seen humor in the petty theft, but that didn't mean I was off the hook.

I went back to bed, finding it hard to sleep now that my moral wound had been reopened. Not surprisingly, my mother was ready to confront me the next morning.

"Was it you who bought the bag of peanuts on credit?" she said, looking deep into my eyes. She already knew the answer. The rhetorical question was merely an invitation to come clean before she decided on a suitable course of action.

"Yes, but it was only a five-cent bag," I replied.

"You can't do that!"

"I know, but I was curious."

She hesitated for a moment. "Well, don't ever do that again," she said. *That's it?* My guilt evaporated into thin air as I walked away, heaving a huge sigh of relief.

Now that my career as petty thief had been permanently derailed, I decided to become an entrepreneur instead. This move was again inspired by my school chum Richard. He had taught me that empty soda bottles were a virtual goldmine. Large glass bottles would fetch up to a nickel apiece; it sounded almost too good to be true.

Drawn by the prospect of big profit, I decided to get into the business of collecting empty soda bottles. I could use the proceeds to buy store candy, a persistent source of enticement. But my entrepreneurial scheme was already off to an inauspicious start. We rarely drank soda at home—my parents bought it only when we expected weekend guests. So, we had no empty bottles to return—a slight hiccup in my plans.

"But your grandfather does drink soda," Maman said. "Ask him for the bottles." Hope returned as the dollar signs floated before my eyes once more. Driven by greed, I wasted no time traveling the short distance to Grandpapa Côté's.

"Do you have any empty soda bottles I might have?" I asked him bashfully.

"I throw all my bottles behind the house. You can have whatever you find."

Thrilled with his cooperation, I wasted no time making my way to the backyard. I could see small piles of buried bottles, but many were broken and others were of the non-refundable variety. I started digging with my hands, a nearby wagon waiting to hold my precious cargo. It was hard work, but I managed to salvage about a dozen bottles.

Back at the house, I washed the big soda bottles in the summer kitchen. Most were filled with sand, the result of exposure to many seasons in the great outdoors.

Eager to reap the fruits of my labor, I asked my father if he could drive me someplace to cash in the bottles. He agreed to bring me along the next time he went to town on errands. The following Saturday, I packed up the empty bottles in a cardboard box. Papa parked the car in front of the tavern in St-Gérard, pointing to the entrance. The tavern was located in the lower level of the only hotel. I struggled to open the heavy tavern door, careful not to damage the fragile package clinking in my arms.

The place was dark and dingy. A few men were sitting at the bar drinking beer, smiling at the odd little boy who'd just entered the adult premises.

"Can I cash in these bottles?"

He seemed amused to see me standing there. I lifted the box onto the polished bar, and my efforts were soon rewarded with a handsome sum of sixty cents. I was rich.

I spent part of my newfound wealth at the country store, where my father had stopped for groceries. I bought a chocolate bar and a plastic toy, leaving with change to spare.

French grammar was quirky, and learning it could be tedious. Nouns were assigned genders that dictated the articles that preceded them. And the same verb could end with *e*, *é*, *er*, or *ez*, depending on context. The plural form of verbs could also change dramatically between first, second, and third person. There were compound tenses with maddening rules of their own, and stressed pronouns that drove you nuts deciding whether to use *toi*, *lui*, *elle*, or *vous*. To top it off, you had to figure out where to stick all the queer accents like the cedilla (ç), circumflex (â), acute (é), grave (à), and dieresis (ä).

Despite its troublesome rules, grammar was still easier to grasp than Catechism. The only way for a child to learn all the Catholic doctrines was to commit them to memory. There were no patterns to leverage, only endless precepts on faith and morals.

Catechism required a supernatural sense of faith—this was a difficult imposition on a pragmatic farm boy like me. I racked my brain to make sense of the dogmas but rapidly grew frustrated with their ethereal nature. I gave up trying to comprehend the dry facts, settling for rote memorization—I could at least spew them back out on tests.

I found the Ten Commandments easy enough, but other Catholic doctrines flew right over my head. The mystery of the Most Holy Trinity was a riddle to me; I struggled to conjure up a physical image of the Father, Son, and Holy Spirit as one entity.

I reacted to the transformation of bread and wine (into the Body and Blood of Christ) with disgust. *So now I have to eat the flesh of some dead guy?* I thought. But the Catholic doctrine of transubstantiation was not to be taken lightly. Martin Luther had contested it as a form of idolatry back in the sixteenth century, contributing to the history-making split between the Protestants and Roman Catholics. It's not surprising that our religious teachers sought to guard this particular dogma with Gestapo-like zeal.

"You must believe that this is truly the body and blood of Christ," we were told. We'd nod sheepishly, afraid to offend the divinities with our juvenile heresy.

Kids had to endure four sacraments before reaching adulthood. The sacrament of baptism was administered right after birth, penance and holy communion were next, and confirmation was administered later. I made my first penance and first communion while in first grade, and my confirmation at the ripe age of eight.

Our first-grade teacher collaborated with the parish priest to prepare the class for first confession. I found the whole thing intimidating. The idea of spilling your guts to a perfect stranger while kneeling inside a confined space sounded quite distasteful.

A six-year-old doesn't have much to confess either. After racking my brain, I came up with three venial sins that I could confess each time. I could always count on losing my patience, arguing with siblings, and disobeying my parents. These became regulars. The confession had a predictable format involving a memorized formula.

"Father, it's been a month since my last confession. I accuse myself of being impatient five times, arguing with my brother three times, and disobeying my mother twice." This was the typical format and content of my confessions at the start. But the nature of my sins would escalate significantly by the age of eight.

It was unfortunate that frequent illnesses had hindered my religious training. The consequence of missing weeks of school was remedial classes at the rectory. There were two dispiriting problems with the make-up sessions. First, Father Berger was the central figure, an austere priest who'd been dispossessed of smiling at birth. His words would send chills up my spine, and his glare would make me quiver. Every time he visited our classroom, we had to bow our heads before God's representative.

Father Berger also made it a point to visit the home of every parishioner once a year over the warmer months. He'd stroll to our house wearing his authoritative-looking black cape, while we watched him approach with great agitation.

My mother would turn into an insecure wreck as soon as she knew he was coming. She feared that her nervous words and gestures would incite his reproach. In the tradition of the Jesuits who had dominated New France in the seventeenth century, Father Berger was not just a representative of the Church; he was also the most powerful man in town.

Lucette had assigned Father Berger the unflattering nickname "*petit cul baiser,*" which loosely translates to "little ass kisser." This crude but apt appellation referred to the shape and movement of his lips. They were always pinched tight, forming little white wrinkles that opened and closed with repulsive motions.

The second problem with the remedial sessions was the students—they were all morons. There were only three other boys in the make-up class, but they were all quite conspicuous. These were hapless rejects who'd failed to show even a faint understanding of religion.

Serge looked almost as tall as Father Berger. His colossal size suggested that he might have repeated first grade about seven times. I suspected that he already shaved his face twice a day. But I felt pity for Serge. He had a bad stutter, a vacuous look in his eyes, and a steady supply of foam bubbles at the corners of his mouth.

"Who is God?" father Berger asked with a stoic face, his lips quickly resuming their tightly pinched form. There we were in his office, a group of slow-witted kids sitting in a decrepit little circle, and nobody knew the answer to this most basic question. Except for me, that is. But my devouring fear of "little ass kisser" was inhibiting my speech. To Father Berger, I too had a guaranteed lifetime membership to the Dimwit Club.

"It-it-it's the devil!" Serge finally blurted out with great difficulty, spitting foam bubbles at the priest in a feeble-minded attempt to supply an answer. Father Berger's bald forehead turned red in anger, his beady eyes staring back like two rifle barrels.

I bowed my head in shame, covering my eyes with one hand to block out the pathetic scene. My regrettable association with the Three Stooges was hurting my pride and filling me with a deep sense of humiliation. I just wanted to be back in class.

I managed to make it through the humbling remedial sessions, receiving first penance and communion with the rest of the first-graders. And I learned that confession shares common elements with acting in school plays: the anticipation is terrible, the delivery is not usually too bad, and the resulting high makes you want to go again.

By the time confirmation came around, school had been a routine part of my life for the better part of three years; I was an old pro. The sacrament of confirmation was special because it was administered by the grand poobah of priests, the bishop himself.

The most worrisome aspect of confirmation was the anticipation of getting slapped by the bishop. This was standard procedure, intended to remind us that we must endure adversities in the name of Christ. Horror stories on the severity of these slaps abounded in the schoolyard, spread by cocky boys who'd been previously confirmed.

Since the bishop only visited St-Gérard every three or four years, several age groups were always confirmed at the same time. The small church was filled beyond capacity on the day of my confirmation. It seemed like entire clans had come down from the hills to witness their little brats receive their high-profile slap from the bishop.

The bishop stood up to confer the sacrament, and our coach soon gestured for us to approach the altar. The air became filled with flesh sounds, as the bishop first anointed our forehead with oil and then slapped our cheek mercilessly. Maman knew the moment I was confirmed; she heard the crisp smack from the back of the church. I walked back to my seat with a sore cheek, resentful of the adult smiles I noticed along the way.

I may have been shy, but that didn't prevent me from being naughty. My shyness simply made me more discreet and careful in my execution. A guilt-induced chill ran up my spine whenever I heard an adult say, "It's the quiet ones you have to watch out for." This rang true for me.

My calculations weren't always successful though, and I sometimes got busted. That wasn't hard to do in a Catholic institution run by ninja nuns who were trained to root out ungodly behavior. All it took was one careless whisper or misplaced smile, and you could be court-martialed. Not surprisingly, the majority of repeat offenders were boys.

The choice of punishment was left up to the teacher, but you could always count on a swift sentence delivered in full view of classmates. The penalty for small violations usually took the form of public humiliation, like standing or kneeling in the corner. But greater offenses were treated with corporal punishment, adding pain to humiliation.

Physical punishment was often administered with the aid of blunt instruments; a simple slap on the behind apparently lacked the theatrical effect sought for deterrence. The choice of weapon depended on both the teacher and severity of crime. Belts, rulers, clackers, blackboard erasers, and books could all turn into penal instruments.

An unlucky boy in Lucette's class once felt the punitive power of books. The book in question happened to be in the hands of his lay teacher at the time of the incident. The boy had two strikes against him: he stuttered badly and learned slowly. As he stuttered the reply to a topical question, the teacher became frustrated with his incessant stammer. She walked up to his desk, lifted the heavy textbook in one hand, and slammed it down on his head. His eyes rattled around his skull like two ping pong balls as he caught a fleeting glimpse of shimmering stars in a distant galaxy. The ruthless blow didn't do much to cure his stuttering, but it did add chronic drooling to his list of problems.

If a kid was charged with a serious crime, like disobedience, it meant a sorry trip to the dreaded principal's office. I was convinced that the principal indiscriminately gave the strap to every child who had the mischance of stepping into her office.

I once witnessed my cousin Rénald being dragged to the principal's office when we were both in the second grade. It made an impression that I never forgot.

Our second-grade teacher was Sister Bernadette Sophie. She was a tall and skinny nun with a pale complexion and stern appearance. We were making paper cutouts when one of the girls broke out in tears. It turned out that naughty Rénald was the source of her considerable distress. Sister Bernadette quickly judged that Rénald had misappropriated scissors to cut diagonal slices through the hem of the victim's pretty dress.

My cousin incriminated himself even further by wearing an audacious smile while the angry nun was charging him with the criminal offense. I had the impression that the nature of the case exceeded the jurisdiction of Sister Bernadette, because she briskly ordered Rénald to accompany her to the principal's office. He adamantly refused.

Rénald had probably heard the same inflated rumors about the principal and feared for the safety of his unruly butt. When Sister Bernadette reached out to grasp his hand, my cousin dropped to the floor on his back, screaming bloody murder.

"No, no, no. I don't want to go!" he howled through copious tears. The arrogant smile he'd sported earlier had vanished; a look of primal fear had taken its place.

The kids watched the awful scene with pale faces, while my heart sank to the pit of my stomach. *Nobody deserves this punishment*, I thought—not even Rénald.

But Sister Bernadette was not about to be dissuaded. She managed to lift Rénald to his feet, dragging his body toward the exit and the hallway beyond. Rénald continued crying convincingly while we all watched the tragedy unfold in horror.

I'd never seen a nun wrestle with a kid before; it seemed as though black cloth was flying everywhere. When their pathetic courtship reached the door, my cousin cleverly locked his arms around the door jam. As Sister Bernadette sought to dislodge his limbs from the frame, Rénald's flailing arms accidentally hit the good sister in the head.

The sudden blow knocked her veil back into an unflattering angle, exposing forbidden bits of hair in the process. The kids gasped in unison. Until that disgraceful moment, I seriously doubted that nuns had any hair at all. Sister Bernadette paused for just a moment to adjust her bonnet, and then she jumped back into the ring.

Our teacher eventually prevailed; we heard Rénald's screams languish as his body was dragged down the hallway to the principal's office. Sister Bernadette came back alone, confirming our suspicion that we'd never see Rénald again.

But Rénald did come back—with a big smile. I questioned him over lunch, curious to learn the extent of his punishment. It seems that the principal never touched him. She merely tried to make him understand the consequences of bad behavior. Big deal!

My first-grade teacher may have been easy going, but she still punished me from time to time. Even minor rebukes could ruin my day, leaving me distraught for hours at a time.

Mrs. Brunelle had kept us in class over recess on a blustery winter day. A group of boys had gathered near the front of the class to exchange views on wild animals.

"Bears aren't dangerous," my friend Gérard said.

"Yes they are," I corrected. I knew all about black bears; they kept mauling me in my dreams. The ending would always be the same. I'd find myself lying on my back in the backyard, paralyzed with fear. The bear would approach slowly, sniff my face, and start biting at my head. I'd watch in horror as sharp teeth ripped the flesh off my bones.

"No they're not!" he said more loudly, his little ego offended by my troubling retort. Several kids nodded in approval of his more gentle perspective.

"My father says they won't hurt you if you leave them alone," another boy said in support of Gérard. These opinions struck me as preposterous. They were all wrong; I'd have to set them straight. Anger rose inside my chest and my face turned hot with rage.

"You're all crazy…bears kill people!" I yelled with conviction. These kids were obviously deluded; imposing the truth could actually save their lives.

Mrs. Brunelle heard my angry voice and responded swiftly, taking hold of my arm and pulling me to the back of the class. My antagonists watched with glee as she dragged me away from the heated conversation. The class suddenly turned silent.

Where is she taking me? It became apparent that we were heading for the door. "Please, not to the principal's office," I prayed. She stopped in the hallway outside the classroom, turning my shoulders to face the wall at the base of the stairs.

"Stay here until you can behave. I'll come back when I think you're ready," she said with an austere look on her face. She closed the classroom door behind her and called an end to recess. Class activities resumed as I stood disgraced in the main hallway.

The main hallway was empty. Since classes were in session, there was no good excuse for stragglers. A kid who was caught outside class was akin to an escaped convict. The only person who could freely roam the hallway was the principal herself.

I'd been staring at the wall for about fifteen minutes when I heard the footsteps. They originated from the second floor, where the nuns took residence. The unmistakable rattle of wooden rosary beads and crucifix—dangling from waist down to ankles—told me with reasonable certainty that it was the dreaded principal herself.

The heels were clumping toward the staircase where I stood. I broke the rules and turned my head to peek at the top landing. I could see nun shoes and the hem of a long black dress. I was doomed. There would be questions, verbal reprimands, and an involuntary visit to her office. I resumed facing the wall, resigned to my fate.

The footsteps began traveling down the hardwood staircase. I wondered how much pain her strap would inflict on my butt. *Would she ask me to pull down my pants?*

Just a few seconds before the principal would reach my position, the classroom door opened unexpectedly. Mrs. Brunelle grabbed my arm and quickly pulled me inside. I had the impression that she had heard the principal and was acting to avert my demise.

My eyes were wet and frightened. The teacher took hold of my hand and walked me back to my desk. The other kids were sitting down, tracing the alphabet.

"Keep your eyes on your papers," she warned those who stared my way.

Back at my desk, she leaned down and gently guided my hand over the first few letters of the alphabet to get me caught up with the rest of the class.

"That's very good," she praised. "I shouldn't have punished you after all. Maybe you can lower your voice next time."

So she doesn't hate me after all? I smiled back at the loving face; I felt better now. But I was left with the indelible lesson: *Never express strong opinions in public.*

It wouldn't be the last time that I faced the wall for misbehavior. Miss Léonelda Lebrun supervised the lunchroom to relieve nuns and teachers over the lunch hour. Standing barely four feet tall, she'd watch over her charges with hawk eyes.

The lunchroom was in the school basement. The room was lined with long wooden tables and hard benches, where we ate the bagged lunches our mothers prepared. Excited voices and laughter filled the air, amplified by the low ceilings.

There was a wall-mounted water bubbler at the entrance of the lunchroom. A fragile wooden crate was nudged up against the base to assist the shorter kids.

Partway through lunch one day, several of us headed off to the bubbler. When my turn came, I jumped up on the orange crate with an exaggerated hop to be silly. My feet crashed through the top of the crate, shattering it beyond repair. I was flabbergasted.

Miss Lebrun heard the commotion and arrived on the scene in a flash. My feet were still entangled in the ruined crate when she emerged like an angry gnome. She instantly judged my misdeed, probably concluding that I'd been planning the destruction of that fragile crate since the age of five.

She squeezed my arm and dragged me to the center of the room while sputtering rebukes in my ear. I stood there staring at the floor, averting my eyes to hide my intense shame and humiliation. She asked for my right hand and proceeded to slap it repeatedly, her stiffened hair bobbing up and down to the rhythm. My friends stood nearby, watching the show with a distinct "better you than me" look on their faces.

When she was done, she left me facing the wall at the bubbler. For the remainder of that lunch period, every kid approaching the bubbler bore witness to my punishment, seeing my remorseful head bowing down at the wall. I left the humbling post only after the bell rang to resume classes. The day was ruined.

My third-grade teacher was Mrs. Brière, the wife of a local farmer. They lived in an unpainted old house at the end of an isolated dirt road surrounded by apple trees.

Mrs. Brière had the distinction of being the largest woman I'd ever met. She was shaped like a giant milk-fed pumpkin, the kind that wins ribbons at the county fair. When she walked, she waddled from side to side like a penguin, shifting her weight left and right. Her rotund shape made all her dresses appear bell shaped, as though supported by a gargantuan crinoline. Her turkey neck contained more chins than I could count, and the underside of her upper arms swayed like the full udder on a cow.

Mrs. Brière and her son once paid a memorable visit to our farm. I was seven years old at the time; this was about a year before I joined her third-grade class. It was Saturday night, and dusk was falling on the unlit dirt road that led to our farm.

Her arrival had been momentous. Her son, one of the town yokels, was driving the family tractor, pulling an old hay wagon behind. Mrs. Brière was sitting alone in the flatbed wagon, occupying the only rocking chair that could lodge her oversized butt.

I found the scene rip-roaringly funny. We were standing in front of our house when the dunce-parade float pulled into the yard. Her toothless son had brought an old stepladder to facilitate his mother's descent from her humble carriage onto solid ground.

"Stop laughing," Lucette warned, trying hard to control her own snickers.

Mrs. Brière ungracefully climbed off the farm wagon, all the while chiding her son with unflattering comments. The whimsical procession then moved inside the house. They settled in our small living room; several of us chose to remain outdoors.

We kept an old baseball bat in the garage alongside a lonely hard ball. We didn't play ball very often, yet these items had been around the family forever. On this memorable evening, my brother Pierre and I decided to play catch for some reason. We settled on the front porch, scampering down every few minutes to fetch foul balls.

I lost control of one of my throws and sent the ball smashing through the living room window. The sound of shattering glass was unnerving, but it was the high-pitch screams that pumped buckets of adrenalin into my veins. *Uh oh.*

I reacted as I always did when facing the prospect of parental retribution: I ran like hell. Pierre was at my side as we settled behind a sizable rock in the apple orchard. We'd barely reached our hiding place when my mother stepped out on the porch, calling out our names loudly. It was not a happy voice. When we failed to comply with her repeated demands to show ourselves, her anger became more pronounced.

But I was determined to go nowhere. I knew enough to avoid peak emotions and to make my appearance only after her anger had safely dissipated. But Pierre's resolve was beginning to weaken under the weight of my mother's threats. I saw him waver.

"Don't stand up!" I whispered as he started to fidget.

But it was too late. He was on his feet, walking toward Maman like a timid sheep. Her face was scowling and her hands were poised on her hips—both bad signs.

I was really upset. Not only had Pierre crumbled under pressure, but even worse, he'd endangered my self-centered ass by revealing our hiding place. Much to my surprise, though, Maman aborted all attempts to flush me out of the apple orchard.

Mrs. Brière had inadvertently saved my butt. My mother had let politeness take precedence over punishment. She returned to socialize with our visitors as my father cleaned up the mess and boarded up the damaged window with cardboard.

I stayed in hiding until dark, peeking over the edge of my rock to watch Mrs. Brière remount her lowly chariot for the return trip. But the spectacle wasn't funny anymore.

When the coast was finally clear, I guardedly entered the house through the kitchen door and headed up the stairs to my bedroom. But my mother caught me; she administered a verbal reprimand as I stared remorsefully at the floor.

"So, what happened?" I quizzed Pierre when I reached the bedroom.

"She broke the yardstick on my back," he said with a smile. I gasped, feeling terrible that he'd suffered the brunt of her anger while I had escaped unharmed.

"I told you not to stand up."

"She would have caught up with us anyway," he said. He then proudly retrieved the broken yardstick to show me proof of his endurance. Sure enough, it was split in half.

Despite her odd shape and size, nobody *ever* laughed at Mrs. Brière at school—at least not if they wanted to survive another day. She was our teacher for two years in a row, and I never once saw a child so much as dare a smile in her presence. Even recess seemed off limits to jokes, the kids petrified that their mockeries would be dutifully reported.

I only heard one indignity spoken about Mrs. Brière in the third grade, and it came from my smart-aleck friend, Richard Pruno. His face was grinning naughtily while he painted a vivid and funny image of Mrs. Brière in the schoolyard.

"She punishes kids by sitting on them," he said. "Why, there could be a dozen kids up her butt crack by now," he said with a naughty laugh.

I found this brazen joke hilarious and had a tough time controlling my funny bone in class over the next few days. Every time she turned around to face the blackboard, I could imagine her pumpkin butt hiding untold kid carcasses. I snickered to myself as I visualized little arms protruding below her dress hem.

Once she'd established her authority, Mrs. Brière became an interesting and mostly pleasant teacher. But she was quick to anger, so it was only a matter of time before I would test her patience. Not surprisingly, my friend Richard would lead the way.

We attended third and fourth grade in an overflow classroom above a country store. This private house—Mater Domini occupied the top floor—was adjacent to the school, its rear staircase providing convenient access to the main school-yard.

The seats in our third-grade classroom were laid out in pairs; two kids would sit together at abutting desks, and an aisle separated the pair on both sides.

As luck would have it, Richard became my "buddy." He sat to my immediate left. We'd just come in from recess one day when he started taunting me. Every time Mrs. Brière turned her back, he'd poke me in the ribs and smile. Not wanting to alert the teacher, I sent disapproving looks in return. But his teasing was relentless. I tried to pay attention to class, but he'd poke me at every chance, causing me to twist in my chair. This seemed to amuse him greatly, his white teeth sparkling with delight.

Mrs. Brière was busy writing on the blackboard when I decided to end the roguery once and for all. I waited patiently until Richard had turned his head away before delivering a hefty punch to the pit of his stomach. The punch took his breath away, causing him to bend over in pain and cough like a drowning man. *Oh shit.*

"What's the matter, Richard?" the teacher asked, turning back abruptly.

Richard spoke the truth. "Michel punched me."

"Come here," she said, glowering at me with vengeful eyes.

"Put out your hands," she said, reaching for the wooden clackers that rested in the top drawer of her desk. I stood in front of the class, resigned to my punishment.

She extended the wooden clackers—they were shaped like a pair of dentures—and slammed them down across my fingers. She was visibly upset. Her face was flushed with rage as her bountiful jowls quivered with every blow.

I kept my fingers extended as the wooden weapon bludgeoned the fingers on both hands. She was soon out of breath from the strenuous labor and ceased hitting. My fingers were stinging from the blows, but my pride insisted that I keep a stoic face.

"Now go stand in the corner," she said, pointing behind her desk. Her goal was to humiliate me in front of the class for the rest of the morning. Silent tears dribbled down my cheeks as I faced the wall. I hated Richard with a passion.

At lunch, I kept to myself, giving Richard the cold shoulder, even refusing to look in his direction. Expecting to be jeered by ruthless kids, I avoided my classmates altogether. They could all go to hell, with the big pumpkin piloting their descent into the fiery pit.

"I'm sorry, but your punch caught me by surprise," Richard said. He'd caught up with me in the schoolyard, persisting in spite of my attempts to avoid him.

"You started it—and you didn't even defend me," I protested.

"Hey, I'll make it up to you. Now come and play," he said with a beckoning smile.

His natural charm quickly restored my confidence, and I was soon playing with Richard as though nothing had happened. And he did try to make it up to me. Whenever he heard somebody talk about the clacker episode, he'd come to my defense. Richard could have run for political office and won by a landslide.

It was in third grade that I also experienced the bitter taste of inequity. It was winter, and we were heading out for recess. The back of the classroom was in turmoil, as kids donned their coats, hats, mittens, scarves, and boots in a rush to maximize playtime.

The country store below our classroom belonged to Lorenzo Doyon. It just so happened that his darling daughter was in our class. Miss Doyon was a spoiled and temperamental girl—I had the impression that all store owners pampered their kids.

I was almost out the door when I hear a loud sob coming from the back of the room. It was none other than Miss Doyon, who was sitting on the floor in a puddle of tears. Mrs. Brière approached the coddled child and asked about her emotional display.

"One of the boys hurt me," Miss Doyon said amidst a flood of baby tears.

"Who hurt you?" the teacher asked with furled eyebrows.

"Michel. He stomped my feet on purpose," she said, flaunting more tears.

I couldn't believe my ears. I'd been dressing on one side of the room while she was sitting on the floor on the opposite side. Yet the little brat was incriminating me before our impatient teacher. I had no choice but to defend myself.

"I didn't even go near her," I said, my words coming out hollow.

"That's enough! I want to see you here at noon," Mrs. Brière snapped. There was to be no more discussion. I'd been accused and tried, and would be sentenced at lunch.

At recess, the boys in class jokingly speculated on my fate. But I wasn't amused, expecting to be again brutalized by the stupid clackers.

I ate my sandwich half-heartedly, lost in dreary thoughts about injustice. When the rest of the class trampled outdoors to play in the schoolyard, I stayed in my seat.

"Do anything you want," Mrs. Brière said. She was no longer angry. On the contrary, her mood seemed downright cheerful, as if she'd temporarily switched off the stern teacher act to restore her batteries. I decided to speak up.

"I didn't do it," I said.

"Miss Doyon is spoiled and cries for nothing anyway. Just avoid her."

It dawned on me that maybe I'd been a political scapegoat. The school depended on the Doyon family for the overflow space. I had the impression that Mrs. Brière had feigned reparation just to shut up Miss Doyon. There was to be no punishment.

Our poor Mrs. Brière was nearly killed in the summer of 1961. It happened just a few months before we were to rejoin her fourth-grade class at Mater Domini.

Her blockheaded son—the same one who'd once driven her to our house—had bought an old pickup truck that served as their primary mode of transportation. They were returning home from town one day with Mrs. Brière in the passenger seat. The passenger door had been improperly latched, a clear invitation to disaster.

As her son negotiated a sharp bend in the road, Mrs. Brière was shoved against the door and tumbled out of the moving vehicle. She slammed down on the pavement and rolled like a tenpin bowling ball on a polished wooden alley.

Her injuries were severe and life threatening. She had broken bones, a concussion, and severe bruising all over her rotund body. She barely survived.

But Mrs. Brière did return to teach our fourth-grade class. Her arm remained in a sling and one side of her face was the color purple. We welcomed her back to class, partly out of sympathy but mainly because we'd grown fond of a good teacher.

I hated Monday mornings. It was always drudgery to return to school after spending a pleasant weekend on the farm. Monday morning always came too soon and too often.

I was nine years old when I became a truant. It was a lazy Monday morning, and I'd skipped my usual chore of milking one cow, choosing instead to remain in bed. My contributions added little to the farm routine, so my family rarely missed my services.

As I lounged in bed that morning, I made the bold decision to feign illness. It was something I'd never done before, so I was naturally nervous about my ability to pull off the lie convincingly.

My plan was simple. I'd start by ignoring my mother's beckoning calls until she came upstairs to check on my whereabouts, at which time I'd pretend to be sleeping. When she woke me from my bogus sleep, I'd put on a sick face and moan about a headache and stomachache. Once my siblings were safely off to school, I'd wait a credible hour before announcing my miraculous recovery, no doubt a result of the innocuous aspirin she would have prescribed by then.

But would Maman fall for my shifty story? Would my acting be convincing enough to keep me home for the day? These questions worried me considerably. If my little charade failed, it would lead to lasting distrust and increased parental vigilance.

But the plan worked beautifully. My close bond with Maman had enabled me to predict her response with exactitude. She left me to lie in bed, fetching some aspirin to relieve my symptoms. I knew I'd succeeded when I overheard her instruct my sister to notify the teacher. I smiled to myself, bloated with self-satisfaction.

While I was waiting in bed for my "recovery," Maman brought me some milk and toast in the hope of abating the vague ailment. She asked me questions, no doubt trying to diagnose a familiar illness from my symptoms. I ate my food slowly to conceal the delight.

Not long after my siblings had gone off to school, Mrs. Gagné, our friendly neighbor and the mother of my playmate Jean-Marie, stopped in to see my mother. It wasn't long before the good neighbor joined Maman at my bedside to assess my condition.

"He seems to have a fever," my mother pronounced after placing a hand on my forehead. I sat up in bed. *She must be imagining things*, I thought. I felt fine.

Mrs. Gagné reached down to feel my throat. "His glands are swollen. I think he has the mumps," she said. Her medical opinion caused a thousand shivers to shoot up my cheating spine. Praying for a misdiagnosis, I touched my throat and felt bumps. *Uh oh.*

The scene suddenly turned surreal. My mother ran downstairs to concoct a more appropriate potion for the mumps while Mrs. Gagné kept me company.

"It looks like you'll be out of school for a while," she said, daring a good-natured laugh. But I wasn't laughing. *How could this happen when my illness was a sham?*

Then I came up with the answer: God had punished my truancy. It was true what our religious teachers had said about His omnipresence. The conclusion stunned me.

The women returned downstairs, leaving me depressed and guilt ridden. Turning my eyes to the ceiling, I made the sign of the Cross and prayed in a whisper.

"God, I'm sorry I skipped school today. I know it was wrong. I'll never do it again." I repeated this several times to make sure He got the message. I really *was* sorry.

It did turn out to be the mumps. My salivary glands swelled, giving me the appearance of a chipmunk whose cheeks were filled with acorns—and giving my siblings a little comic relief in the process. And I endured a high fever and a big headache—both real this time. Swallowing was painful and talking yielded only a muffled squeak that added to the humor.

I stayed home for more than a week. Before it was over, I was begging Maman to go back to school. The mumps had altered my perspective. I never feigned sickness again, nor did I miss another day of school. After all, God was watching.

8

Grieving Little Mario

I met Mario after school one memorable September afternoon. Earlier in the day, my sister Doris had nudged me as we passed each other in the hallway.

"Can you walk me home after class?" she asked with a twinkle in her eye.

"Sure, what time?"

"I'll be a little late. Wait for me in the schoolyard."

I liked Doris. She was usually approachable and friendly, and her gentle words made me feel special. This was in contrast with my other siblings, who seemed to think I was an annoying pest in need of more parental control. They were more than happy to provide the extra dose of castigation I deserved.

I was loitering around the playground waiting for Doris when I heard a young voice call out in my direction.

"Hey, come here!"

The voice was coming from under the stairs near the brick wall of the school building. I walked over cautiously, still shy and wary of strangers.

"*Salut*, do you want to play marbles?" the young boy said. He was kneeling on the ground with a handful of marbles at his knees. His face was streaked with dirt from dusty fingers, giving him the appearance of a street urchin.

"I have no marbles," I replied.

"It doesn't matter. I can lend you some of mine."

I accepted his invitation to play, removed my backpack, and kneeled on the opposite side of the makeshift marble court. It was a simple game. Ten or twelve marbles were placed inside a circle drawn in the sand. We'd take turns throwing a marble, keeping all those we succeeded in knocking out of the circle. The objective of the game was to win as many marbles as possible.

"My name is Mario," he said. He was a handsome blond kid with short hair and a round face. He seemed confident and outgoing for his age; I liked him already.

"Mine is Michel," I replied.

Mario and I played a few carefree games while exchanging silly pleasantries.

"Where do you live?" I asked.

"Just down the street, near the hotel."

Our lighthearted game was soon interrupted by Doris, who came walking out of the school building beaming a warm smile. I returned the borrowed marbles, bid Mario goodbye, and started for home with Doris. Little did I know that my chance encounter with Mario would teach me a lesson I'd never forget.

It was a cold Monday morning in December 1960. I was walking to school with my brother Pierre, experiencing the usual letdown that accompanied the end of another pleasant weekend. The morning air was crisp, causing us to exhale puffs of elusive fog. The chimneys sent up white plumes of twisting smoke that ascended in slow motion. The bright snow everywhere painted a sharp contrast against the clear blue sky.

We were shaken out of our sleepy state while approaching the center of town. The little wooden house near the only hotel in town was smoldering like a witch's cauldron. The outside was charred black like the charcoal we picked up on the railroad tracks. Some of the walls and part of the roof had collapsed.

I expected to see a huge crowd of curious bystanders gawking at the house, but the street was curiously empty. This should have been big news in a town where the only events worth reporting were automobile and farm accidents. But town dwellers were staying away for some reason, as though silently mourning the devastation.

The house stood alone, spewing lazy white vapor into the cold morning air. We stopped in front of the house to survey the damage; Pierre and I stood there staring at the scene. I'd never seen a burned house before.

"Come on, we'll be late for school," Pierre said, running up the street.

I followed him slowly, but frequently turned back to steal glances at the charred spectacle until it became obscured by a bend in the road.

When we entered the schoolyard, the place was abuzz with news about the fire. It seemed to be the only topic of conversation. I walked up to my friend Gérard.

"Did you hear about the fire?" he asked excitedly.

"Yeah, I just walked by the house. It's still smoking. Who lives there?" St-Gérard may have been a small town, but I knew little about its residents. We attended school and church and visited with relatives, but I knew little else about the town. I never visited my school chums at home; farmers had no time to chauffeur their kids around town.

"It's the Roy family," Gérard said. I was unable to put any faces to the name. "I heard that the father set the fire on purpose," he added.

"But who would set fire to his own house?"

"The type who wants the insurance money."

The bell rang, and we lined up according height, as always, marching off to class like little soldiers. After removing our coats and boots, we took our normal places. Our third-grade teacher, Mrs. Brière, then stood up to address the class.

"I'm sure you've all heard about the terrible fire," she said. "It breaks my heart to tell you that a child died in that house," she continued.

A hush descended over the classroom as we held our breath, wondering who it was. We knew that it wasn't anybody in our class—all the available seats were taken.

"Mario Roy, a first grader, lost his life in the fire," she said with sad face.

My head was swirling. *Mario? The nice kid who asked me to play marbles?* Surely, it couldn't be *that* Mario. My mind sought to expunge the dreadful thought.

But it did turn out to be Mario. The rest of the day was a blur, and I found it almost impossible to concentrate on schoolwork. At recess, the playground was overflowing with horrid stories about the fire, sending electric chills up and down my spine.

It seems that Mario hadn't just perished in the fire; he'd suffered a terrible death. The fire had started on the first floor of the house at around two-thirty in the morning, ignited by hot ambers in the woodstove located at the base of the stairs.

The eight children slept upstairs, in cramped rooms under the eaves. As smoke filled the house, the parents had escorted their children outdoors, ordering the older children to care for the younger siblings. But Mario had panicked and hidden upstairs.

By the time the family realized that Mario was missing, it was already too late. The father made repeated attempts to climb up the flame-engulfed staircase to fetch his son; he had to be restrained by relatives when the fire raged out of control.

Witnesses could hear Mario crying out for help as he stood trapped at the top of the stairs, frightened out of his hiding place. His father begged him to jump down the stairs in spite of the scary tongues of fire, but the young boy said he couldn't. He stood there frozen in fear while his father frantically pleaded with him to jump.

One of the neighbors finally put a ladder up to a side window near Mario's location, intending to rescue the boy through the window. But the instant the glass was broken, the fire spread with the force of hurricane winds. Mario ceased crying.

They found his charred body at four-thirty that morning, on the landing at the top of the stairs. Six inches further and he would have tumbled down the stairs, hurt but alive.

I felt sick to my stomach. *How could a little boy suffer such a horrible death?* I could envision Mario frantically brushing off the flames with his hands as they consumed his flannel pajamas, feeling his skin burn before lapsing into unconsciousness.

My mind reeled in horror, replaying the script of his death over and over again, each time more terrifyingly than before. His death made no sense at all.

Mario's death suggested that I too could die. Until that moment, I'd felt almost immortal. Only old people died, I thought. But this was an innocent boy, just like me. *What sort of god would let a child die like that? Isn't God supposed to love us?* To an eight-year-old boy, the answers were no longer apparent.

My mother was baking a cake when I walked in the house later that afternoon. She already knew about the fire and had heard all the details about Mario's last minutes. She offered me a beater from the blender that was dripping with yummy cake batter.

"I'm not hungry," I said.

She sensed my mood, handing me the beater in spite of my words. I took it, but licked it with disinterest. I had more important things on my mind.

"Maman, why do children die?" I asked.

"Oh, I guess God must have needed another angel."

"But could it happen to me?"

"Well, it *won't* happen to you," she replied, avoiding the question.

Nevertheless, her confident words made me feel safer, and I believed her. The rumors on the origin of the fire suggested that Mario's father had been negligent in disposing of the ashes in the woodstove. I knew that my father would never be careless like that. So, it seemed to me that my mother might be right; this would never happen to me.

"Do you think Mario suffered?" I continued. His death was bad enough, but the idea that he might have suffered unbearable pain made it much worse.

"The smoke probably got to him before the flames," she said.

Her words made me feel a bit better. Maybe he hadn't been burned alive after all. But there could be no doubt that he must have been terrified to be stranded alone upstairs, with flames shooting up at his feet. That itself would have been slow torture.

That evening, I knelt by my bed to say a prayer as usual. But this time, I thought about Mario and the Roy family. I couldn't imagine what his siblings must be feeling, having escaped the burning house while their little brother stayed behind to perish.

I found it impossible to sleep, my mind reliving the bad events of the day. I decided to engage Mario in conversation. Since he was an angel, I figured that he'd be able to hear me. So, I lay on my back in my bed and addressed him as if he were somewhere above me. Once the greeting was over, I moved on to specific questions.

"Did it hurt to die?" I asked.

I sensed that he replied, *"Not very much."*

"What's it like to be an angel?"

I thought he said, *"Not too bad."*

"Is it embarrassing to be naked?"

It felt like he might have replied, *"You get used to it."* This last question troubled me, because all religious paintings and statues showed little cherubs naked. I assumed that this was the natural order of things, and that Mario would have to abide by the same clothing restrictions. Religious statues depicted cherubs with short wings and tiny weenies. I guessed that this was to avoid scandalizing scrupulous old women.

"Do you play marbles up there?" I asked. I heard him say, *"Yes and much more."*

This imaginary banter went on for about an hour. It would become part of my bedtime ritual for the next few weeks. I would imagine Mario sitting up on a fluffy cloud, flying around like Peter Pan and playing carefree games with fellow cherubs. This time with Mario helped me come to grips with both his loss and my own mortality.

The day after the fire, I walked home from school with my brother Pierre. But before leaving town, we followed my cousin Christian to the burned-out Roy residence. By the time we arrived at the scene, the street was deserted. Ever an adventurer, my cousin boldly walked up the front steps to the house; we followed solemnly.

The place was a disaster. The first floor was strewn with charred furniture. As we stepped over the threshold, I glanced to my left and noticed the woodstove that had allegedly caused the tragedy. The rest of the first floor was impassible.

We then climbed up the charred steps to the second floor. The roof had partly collapsed, raining debris on the staircase and exposing sections of the house to the elements. I was worried that the steps would collapse under our weight, but they held up.

The upstairs bedrooms were littered with clothes and remnants of furniture. Bureau drawers had been left open—vivid reminders of the desperate scramble to exit the burning home. I looked around the room wondering where Mario might have hidden. *Was it under that bed?* A partially burned twin bed stood in the middle of the room.

Glancing wide-eyed around the room, I inhaled the pungent odor of burned wood. Our visit felt entirely wrong, like violating some sacred memorial to the dead. After all, we *were* trespassing in the private home of a family who'd just lost a child.

My brother and cousin were at the top of the stairs brushing snow off the landing. Linoleum flooring had covered the bare wood planks, but the fire had turned most of it black. That is, except for the place where Pierre and Christian were removing snow with their hands. On that portion of the unburned linoleum, they exposed a horrific sight—the silhouette of a child. A chill ran up my back so fast that I felt dizzy.

Pierre and Christian were soon bored with the adventure, and they wandered back downstairs and into the street. But I remained at the top of the stairs a little longer, kneeling on the landing to touch the portion of the unburned flooring where Mario had perished. The shadow on the floor clearly defined his arms, legs, and torso. Tears welled in my eyes and spilled onto the floor. I'd never been so sad in my life.

Pierre yelled up that he was heading home. I was suddenly petrified to be alone in that house of suffering and death. I bounced down the stairs to the safety of the outdoors, wishing that Mario could have done the same the night before.

The rest of our walk home was a big blur, my mind revisiting the scene of the fire over and over. I'd now seen Mario's death imprinted in linoleum; it had made a ghastly impression on the brain of an eight-year-old boy.

That same afternoon, my sister Lucette came home from school looking pale. She was a classmate and a good friend of Mario's sister, Ghyslaine. Their teacher had offered the students the option of attending Mario's wake, and Lucette had gone.

As she described her experience in ghastly detail, I trembled in disbelief. Her report of the wake was even more astonishing than the eyewitness accounts of the fire.

Despite the severe damage to Mario's body, his mother had insisted on an open coffin. Family members had cleansed the body, scrubbing Mario's charred skin with Brillo pads in a futile effort to restore his light complexion. His body was not embalmed.

Mario's open coffin was then placed in the living room of his uncle's house. The ranch-style home was situated beyond the entrance of the only cemetery in town. Even the location of his wake sounded eerie to me, in full view of the cemetery.

A thin, sheer fabric had been laid across the coffin lid to obscure the dreadful appearance of the dead child. But without hesitating, thirteen-year-old Ghyslaine moved the fabric aside to give her friends a closer look at her little brother's body.

His hair was scorched, his face was black like charcoal, his mouth was gaping in a last gasp, and his eyelids were weighted down with coins to hold them shut. There were also white cotton swabs inside his mouth; Ghyslaine removed them to show her peers that the intense heat had fused his lips and tongue inside the mouth cavity.

Moving on to the torso, Ghyslaine rolled up her little brother's shirt sleeve to reveal melted skin, exposing the fleshless skeleton fingers. She then loosened his little tie and unbuttoned his white shirt to expose the deep fissures in his chest. The skin was split open, with crevices that resembled those seen on overcooked hotdogs.

Lucette had been visibly marked by what she saw at the wake, as her classmates no doubt were. The ghastly details of that day would haunt her brain for a long time.

"They should have closed the coffin," Maman said in a disapproving tone. We knew she was right; our memories of the blond boy had been forever ruined.

Her emotion-packed report caused me to cringe; Mario had been horribly defaced in death. Despite my trepidation, I made the bold decision to attend the wake the next day. That would be the day before the funeral, my last opportunity to bid farewell.

The kids in the lower grades were not invited to attend Mario's wake; the teachers knew that the experience would be too traumatic for young children. So, I told nobody of my intention to visit Mario that day. I skipped lunch and sneaked out at noon.

Mario's uncle owned a house at the end of the cemetery road, and I had to walk the length of the creepy cemetery to reach my final destination. As I approached the house, I could see the living room windows, with shadows of people inside.

I thought I could see the coffin lid through the curtains; my heart began beating at a frenetic pace. I paced the front of the house in a zigzag pattern, but my wobbly legs refused to take me up the front walk. I mumbled encouraging words under my breath to rally my courage, but the self-talk did little to assuage my fear.

"You owe it to Mario," I whispered to myself when my legs refused to carry me to the door. I wanted to pay my last respects, but my brain was crippled with fear.

The hour was fast approaching one o'clock; I knew it was time to go back. I sobbed all the way back to school, ruthlessly cursing my cowardice aloud.

"*Maudit pisseu*" ("damn chicken"), I cursed. We always reserved this unflattering rebuke for the worst of wimps. I'd blown my last chance and let Mario down.

His funeral was held the next morning. The upper classes attended the funeral Mass, but the lower grades did not. I was deeply disappointed. The principal apparently felt that the macabre affair would be too difficult on young children.

We were outside for recess when the funeral procession pulled up to the church. The church building was next door to the school, so we were able to observe the cortege from the schoolyard. I saw family members enter somberly, and then watched with heavy heart as Mario's small coffin was carried up the steps and into the church.

The school bell rang to announce the end of recess, and we climbed back up the stairs to resume class in our second-floor schoolroom. But I found it impossible to concentrate; my eyes were glued to the windows facing the little church building.

The church bells soon tolled their solemn timbre to announce the end of the funeral Mass. I turned my head just in time to see Mario's coffin being carried out of the church. The cars of family members and friends slowly vacated the church parking lot, heading for his final resting place at the cemetery. Mario was no more.

I never forgot little Mario. Over the years, I've often wondered what he might have become, and whether our paths might have crossed later, in our adult years. Mario's death had taught me an important yet horrifying lesson: *Kids die too.*

A few days after the funeral, his family moved to the United States. This had been their intention all along, and the father was already working in New Hampshire. It was also the source of the callous rumor alleging that the father had set fire to his house for insurance purposes. My sister Lucette never saw her friend Ghyslaine again.

Some forty years after his death, I stopped at the little cemetery in St-Gérard to visit to my father's grave, much like I'd done on prior occasions. I walked through the cemetery alone, taking time to stroll leisurely among the tombstones.

About twelve feet from my father's grave, my eyes rested on a tombstone that was inscribed with the name "Samuel Roy." I knew that this was Mario's grandfather. But as I looked down at my feet, I was stunned to find a small stone measuring some twelve inches wide, inscribed with the word "MARIO." It sat flat on the ground, its dull edges covered over with grass. A chill ran up my spine—it was little Mario.

I crouched down to feel the tiny stone that irreverently covered the child's grave. It contained no date or religious images. As I passed my hand over the unpolished gray stone, my mind traveled back in time to December 6, 1960. For a moment, I was back in that house, touching the unburned piece of linoleum that outlined Mario's profile. My eyes welled up just like those of an eight-year-old boy, dabbing his gravestone with tears.

Mario Roy's gravestone.

On my next visit to the cemetery, I came better prepared. After visiting my father's gravesite, I returned to see Mario's. Kneeling in the grass, I reached into my pants pocket and deposited three beautiful glass marbles on his stone.

"Hold onto these. I'll be back to finish our game someday," I whispered.

9

Physical Education

My parents never dared discuss human anatomy with their kids, never mind sex. They treated the subject as though the mere acknowledgement of genitalia would precipitate sprees of debauchery that could shatter family reputations and lead to eternal damnation. Ignorance was bliss, or so parents and religious educators believed.

Sex cast a shameful and dirty aura even upon its married practitioners. The "act" was an abominable and despicable routine to be performed as infrequently as possible, and even then, only for the purpose of procreating little brats like me.

Faith was the only acceptable excuse for sex. The heated sermons at Sunday Mass warned us repeatedly to avoid sins of the flesh. The religious lesson was crystal clear: *Your body must never be used for pleasure.* In fact, it seemed a fluke of creation that pleasure existed at all, as if God had invented sex on a bad day.

I never had one of those father-son talks about the birds and the bees. None of us did. If Papa had been forced at gunpoint to choose between teaching sex to his boys and getting his fingernails ripped out with instruments of torture, I'm quite certain that he would have opted for the torture. It was easier.

It's not likely that the idea of instructing his sons ever entered his scrupulous brain. Fathers believed that sex was something the boys would learn when they became men. Exactly how this would happen remained one of the great mysteries of life, like one of those divine revelations that you get to figure at death.

Like most men of his time, Papa relegated all child-rearing responsibilities to my mother; it would have been up to her to sit us down for a chat about sex. But my mother's generation believed that kids would build up the nerve to ask questions when they reached "the age"—whatever that meant. This would be the cue for parents everywhere to dish out evasive answers, the kind that send the kid staggering back in juvenile confusion after learning that love makes babies. *Huh?*

Kids had their own quirky lingo to refer to their private parts. We had no choice; I didn't even know the correct names for male and female genitalia until I was a teenager with an unabridged dictionary. Both family and church deemed the clinical terms for these sinful body parts off-limits to children. This ignorant stance was rooted in the moralistic concern that enunciating words like "penis" or "vagina" might place unbearable pressure on parents to explain their reproductive roles to children worldwide. And that could never happen. So, parents, clerics, and teachers banished the nonessential words altogether. Kids got the message: *You must never refer to your private parts.*

Although we used forbidden slang terms among playmates, those naughty words could never be spoken in the presence of adults. At least, not without risking a sharp slap on the ears—the kind that makes your world echo for hours as if spoken through a tin can.

We often used the word *guidoune* for penis. It bears a close resemblance to its English cousin, the diminutive "dink." *Pinouche*, a multi-purpose word that means "little thing," was also used. And testicles were called *la poche*, which translates to "the sack."

Our impoverished vocabulary for female parts included *téton* for breast, and *la craque* for vagina—a dimwitted term attesting to our near-total ignorance of female anatomy. The vagina was sometimes called a *pissette*, a lamebrain reference to peeing.

Buttocks were called *fesses*, one of the few acceptable terms we could utter in the presence of adults without reproach. And *trou-de-cul* was crude slang for anus—but it could also be applied to an offensive human.

"*Maudit trou-de-cul!*" ("Damn asshole") was a popular curse.

"*Mange de la merde!*" ("Eat shit") would be a justified reply.

The absence of labels for our private parts sometimes created awkward moments between parent and child. On those rare occasions when it became absolutely necessary for health reasons, we simply pointed. The index finger would be held waist high, curved slightly to show the general path of our ailment, and the words "down below" would be added for clarification. If you pointed toward your butt, the message was clear and unambiguous. If a boy mumbled "underneath" while pointing in the vague direction of his crotch, it referred to his testicles. By means of these Neanderthal interactions, we managed to avoid uttering offensive terms while trying to solve our dilemma. It was quite efficient, a form of shorthand that compensated for the deficiencies in our vocabulary.

City folks tend to think that growing up on a farm guarantees an early sex education. Large animals parade their over-endowed private parts for all to see and unabashedly engage in their primitive mating rituals under open skies. Add a touch of deductive reasoning to the visual effects, and you've got yourself worldly knowledge.

Any kid with half a brain would reach the logical conclusion that human adults must engage in equally gross mating rituals, but not me. I exuded an unflattering rural stupidity. The large appendages dragging under the bellies of the horses and bulls were obviously for peeing; you'd have to be a nitwit not to know that. And the backend of a cow was just a big, ugly butt to me—nothing more.

From time to time, I'd witness a mating bout in the bullpen, but I always thought the animals were just fighting—the equivalent of an unfair wrestling bout between humans. It riled me no end to see the bull mounting a cow. The pathetic mooing sounds that emanated from the helpless female spoke of pain and anguish. We knew these cows on a first-name basis, so these acts of bovine aggression begged for justice.

Like Mighty Mouse sent to the rescue, I felt obliged to separate the animals but almost always failed my mission. My weapons were small rocks, aimed at the most sensitive parts of the bull. Even when I hit my target, the bull barely acknowledged that he'd been hit. With an evil and maniacal look in his eyes, the bull was oblivious to all except his partner.

It also bothered me that my father did nothing to stop these wrestling matches between the stronger bull and more timid cows. I could never understand why he seemed to lack sympathy for the helpless animals.

One day when I was about seven, I ran up to the farmhouse in full gallop after witnessing another brutal episode of bull-on-cow violence. On this occasion, my empathy for the cow was particularly intense, because its mooing cries had reached ear-piercing decibels that scared the crap out of me. I was sure that the bull was committing bovicide. I ran up the hill from the barn, crashed through the front door of the house, and ran to my father, who was sitting in the living room.

"Papa, come quick! The bull is hurting the cow real bad," I said, short of breath.

"I'll be down to check in a minute," he said in his usual monotone voice.

In a minute? That part of his reply really bothered me. *Shouldn't we be sprinting down there in a synchronized trot this very second?* I hightailed back to the barn alone, heading for the nearby bullpen. Things had gotten worse. The bull was digging its front hooves in the soft sides of the cow, while its rear legs shuffled diabolically to the left and right in an effort to remain balanced on her rump.

I hated that bull with a passion; the hoarse-sounding moos from the cow told me that it was in full agreement. I wasn't much impressed with my father's responsiveness either. I ran back up to the farmhouse hoping to light a fire under Papa.

"Papa, the bull is on the cow's back!" I yelled, as if this was an abominable transgression of cattle regulations.

"The bull is not hurting it," he said flatly, without even looking in my direction.

Huh? How could he possibly know this? I'd been the only runt there to witness its blood-curdling moos just moments ago. I was bitterly disappointed. *Doesn't Papa love his animals?* I cursed him under my breath and stomped my feet back to the pasture.

By the time I had returned to the crime scene, the wrestling match was over. The bull had parted ways and the not-so-innocent cow was calmly grazing in the field as though nothing had happened.

My father never offered an excuse for the animal behavior or for his own inaction. The garbled message I processed that day was, *Bulls can abuse cows without recourse.*

These antics of cattle abuse soon ceased. The bull was dismissed and sold, his generous balls summarily removed from our midst. Papa had never been comfortable having a temperamental animal around his kids. In place of the mean bull, a nice veterinarian now started making periodic visits to the stable. The clipboard containing his unintelligible scribbles was kept inside a little wooden cabinet that was affixed to the stable wall, like some miniature shrine to the cattle gods.

This man had no scruples. I'd watch him treat the cows just because it was so curiously disgusting. Wearing a single disposable latex glove that stretched up to his armpit, he'd insert a foot-long syringe in the backend—or so I thought—of the cow. As his arm slowly disappeared in the abyss of the cow's derrière, we could hear audible sucking and slurping sounds reminiscent of a man drowning in Australian quicksand.

From time to time, the cow would glance back at the strange man with an annoyed what-the-hell-are-you-doing-back-there sort of look. The funny sounds combined with the befuddled cow expression always drew laughter from the kids.

When his entire arm had vanished inside the cow rump, the veterinarian would empty the syringe and slowly retract the arm with the same sucking and slurping sounds repeated in reverse. I had no idea that I was witnessing artificial insemination. I just thought he was administering medicine—the equivalent of those unpleasant shots I periodically received in my *fesses* to immunize me against polio, diphtheria, and tetanus. Yep, this lesson was way over my head.

My first recollection of feeling embarrassed about nudity was at the age of five. It was a warm summer afternoon, and my mother was about to give me a bath.

My bath routine was always the same. She'd fill up the kitchen sink with warm water, and I'd sit naked on the edge of the bowl with my feet dangling in the sink. From this position, Maman would attack my ears, neck, face, and feet with vigor. She always seemed especially frustrated with my ears and neck, scrubbing them with the resolve of a priest exorcising demons. At times, that washcloth felt a lot like steel wool.

Once the top epidermis layer had been rubbed off my face and the skin had turned a vibrant blush color, she'd turn her attention to the torso. I'd stand on the kitchen counter, pivoting to the left and right as Maman scrubbed my chest, back, butt, and legs.

One pleasant summer afternoon, one of my mother's cousins stopped by our house with her young daughter for an unexpected visit. The cute little girl was about my age. She had wavy brown hair and was dressed in a pretty skirt and blouse. They walked in just as my mother had started taking off my clothes.

"Oh, don't interrupt his bath for us," Cécile said apologetically. "We won't be long." After exchanging amenities, Maman continued with my bath as planned.

My mother's cousin sat on the rocking chair in the kitchen while her daughter settled nearby, closer to the kitchen counter. They chitchatted while Maman bathed me.

When it came time for the torso, I stood naked on the counter as usual, except that this time I had an audience of strangers, and all eyes were turned in my direction. That little girl was showing a lot more interest than I would have liked, too. Her gaze was focused on my naked form, her eyes making frequent trips down to my front midsection.

My mother scrubbed my back as I faced our guests, the soft parts of my anatomy jiggling in full view. It made me blush, but I resisted the urge to cup my hands over my private parts. That would make it even worse, I thought. So, I just stood there giving the little girl a frontal view of bouncing genitals.

"That little girl was looking at me," I said once they were gone.

"She's just a little girl," Maman replied as if we were too young to fret over nudity. But I hated the idea that my springy display had been a source of amusement.

My first graphic lesson in male anatomy came at age six. It was a Saturday morning and I was playing alone in the space above the stairs that doubled as the boys' bedroom. My eldest brother, Réal, now seventeen, was sleeping late in one of the back bedrooms.

I had to fetch something—I don't remember what—from the closet. I opened the bedroom door where Réal was sleeping late, and entered on tiptoe to avoid waking him. He was sleeping fitfully on his back, free of blankets, wearing only a pair of white boxer shorts. I glanced over at the bed as I tiptoed past. *What the hell is that?*

A hideous object had taken the place of my brother's *guidoune*. In its place, there was a ghastly growth rising out of his fly. This thing was huge! To me, it looked like an ugly little arm with a purple fist on the end.

I stared at this unnatural phenomenon for a moment, glancing back at his face to check for visible signs of distress. But the face was peaceful, blissfully unaware that something even more terrifying than the mumps had infected his body overnight.

I went bouncing down the wooden stairs at high speed. I found my mother working in the kitchen, as usual, and blurted out my terrible discovery.

"Maman, come upstairs right away! There's something wrong with Réal."

"What's the matter with him?" she said, alarmed by the tone of my voice.

"He's all swollen down there," I said, pointing a finger at my crotch.

"I'll come up to check on him in a minute."

Proud of my vigilance and pleased to have initiated my brother's recovery, I ran back upstairs to await my mother's medical assessment. While sitting on the floor outside Réal's bedroom, I tried hard to resume playing, but the disturbing memory of that little protruding arm kept popping into my naïve brain.

I was getting annoyed with my mother. Despite my urgent report, she still hadn't come upstairs to check on Réal. I decided to look in on my brother one more time, with the intention of reporting this latest reconnaissance to Maman. Maybe she'd take action this time. I opened the bedroom door slowly and peered in the direction of the teenager lying supine in bed. Even from the doorjamb, I could still make out the shape of the offensive pillar, a bare arm stretching toward the light bulb on the ceiling.

I'd seen horses and bulls with sizeable organs under their bellies many times, but this was different. This time, the host was my short and skinny brother who weighed around one hundred pounds sopping wet. Surely, this was abnormal, I thought. I made a quick exit and barreled down the stairs in search of my mother once more.

"Maman, Réal is still swollen. I checked again."

"Stay here while I go take a look."

I breathed a sigh of relief as she climbed the stairs; she returned a moment later.

"It's nothing. Just leave him alone. And stay out of his room."

What?

I knew Maman well. The inflections in her voice, the motion of her eyes, the shape of her lips, and the sway of her hips told me everything. I constantly sensed her moods, her quiet opinions, her gentle reprimands, and her motherly love flowing through these subtleties. As she spoke these last words, I could discern a tiny smile on her lips, mixed with a slight touch of embarrassment that she was unable to conceal.

I knew it even before she'd finished with her words: she hadn't entered Réal's bedroom at all. She'd climbed up the stairs, waited a minute, and walked back down just to shut me up. And I knew that the grotesque form I'd seen levitating above my brother's body was not a diseased organ. Her hint of a smile had said it all. The disheartening lesson for that day was, *Big boys grow huge, non-pliable guidounes.*

My next brush with sexual misconduct would involve a horny thirteen-year-old boy who lived half a mile from our house. Aside from my grandparents, the only other family who lived on our road at that time was the Moreau family. Alfred Moreau, his wife, Florence, daughter, Paulette, and son, Jean, were our second and farthest neighbors.

Mr. Moreau was an enigmatic man with a dubious reputation. He'd earned this distinction by being a non-practicing Catholic. In other words, he never went to church. His heretical behavior was both a mortal violation of God's laws and a clear indication of a hopelessly corrupt moral character. I feared him like the boogieman.

In keeping with the old adage that opposites attract, his wife was a warm, ebullient, attractive woman who also happened to be a close friend of my mother's. She'd hug us, laugh good naturedly, and feed us cookies till the cows came home. Florence's only flaw was poor judgment, evidenced by her choice of husband, Alfred.

Paulette was five years older than me. Everyone seemed to like her, too.

The problem was Jean. He was in puberty, and testosterone was rushing in his veins like April sap through a maple tree. He was the Dr. Jekyll and Mr. Hyde of our rural route. At times, he could be the nicest kid around, oozing charm and smarts that he must have learned from his nice mom—although they no doubt masked dubious intentions.

He was a handsome boy with a light complexion and sharp gray eyes; he could have easily passed for a choirboy. He was soft spoken, his cheeks were often crimson from shyness, and his speech was sickeningly polite. This good behavior was usually reserved for impressionable adults, who treated him like the prodigy of his saintly mother.

But I knew the other Jean, the bully who liked to beat on little kids to allay his boredom. This was the boy with the malevolent dog, Spotté, who had murdered our little Princess in front of our watery eyes. I feared him even more than his father.

We passed by the Moreau farm almost every day in the summer. Their property was a milestone on the path to adventurous treks through woods, hills, and creeks. He often waited for me like a cougar stalking a mule deer. Fear and trepidation would knock at my chest every time I approached their house. *What will he do this time?*

He'd threaten, shove, slap, and kick me—not necessarily in that order. A forty-pound weakling was defenseless against Jean, and he knew it. He'd sometimes sic his murderous dog on me for his sadistic pleasure, sending me running home at breakneck speeds that can only be achieved on a flood of adrenalin.

One time, Pierre was pedaling his bicycle past the Moreau farm, while I was sitting sidesaddle on the center bar—my customary position. My heart nearly thumped out of its ribcage when I noticed Jean standing in the middle of the road with menacing eyes. His face beamed a devilish smile that seemed to say, "Here comes some fresh meat."

Moments later, his homicidal sidekick, Spotté, came rushing out to thwart our approach. I quickly pulled up my legs to escape the mongrel's teeth.

Trained from birth in the intelligent art of gnashing tires, the idiot dog soon turned its degenerate bicuspids on our bicycle. The hissing sound of escaping air and the tilting of our bicycle are parts of the disturbing image that remains. Jean eventually called off Spotté. The dog wandered off, no doubt to mutilate baby animals in their dens.

Much to our surprise, Jean offered to repair the damaged bicycle tire—although we knew this seemingly noble deed was rooted in the interest of self-preservation, namely to escape parental attention. A deflated tire was tangible evidence that could be brought before a family court of justice. Such incriminating evidence could lead to phone calls, confessions that damaged reputations, and parental rules that constrained mobility for…hours.

In autumn of 1959, Alfred Moreau died after a long and terrible battle with colon cancer. I wondered if this might be God's way of ridding the world of people who didn't go to church on Sunday. Nevertheless, I felt sad for his wife and his children. I even felt bad for Jean; in times of personal loss, abusive bullying tactics can be forgiven.

About two weeks before Mr. Moreau passed away, my mother received a troubling phone call from his wife, Florence. It seems that he was asking for me.

"But why does he want to see *me?*" I asked.

"I don't know. Just go see what he wants," Maman replied.

I walked the half-mile to his house like an inmate on the final stretch to the electric chair. I kept asking myself why Mr. Moreau would want to see a seven-year-old runt from two houses down. Given the man's dubious reputation, it couldn't be good.

When I arrived at his house, Florence was waiting at the door with a generous smile. She put her arm around my shoulder and escorted me toward the ill-reputed Alfred.

Mr. Moreau was lying on the sofa in the small living room. The entrance to the room was through an arched opening off the kitchen. I halted at the threshold, my legs refusing to carry me further. I could feel the blood drain from my face as I stared at the emaciated form. I'd never seen a dying man before. He was lying on his back, his pale skin stretched over protruding bones, wearing nothing except a gigantic cloth diaper.

"Are you afraid of me?" he said.

"No," I lied, still frozen with fear.

"Come closer then. I won't bite," he said, forcing a weak smile.

Florence gently squeezed my shoulders from behind in an encouraging gesture. My legs finally started moving toward the frightening man in the Gandhi loincloth.

"What grade are you in?" he said

"Second grade."

"How are you doing in school? The nuns aren't too tough, are they?"

These questions caught me by surprise. I never expected to engage in small talk with a dying man. "I like school…my teacher is good."

"What do you want to do when you grow up?"

"I don't know. Maybe a farmer."

"Like your father?"

"I guess so."

"Well, you have plenty of time to figure it out," he said with a smile. "In the meantime, can you do me a favor?"

"Yeah, sure." I was beginning to feel more relaxed. This man seemed nice; he certainly didn't match the dreaded reputation that I'd feared most of my life.

"I'd like you to take out a salt block for my cows."

"Sure, I'll do it right away."

He then shook my hand, smiled, and wished me goodbye with caring eyes. It seemed strange to me that the man had gone out of his way to make such a simple request, especially when he had a thirteen-year-old son living under his roof. It took me less than five minutes to retrieve the salt block and install it in the field.

"What did he want?" my mother asked when I returned in a better mood.

"He wanted me to take out a salt block," I explained.

"He probably just wanted to say goodbye," my mother said. The thought had never occurred to me until that moment, but I sensed that she was right. Mr. Moreau had called to bid me farewell. I never did find out why he chose me in particular, but my visit forever changed my opinion of the man; maybe that had been his intention all along.

I was too young to attend his wake in the lower level of the school building, but my parents and older siblings went. When they returned from town on the first evening of the wake, Jean was trailing behind them like a homeless puppy.

"Jean is sleeping here tonight," my mother announced. The sympathetic look in her face bespoke of "poor little Jean." It was apparent that Jean was playing up the part of the injured choirboy; the whole world was on his side. "He'll sleep with you, Michel."

What? My tormentor is sharing my bed? Why can't he sleep with Pierre? My mother seemed to think that this arrangement would be more comfortable for angelic Jean, since my puny frame occupied only a fraction of the mattress. I knew that Jean must have been sad for the loss of his father, his ugly claws rendered impotent with grief. So, I accepted my mother's decision without as much as a stern look.

I never wore pajamas. None of us boys did. My parents couldn't afford them. So I went to bed in my white briefs, like always. So did Jean. I lay on the right side of the bed as he settled on the left. The house was dark and quiet when Jean shook my shoulder and whispered something strange in my ear.

"What?" I mumbled.

"Can you keep a secret?"

As far as I know, nobody in the history of the universe has ever turned down this offer. This test of trustworthiness has drawn the same primal response since prehistoric times. In spite of my innate distrust for Jean, childish pride provoked me to answer the timeless question in the affirmative.

"Of course," I said as I wiped my eyes. I could see his silhouette in the dark.

"Give me your hand. I won't hurt you."

What was he doing? I felt a prank coming, but didn't want to appear weak and intimidated. My naïve brain was curious as to what he would do.

He extended his hand to my side of the bed in a friendly gesture, and I hesitantly took it. The next thing I knew, he was dragging my hand under the blankets toward his side. He slowly unfurled my fingers from his hand and wrapped them around his…*guidoune*! My mind immediately flashed back to the horrific shape of my brother Réal the year before, and I understood perfectly well.

"Stop it!" I said in a harsh whisper, careful not to alarm my brothers in the next bed. Just when I thought it was safe, Jean had added a new dimension to his threats. Apparently bored with the assaults on my body, he was threatening my sacred morality too. And he chose to do it on the day his father lay dead in the school hall.

I retracted my hand, but he had anticipated my move, pressing his hand on top of mine to block the retreat. I struggled to free myself, but this boy was obviously powered by high-octane testosterone. I yanked hard, managing to slip out of his clutch and shimmy back to my corner of the mattress.

But the wrestling match was not yet over. Undaunted by my blunt rejection, Jean crawled up behind my butt, wrapped his left arm around my tummy to pin me down, and slipped his right hand under the elastic of my briefs to reach my crotch; he was groping.

It was now *my* turn to play the part of the cow to his bull. I responded to the attack like a boy with fire ants crawling up his ass. The rapid friction of my feet against the bed sheet might have lit a Boy Scout fire in the pouring rain. I elbowed, shuffled, and pleaded for release—always in a harsh whisper—as Jean laughed in my hair. I felt like an African gazelle in the jaws of a crocodile, yet he seemed amused.

But he underestimated me. Skinny runts have to develop unorthodox defense mechanisms to survive the assaults of their older siblings. In my case, the expert skills took the form of shin kicks and pinches. My kicks were like karate chops; they were lightning fast, bony hard, and aimed at the most susceptible places. And my pinches were so effective that they might have qualified as a new Olympic sport. My little bony fingers had the agility to twist and maim small morsels of flesh the victim didn't know he had, bringing him down in seconds, whimpering like a baby in bad need of a diaper change.

My brain was jolted back to reality, and I decided to pull out all the stops. *Bam, bam, bam.* I alternated between pummeling his shins with goat-like heel kicks and twisting the crap out of the skin on his arm. He finally loosened his grip, and I leapt out of bed like a frog springing from the mouth of a hungry snake.

"Stop it or I'll tell Maman right now!" I said in the meanest whisper I could muster. This latest admonition had the impact of a pistol shot fired close to his ears.

"No, you don't need to do that," he said. "I'll stop." I stood next to the bed stupefied, watching him slither across the sheet and back to his own side of the bed.

I was relieved to see his reaction, although I never had any intention of carrying out the threat. I had no idea what I would have done if he'd persisted. The only thing I knew for sure is that I could never report the embarrassing episode to my family, for the same reason that I'd chosen not call out to my brothers who were sleeping in the next bed. Kids were ruthless, and I thought my siblings would make a rip-roaring comedy out of the ridiculous episode at my expense. *Nobody will find out about this.*

But Jean was right to fear my mother. She was close to his mom, and he knew that Maman turned into a fierce lioness whenever her cubs were threatened even slightly. He would have been emasculated like a pig before the slaughter, stripped of his phony choirboy image forever, his teenage reputation shattered.

I slept badly that night, rolled up in a fetal position on the edge of the precipice, wrapped in the bed sheet like an Indian maharishi. Jean was unpredictable, and I was hell-bent on averting any further molestation attempts.

Strangely enough, the episode improved Jean's behavior. I now had leverage, as he knew that I could blow the whistle anytime. So, he never bothered me again, and I never looked back on that night with animosity. The episode was an ugly feather in my cap, another one of life's little lessons: *Big boys are pigs.* I accepted this bit of wisdom as fact and moved on. Jean and his family soon moved on as well, packing up their belongings and leaving the farm for the city of Sherbrooke. The bully was gone.

My knowledge of male physiology was primitive at best, but my understanding of girl parts was undeniably pathetic. My sisters were all older than me, and so, unlike many privileged kids, I had never had the opportunity to closely observe diaper changes.

The only thing I knew for sure about girls is that they had no *pinouche* and that their *fesses* seemed to reach to the front. I knew nothing else. If somebody had asked me to explain how girls peed, I would have just stood there, stuttering incoherently.

I became intensely curious about girls around the age of seven. This created much angst in my prepubescent mind, since our Catholic God was highly intolerant of impure behavior. Every immoral digression in thought or action brought my boyhood curiosity in direct conflict with our religious teachings.

The guilt induced by immoral actions could only be eradicated by facing the priest once a month and admitting all. For a child of seven or eight, this was a significant emotional event. Despite my innate fear of priests, the idea of telling lies in the confessional never entered my mind; this would have surely doubled my sentence in purgatory. Instead, I chose to lump the sins into vague categories that were deliberately imprecise. This made them easier and less embarrassing to confess.

My sin buckets included impure thoughts, impure looks, and impure touches. These were sufficient to cover most of my transgressions while avoiding the embarrassing details.

In addition, the monthly confessions required bookkeeping. We'd been taught to report an approximate count of each offense in order to receive the proper absolution. So, I also kept a mental tally of the number of sins in each bucket.

"Father, it's been two weeks since my last confession. I accuse myself of having been impolite to my mother three times, of arguing with my brother four times…"

I would always tell my dirty sins last, hoping that the priest had fallen asleep while I rattled off the boring venial sins. Then, I'd deliberately rip through the more serious sins lickety-split so that they'd sound as incoherent as possible. I usually succeeded. Sometimes, the priest asked me to repeat them more slowly, but the pressure to hear the confessions of the long line of faithful waiting in the aisle usually prevailed.

The Catholic cycle of sin, confession, absolution, and forgiveness was wonderful. You could commit atrocities one day, confess them the next, and be rid of the guilt forever. Just in time to start the cycle all over again.

Feeling like a rural nincompoop, I decided to pursue a sex education before reaching the mature age of eight. My plan was brilliant.

My three sisters shared a bedroom on the second floor. At calculated intervals, I'd go upstairs and pretend to play on the floor outside the bedroom door. When one of the girls would enter the room and close the door, that would be my cue. I'd kneel at the door quiet as a mouse and peer through the keyhole.

It turns out that my plan had more than a few glitches. First, it assumed that my sisters would disrobe entirely, which never happened. Second, it assumed that they'd pose in my field of vision, which only covered a small fraction of the room. And third, it assumed that they'd face the keyhole long enough for me to study the intricate details of their anatomy. Like I said, it was a brilliant plan.

After squinting through the keyhole for a few days, I'd seen absolutely nothing. Then one day, I got very lucky. After arriving home from school, my sister Doris ran upstairs, entered the bedroom, and closed her door. I gave her a few minutes to settle in before pressing my eye to the keyhole as usual. When I bent down to look, an electric chill ran up my spine, tingling all the way from my tailbone to my scalp.

I was staring at a girl's naked bottom. And against all odds, she was facing the door. *Merde, what's that dark hair doing down there?* My jaw dropped down to my chin when I realized that the hair made it impossible to discern the slightest anatomical feature.

My attempt at self-education had failed. And I felt terrible guilt for having taken advantage of a sister who treated me nicely. When Doris came out of the bedroom, she made pleasant talk, but I avoided eye contact. And for the next several days, it wasn't her face that made unannounced appearances in my remorseful brain.

"Father I accuse myself of looking at girls impurely…"

I had abandoned all hope of studying girl anatomy, left only with the dopy premise that their *fesse* crack extended around the front. Then, one day, my little cousin came forward to rescue me from the depths of boyhood stupidity.

Danielle was one of my favorite little girl cousins. She had short brown hair with soft curls, oval brown eyes, and a little round nose. I was eight and she was six. Despite our age difference, I was still a shrimp of a boy and only a little bigger than she was.

We were inseparable soul mates. She played boy games with me, and I discreetly played girl games with her. She was the little sister I never had, and I was the doting brother close to her age. Her parents lived less than two miles from our farm, so my Aunt Colette paid frequent visits to the country with Danielle and her sons.

In the summer, boys always peed outside. The absence of plumbing made it a necessity until I was six, but the habit had persisted long after we had gotten running water.

One day, I interrupted a game with Danielle to go take a wiz. As I was finishing my business, I noticed her standing to the side, watching me from about six feet away.

"Can I see your *guidoune*? I'll show you my *pissette*," she said.

I couldn't believe my ears. This girl was actually offering to show me her forbidden parts. That was something I would have never dared ask. Boys never got away with direct requests like that. More often than not, they were hastily reported, and a righteous parent would descend on their sorry butt with a broom or yardstick.

But Danielle was asking *me*. That made a difference. And since she was initiating, it also seemed to reduce the likelihood of discovery. It was an offer I couldn't refuse.

"Okay, but make it fast," I said in a nervous whisper.

We walked about ten yards to the back of the house, stopping near the left corner and away from the gaze of windows. But even before I could get my fly down, my whole body was shivering uncontrollably. It was so bad that I could barely talk without quavering, bleating like a lamb caught in barbed-wire fence.

The anticipation of seeing a naked girl bottom was the most intense feeling I had ever experienced. I felt hot all over, and my pulse was beating to a metronome set on *presto*. Unfortunately, this carnal excitement also had some unpleasant company. Thanks to my Catholic upbringing, guilt made an early appearance. And the fear of discovery and parental banishment hovered nearby.

Literally shaking in my boots, I fiddled with my fly with unsteady fingers until I finally managed to pull down the zipper. That's when I realized that my *pinouche* had grown to a clumsy size, making the extraction a troublesome affair. This was embarrassing. It annoyed me that my weenie had become uncooperative. *Why is it standing up on its hind leg? Now Danielle will think it always looks like that.*

Unlike me, Danielle seemed to be perfectly calm; she was waiting for me to deliver my end of the bargain with childish curiosity. *Voilà*, my little turkey finally lifted its neck to peek outside the nest; Danielle eagerly bent down for a closer inspection.

"Can I touch it?" she asked.

"Yeah, but just a little," I barked.

My hawk eyes were frantically searching the horizon for the slightest sign of movement. I was like a nervous deer at the peak of hunting season. The consequences of being caught in this incriminating position would have been deadly.

The deviant act of touching private parts fell under the hideous label of *tapponage*. Once labeled a *tapponeux*, you were in serious shit. The people who were found guilty of this crime would automatically join the ranks of cow thieves and Protestants, the kind of folks you'd naturally avoid for the remainder of their decrepit lives.

I was so busy guarding the perimeter that I had no time to notice what Danielle was doing. I vaguely remember the touches and snickers. *So, she thinks this is funny?*

My body was racked by violent shakes, my *pinouche* was poised in a silly state of alert, and my panicky eyes were scanning the heavens for the lightning bolt that would fry my sinful ass. In that rather fragile frame of mind, I failed to see the humor.

My nerves were getting frayed at the edges, so I abruptly slid my little turkey back in its warm nest and zipped up my fly without warning.

"It'sss myyy turrrnnn," I said in a goat voice.

True to her word, Danielle didn't lose any time reaching for the elastic band on her dainty underwear and sliding them down to her knees. Like a little lady, she then lifted up her pretty skirt to give me an unimpaired view. A boy with a bum ticker would have died with a shit grin on his face at that very moment. My heart almost blew a gasket.

At last, the anticipation of seeing a girl crack was over. And just like that nitwit bull I'd cussed in the field, my attention suddenly turned devilishly narrow. Kneeling in front of Danielle, I stared, marveled, and touched in silence. It seemed like hours, although the moral breach lasted only a few minutes. Then it was over.

Danielle and I resumed normal play, and she seemed unfazed by our indecency. In fact, I thought she might have preferred to have pet a chicken. But our unchaste conduct had left its mark on my brain and soul. For me, this had been a whirlwind of sensations like no other. And I'd learned another important lesson: *Girls have more than a fanny crack.* The shakes were gone, but I was left with a huge pang of guilt.

"Father I accuse myself of having touched a girl impurely..."

Danielle stayed faithfully silent about our little spree, leaving the door open for repeat offenses. Later, our escapades became more daring. They were infrequent but intense, leaving me riddled with God-fearing guilt. As before, Danielle seemed unimpressed. We played "show me yours, and I'll show you mine" behind the farmhouse, inside the barn, and even in my grandparents' out-house—the putrid odor dulled only by my concentration.

To me, her body was a lovely pink tulip, with layers of velvety petals that con-cealed a soft core. To her, I was a miniature catapult. I studied her as intensely as if I were looking at a Leonardo DaVinci; she treated me like an inflatable clown with a sand bottom. She'd pull down hard and let go, causing my weenie to spring back and slap hard against my bare belly. *Ping, slap, ping, slap.* She'd chuckle and go again.

I found her treatment humiliating and painful, often barking at her to stop. But she rarely did. To her, my *pinouche* was a human slinky, fascinating only because of its unnatural poise. In the end, I gritted my teeth and tolerated her rough handling. It was a small price to pay for my private education.

One Saturday evening during the winter of that year, we were invited to visit my Uncle Simon and Aunt Jeanne d'Arc, who lived in the nearby town of Stratford. My uncle was a metal forger by trade, a short and husky man with a serious demeanor. My aunt was a slim woman with a pointy nose, reddish hair, and a perpetual glint in her eye.

These were fun occasions involving lots of cousins. The adults settled in the kitchen to play cards in teams of four. On this occasion, for some reason, I found myself in one of the first-floor bedrooms with my cousins Danielle, Julie, and Susanne. At one point, somebody suggested that we play doctors and nurses, and everyone readily agreed.

The next thing I knew, the three girls were taking turns lying on the bed with their knickers down. The patient would first turn on her stomach and then on her back, as the friendly nurses touched, spread, and poked orifices to examine and dispense medical care. The girls seemed relaxed, laughing their way through the examinations.

My owl eyes were glued to the bed; I was amazed at my filthy luck. I stood back from the action, ashamed to be the only boy present but unable to walk away. The scene looked like one of those infernal paintings that depicted hell as a pool of writhing naked bodies. If this is hell, I thought, it's not so bad after all.

My ears and face felt hot just like all those other times with Danielle. I expected to play the role of the boy patient any minute, since that seemed to be the price of admission. The prospect worried me considerably: *What painful tugs, pings, pokes, and bends will my swollen weenie suffer at the hands of three little girls?*

But my turn never came. I was still engrossed in the perversions unfolding on the bed when I heard and then saw the doorknob turning in its socket in slow motion. The cacophony of cheerful voices and laughs from the kitchen suddenly filled the room.

Gulp. My heart raced like a sputtering chainsaw. I'd be dismembered and thrown to the hungry neighborhood dogs. I was dead at the tender age of eight. And God would finally avenge my despicable sins of the flesh. I felt the blood drain from my face as the door opened and my Aunt Jeanne d'Arc walked into the bedroom.

I swallowed hard, as adrenaline readied my small bony limbs for the flight of my life. *What should I do?* My aunt was blocking the only exit from the room, so running would be futile. Susanne was still lying on the bed with her dainty underwear around her knees, attesting to our obscene game like a neon marquee.

Somewhere in the depths of my frightened pea brain, I decided to play dead. Whenever Puppé wanted to plead for mercy, he'd roll over on his back, exposing his furry underbelly with a pathetic hit-me-if-you-want look. Of course, we never hit him in this remorseful state. If this worked for dogs, I figured it might work for kids too.

So, I leaned my back against the nearby wall and let my butt slip down to the floor while keeping my feet flat and knees at a sharp angle. I then put on the most sorrowful face that I could summon, staring at the floor pitifully. If I'd been a dog, my aunt might have been obliged to shoot me out of sympathy.

My aunt walked across the room with a bounce, seeming oblivious to my promising dramatic talent. She fetched something from a drawer above my submissive carcass, turned on her heels, and starting making her way back toward the door.

"Susanne, pull up your little underwear," she said, addressing the patient still lying on the bed. "Why don't you all join the other kids in the basement? Don't stay cooped up in here all evening." She spoke these words while moving across the room without a hint of chastisement, rather like a good friend making a worthy suggestion.

Is that all? My head was abuzz with alarms, and my imagination was vivid with dreary consequences. She walked out, carefully closing the door behind her, seemingly undisturbed that we'd been violating God's sacred laws. The noisy kitchen sounds abated once more, just in time to reveal the clanking sound of my own heart.

I expected to see slaps on bare *fesses* and promises of parental discipline for the rest of us, at minimum. Instead, she exited the room with the same happy glint in her eyes, leaving behind only a mild disapprobation. I was befuddled.

I found it impossible that my aunt would tolerate the sins of these little cretins without consequence, so I concluded that she'd probably left the room to report our immoral deeds to the other parents. If that was the case, we'd soon receive our share of parental thrashings—if not as soon as we left the room, then when we got home.

I stood frozen by the door, wondering what to do. The girls were still playing on the bed as though they hadn't heard my aunt's subtle warning, but I was now motivated to get out of that room in a hurry—especially since boys were blamed for everything.

If kids were squabbling, it was always the boys who started it. If a girl was crying, a boy must have hit her. And if a girl was caught with her pants down, a naughty boy was surely to blame. Girls were given the benefit of the doubt, while boys were immediately deemed guilty due to their gender. So, this little incident reflected very badly on me; I was the only boy in the room with three girls who took turns pulling down their dainty underwear in my presence. I was guilty by association and gender.

But if I left the room too quickly, I would be admitting my complicity in these acts. My only hope, I reasoned, was to confuse the adults by acting totally innocent. And that meant walking out of the room at a leisurely pace, wearing a non-guilty look.

I waited a few minutes, opened the door, and slowly walked out into the hall while holding my breath. I closed the door behind me and momentarily stopped to check on the sounds coming from the kitchen. I half-expected a giant hush to sweep over the room as my terrified frame made an appearance in the hall, but the overlapping voices and laughs seemed the same as before. *Phew*, I had at least distanced myself from the scene.

But I was still in a state of heightened paranoia, suspecting that my aunt had dutifully reported the dirty bedroom escapades to my mother. The suspense was gnawing at my gut like a rat on a ball of cheese. I just *had* to know.

I was able to read my mother's emotions and body language like Braille, so I decided to confront her immediately and sense her reaction. *No sense in delaying my doom.* She was sitting at a card table in the smoky kitchen, playing cards with three other aunts. I approached her from behind and stood there without saying a word. She immediately noticed me, pressed an arm against my back, and gently pulled me closer.

Even before she said one word, I could tell she knew nothing about my lewdness. She seemed in a blissful state of mind, her eyes and soft touch oozing affection. Her kindness caused my sense of guilt to increase tenfold—she had no idea that my beady little eyes had been transfixed on not one, but three girl cracks in that bedroom.

"What are you doing?" she asked, with a complacent look on her face.

"Nothing," I lied.

"Well, go play with the other kids."

There was one more test I had to perform. Aunt Jeanne d'Arc was standing at the kitchen counter pouring drinks for her guests. Since she was the only adult to witness our indecency, I had to figure out her intentions. Had she *really* forgiven our licentious behavior, or did she plan on reporting us to parental authorities later?

I slowly approached the counter, scrutinizing her face for any sign of judgment. As far as I knew, mothers were incapable of holding back their feelings. If my aunt condemned my actions, she'd send me motherly vibes of scorn and disdain. She noticed me standing there and leaned close to my face wearing a half-smile.

"What would you like, my little man?" she asked. "Would you like a soda? I have strawberry, orange, and cream soda." These were our favorite flavors, and my aunt had them all. But on this occasion, I had no need for a soda; I was looking for peace of mind. I continued watching her face in a daze, my mouth too numb to answer.

"Here, take this one and go play with the others." I stood there with an orange drink in one hand, stupefied at my unbelievable luck. I suddenly felt a deep affection and bond with this woman. She understood us. She seemed to know that kids were naturally curious and tolerated our behavior without feeling she should punish us. I felt like jumping up in her arms and wrapping my spindly legs around her waist to give her a full body hug. But instead, I walked away as she suggested, with guilt stabbing at my chest.

On the way home, I stood on the transmission hump as usual. Feeling lucky to have escaped discovery, I promised myself never to look at or touch girls again. This time, the fear and guilt had been too intense; I'd finally learned my lesson. But I lied.

"Father, I accuse myself of having looked at little girls impurely..."

When spring came around, I was a boiling cauldron about to spill over. The promise I'd made the prior winter had long been forgotten, and my interest in girls had rebounded with a vengeance. In fact, I'd become even more brazen since the close call with my aunt. I now felt invincible; I could escape detection from just about anything.

It was August when Aunt Colette came to drop off Danielle for the day. After tromping over the farm grounds for a few hours, I casually proposed to Danielle that we play a familiar game of doctor behind the tool shed. She agreed.

Danielle looked up to me, and would have done just about anything I asked. It was mid-afternoon, the sun was warm, and the breeze felt like a soft caress on our skin. The tool shed was located near the stable, a few hundred feet from the house.

This time, I asked Danielle to sit down on a wood plank behind the shed, directing her to remove one article of clothing at a time under my watchful eye. She was soon stark naked, with the exception of the little white ankle socks on her feet. There she was, nude under the pleasant August sky like Venus the Greek divinity.

She was lying flat on her belly when I crouched down to begin her physical examination. Suddenly, I felt a sharp pain on my neck, reminiscent of the numerous bee stings I'd received in the past. I'd been chased by swarms of bees on several occasions, which caused me to hop around in frenzy like a kid with a screw loose, waving my arms frantically as though engaged in demented calisthenics.

I instinctively reached for my neck, expecting to brush off another bee. But before my hand could reach the painful spot, I felt another ten needles enter the same place. *What the hell?* I turned my head in panic, mortified to see the blurry form of my mother raising a branch in fury. I'd last seen that uncanny look on a charging bull.

This was cherry season. Maman had been rocking on the porch, eating red cherries from a branch, when she became suspicious of our whereabouts. Descending the hill toward the barn with stealth steps, she'd caught us literally with our pants down.

I saw my life pass before my eyes; it was over. I bowed my head to soften the blows from the cherry branch, holding my hands behind my head for protection.

"Maman, you're hurting me!"

The swinging branch alternated in a rhythm between my neck, head, and back. *Wham, wham, wham.* All this time, Maman was yelling unflattering invectives in a guttural voice that made it clear that she thought I was a disgusting brat.

"But I haven't touched her yet," I blurted out in self-defense.

This was about the stupidest thing I could have said, as it admitted my piggish intentions. *Bam, bam, bam.* My eyes were watery from the stinging pain, my pride crumbling to pieces before the startled eyes of my favorite girl cousin.

Feeling humiliated, I decided to flee—it was all I could do. Running like a whitetail deer, I headed for the back of the barn. I ran so fast that the soles of my sneakers slapped up against my ass cheeks. My hair tossed in the breeze and my vision blurred from the rapid stride. Out of breath, I rested my back against the barn and tried to think.

What should I do? I looked around in senseless desperation, deciding that I needed to put more distance between myself and the house; my mother could easily find me here. So, I headed for Grandpapa's farm, where boulders littered the cow pasture like giant gray marbles. Running from my mother like Adam after tasting the forbidden fruit, I crossed the open field and settled down behind one of the medium-size boulders.

It was a perfect hideout. The location provided a bird's-eye view of the dirt road and farmhouse. From here, some three hundred feet away, I could spy on road traffic and observe all movement into and out of the house.

I sat on the ground with my back resting against the boulder and ranted. The physical pain was gone, but the abject humiliation and shame still stung like crazy.

My guilt soon turned to anger. I raged like a madman, yelling in a harsh whisper at the sky, the ground, and the rock that hid my whereabouts. A torrential flood of tears flowed down my cheeks as I spat curses at my mother, blaming her for keeping me ignorant about girls. Ignorance, I swore, had caused my immoral deeds. I accused all parents of being useless, leaving kids in the dark for the privilege of spanking them at the slightest provocation. And I cursed God for creating the temptations that entrapped little boys like me. I hated God, my mother, and all adults.

"*Maudite folle!*" ("Damn fool") I screamed at the mental image of my mother.

The events of that day had been a devastating blow to my young life. I felt alone. Maman had always been my close friend, and now I'd lost her. Her angry face kept reappearing in my senseless brain, reaffirming that she hated my guts.

I bawled my eyes out until I could produce no more tears, and then my anger turned to bitter indignation. I would not bow down to parental abuse. My mother no longer loved me, and I hated her in return—we were at war. From now on, my behavior would reflect a headstrong and obstinate demeanor like she'd never seen.

This is when I formulated my first plan of action: I'd run away from home. I'd sneak up to my bedroom after dark—not a small feat with nine of us living in the house—and wrap some clothes inside an old bed sheet. Then, I'd walk to the main road like a hobo. From there, I'd hitchhike to Québec City. It wasn't much, but it was a plan.

From my hideout, I saw my father drive up with Aunt Colette, heard the car doors slam, saw Danielle climb back into the car, and watched them drive away. This day had started well but ended in tragedy. Just a few hours ago, I was a happy-go-lucky kid, but now I was an angry runt thinking of running away.

Maman came out on the porch, calling me in for supper. She did this twice within a ten-minute span, suspecting that I was hiding in the barn. But I had no intention of going back to face my angry parents and my callous siblings, who had no doubt been informed of my filthy exploits in vivid detail. They could all go to hell.

I stayed in hiding until dusk. The sky darkened, the trees grew scary shadows, the frogs croaked at a deafening pitch, the twigs creaked menacingly, and the eerie owls shrieked. Before long, I was on the alert for skunks, raccoons, and bears.

The creepy darkness was shaking my convictions; I needed a change of plan. Hitchhiking alone at night no longer seemed such a good idea. There was only one road heading north, so I rationalized that it would be well patrolled by police. I imagined the humiliation of being captured, dragged back home wearing handcuffs like a criminal, and delivered to my parents while my siblings snickered at my well-deserved fate.

In the absence of another plan, I decided to sneak back inside the house, crawl up to my bedroom unnoticed, and get to bed early. I'd think of something better tomorrow.

It was late. I waited until I could see no movement in the house before approaching like a member of some covert military unit. I waited on my stomach in the ditch across the road and then crouched at the base of the porch. I stopped and listened; all was quiet. I then tiptoed up the staircase to the porch, hiding between the living-room window and front door of the house—still nothing. I lifted my head to peek inside the kitchen through the screen door, and I saw nobody there. Luck was on my side. I opened the screen door in slow motion, stepped quietly inside, and gently closed the door behind me, careful not to make a sound. It was going well; I was all alone in the kitchen. I could see the staircase on the opposite side of the kitchen that would take me to my bedroom, so I started crossing the room quietly.

"Michel?" a voice rang in my ears like a bullhorn.

It was my mother. I stopped dead in my tracks but didn't answer the voice. She came out of the bedroom to meet me, raising my suspicion that she'd been carefully tracking my movements all along. (Her bedroom window faced my hideout.) I braced myself to face her wrath, reminding myself to be unbending. I would not give my parents the satisfaction of reacting to their insults and blows.

"Your food is in the oven," she said in a pleasant voice.

"I'm not hungry," I replied in a cold tone.

Maman ignored my belligerence, opened the oven door, reached for the warm plates using potholders, and gently deposited them on the table.

"I'm not eating," I repeated. The delicious aroma wafted up to my nostrils.

"Wash your hands and sit down," she said, ignoring my rebellious demeanor.

I was getting confused; this wasn't the same person I'd imagined a few hours ago. This woman seemed calm, gentle, and understanding. So I decided on a face-saving compromise. I would sit down to eat as she asked, but I would refuse to speak with her. And after gulping down my food with feigned indifference, I'd go upstairs without saying a word and go straight to bed. That would give her a taste of my new attitude.

"I'll eat just a little," I said with disinterest.

That sounded belligerent enough, I thought. And I still had control of the situation too. I washed my hands and sat down at the end of the table. The food was delicious, so I had to force myself to eat more slowly; she would not win this battle. Maman was standing at the kitchen counter washing the last few dishes. I ate everything that was on my plate and then attacked the dessert she'd set on the table.

"It's not right for you to touch girls," she said.

I froze. *Is she actually trying to teach me something?* Her words flowed like a gentle breeze, carrying no hint of blame. I was already beginning to soften at the core.

"It's normal to be curious at your age," she continued.

A chill ran up my back. *Damn*, she was actually trying to talk to me about girls. *Can she know what I am feeling?* I thought I heard the unmistakable sound of a deflating balloon as my arrogance developed a slow leak.

I had barely finished eating when she announced that I needed a bath. My face was that of a camouflaged soldier, smeared by fingers with tears and dirt. I'd been sitting and crawling on the ground half the day, and my clothes were filthy.

I grimaced at the thought of a bath. Our farm had no tub, so these weekday baths were always taken at the kitchen sink.

"I'm sorry I was rough with you today," she said while passing the facecloth over my chest. My head was already swimming in a pleasant haze. She understood my curiosity after all, and was even apologizing for her behavior.

"It's my fault. I'll never do it again," I said.

Feeling small and susceptible, I fell in love with my mother all over again while standing naked on the kitchen counter. By the time she'd finished bathing me, my heart was soft like Jell-O and my eyes were moist with admiration. She *did* understand me.

"You know, you can always ask me anything about girls," she offered. These words were the icing on the cake. I told her how sorry I was all over again and repeated my unwavering commitment never to touch another girl. I was pathetic.

By the time I kissed Maman goodnight, I felt enveloped in a warm glow. I gave her a bigger kiss than usual and told her I loved her. She was my friend again.

My next confession was a big one, filling up almost all of my sin buckets. I entered the confessional with shaky knees and spilled my guts. The guilt was magically gone.

Maman never reported the incident that transpired on that memorable day in 1961. It remained our little secret. My siblings never knew, nor did Aunt Colette as far as I could tell. I suspect that my father knew, but he never mentioned it. Papa had an aversion to talking about sex, so I knew that he'd avoid it like the plague.

The intensity of that August day has remained vivid in my mind. The range of emotions I'd gone through ran the gamut from carefree pleasure to loathsome despair. In five hours, I had experienced sensual pleasure, humiliating pain, incapacitating guilt, uncontrolled fury, and consummate love. Children's emotions are like that. One minute you hate and the next you love. You sob, and moments later you laugh like a hyena.

The realization that my mother still cared was the cure I desperately needed. Despite my naughty behavior, she'd forgiven me and continued loving me just like before. I've often wondered how many kids have experienced similar incidents in their lives without a compassionate parent to heal their wounds at the end of the day. On that August day, I learned a painful lesson firsthand: *Even bad kids need love.*

I did keep my promise to Maman, and my indecent acts became a thing of the past. But it wasn't firm discipline that altered my behavior; it was the displacement of families. My Aunt Colette and her family soon relocated to the United

States after my uncle had found a job in a New Hampshire textile mill. I was lonely, and without an accomplice. My soul mate was gone, never to be replaced. This curious season of my life was over.

10

Origin of a Phobia

Our life was governed by religion. There were daily prayers at school, prayers at home, and mandatory church services to attend year round. With over forty Catholic holidays on the religious calendar, Mass had always played a central role in our lives.

It was next to the church that we once witnessed a ridiculous attempt at fireworks. The mayor had decided to put on a spectacular fireworks display, the first ever in the history of St-Gérard. Every family in town was encouraged to attend the festivities, scheduled for the evening of St. John the Baptist Day. At the appointed hour, we stood in the schoolyard adjacent to the church grounds, anticipating the start of the show. A loud booming voice rang out.

"Fire...fire...run...run!" a man's voice bellowed. We could see several men galloping away from the commotion, gutless sprinters competing in a race to escape the scene in a hurry. We stood there watching with befuddled interest as the cowardly men hightailed out of the field like scared jackrabbits.

"Where are they going?" I asked my father.

"It looks like they're having trouble lighting the fireworks."

There was trouble all right. The nitwit attendants had set fire to the cardboard boxes holding the ill-fated supply of fireworks as they attempted to light their first rocket. And it seems that they'd also neglected to bring water or fire extinguishers.

Seconds later, we were rewarded with a multi-colored explosion, and then another. The flames grew taller, as the pyrotechnic display took flight in an unexpected horizontal direction, heading straight for the baffled audience. People ran in all directions, the scene resembling a scaled-down reenactment of the *Hindenburg* crash.

The sky rockets, shells, pinwheels, Roman candles, and sparklers soon merged into a nondescript mass of light, with intermittent booms accompanying the blinding flashes. The show was over in less than a minute; it was possibly the world's shortest fireworks display.

We were again reminded of the comical scene a few years later while attending another small-town fireworks celebration on St. John the Baptist Day. This one was held in Beebe Plain, a pleasant border town situated eighty miles south of St-Gérard.

This time, the fireworks display did go off as planned—unfortunately. The show would have been lovely had the canons launched their rockets to the pre-scribed altitude. But they didn't. Instead, they spit out their fiery load in a half-hearted toss, causing some shells to detonate low over our heads and others to explode on the ground among the rather distraught audience. It was not a pretty sight.

People were blocking their ears to protect their eardrums. Some ran for cover while others just stood there (as we did), glaring at the sky, trying to foretell the trajectory of the falling shells. For a few long minutes, we were witnessing the London Blitz of 1940, dodging bombs.

"Put out the fire! Put out the fire!" the young boy screamed as he ran past us, frantically pointing at his butt. A rocket had landed on the grass near his location, and the seat of his pants was now smoldering from the heat of stray cinders. The poor kid was in a panicky state; it was probably the only time in his life he'd have to beg strangers to douse his behind.

These early experiences taught me the following lesson: *Avoid small-town fireworks*. Modern regulations make these affairs safer these days, but the troubling memory of the boy with the smoking pants still makes me leery about attending small-town displays.

The little brick church in St-Gérard was torture. It had been erected back in 1905 to eliminate the tedious five-mile walk to Weedon on Sunday mornings. The building could seat around two hundred people. Its straight-back benches were designed to keep us awake, each equipped with a torturous kneeler that united hardwood with human bone. But the hardened furniture seemed only fitting for the sacrificial climate of Mass.

The little church in St-Gérard.

Every respectable family in town paid for a pre-assigned pew in church. Ours was to the left of the center aisle, about mid-way up to the sanctuary. Every Sunday morning, we'd crowd into that stiff pew for the interminable Mass.

Mass was always boring. It's not that I lacked faith; I had plenty of that to go around. I never doubted the existence of God, Jesus, and the rest of the Family. And in addition to the Holy Trinity, our religion also summoned a disquieting army of demons, saints, and spirits to bludgeon our souls, which I also believed in. But even these intimidating figures couldn't alter the fact that Mass was a big yawn for most of us Catholic kids.

Despite our boredom, we could never admit to feeling languid about church. We knew from experience that the parents would quickly correct such brazen admissions with a firm admonition. Plus, the avowal itself risked offense to the frightening divinities. Good people went to church, and bad people didn't—it was that simple. So, Mass became an infliction that we tolerated, much like our Saturday-afternoon bath. The weekly bath cleansed our bodies, while Sunday Mass healed our souls.

Language was a major reason for our boredom: the entire liturgy was celebrated in Latin. The only exception was the homily, delivered in the local French dialect.

"*Glòria in excèlsis Deo et in terra pax homìnibus bonae voluntàtis.*"

Like all Catholics, we understood some Latin words. Everybody knew that the proper reply to "*Dòminus vobìscum*" was "*Et cum spiritu tuo.*" But these tiny fragments of comprehension did little to stimulate my interest in the liturgical ritual.

I suspect that the outcome would have been the same had Mass been celebrated in an African language consisting of tongue clicks and clucks. Kids were fidgety, yawned, played with their fingers, and daydreamed. A brave child might taunt siblings with subtle gestures, but these attempts at unruliness were quickly thwarted by vigilant parents.

It was a bad idea to be naughty in church. Parents would dress their litter in their finest (and only) Sunday clothes, to be paraded proudly in front of the whole community. Each child was a microcosm of the family unit—misbehavior brought not only individual humiliation, but also a lowered opinion of the clan in the eyes of the world.

"My, how your children are well behaved," was perhaps the most honorable and uplifting tribute a mother could hear after Mass. All parents were hell-bent on making sure that their kids lived up to the peaceable motto "I cause no trouble."

Being the youngest member of my family, I endured the privilege of sitting next to my mother in church. She was our sole disciplinarian, the one who ensured my good behavior in public places. My brother Pierre, with whom I competed for her attention, was usually sitting on the other side of my parents, far from my naughty reach.

"Stop that," my mother would warn in a whisper that meant business. These words were rarely repeated; the second offense was usually punished with action.

Maman reserved a unique implement of discipline for church: she pinched. Her pinches were discreet yet lethal. She'd pinch whenever I fidgeted, slouched on the bench, or was otherwise distracted from the religious service. She'd nudge up against my shoulder, her hand slithering across like a snake reaching for its prey. Then she'd twist the first available morsel of flesh on my shoulder, arm, or side. I was rarely prepared for her surreptitious approach, the hard pinch inevitably bringing tears to my eyes.

It seemed to me that the priest went out of his way to make the service uninteresting. Nothing new ever happened at Mass; it was like attending the same play week after week. Every word and action was scripted, regurgitated on cue to the forbearing audience.

"*In nòmine Patris, et Fìlii, et Spìritus Sancti.*"

"*Kyrie elèison.*"

"*Gràtias agàmus Dòmino Deo nostro.*"

Week after week, the priest uttered these familiar Latin phrases, using the same vocal intonations, facial expressions, and hand gestures.

The burning incense would block my sinuses, the holy water would splatter against my forehead like spittle, and the bell would clang obnoxiously, aborting my daydreams before their climactic finish. Even worse, we had to stand and kneel through much of the ceremony; the luxury of sitting was reserved for the long and tedious homily.

From time to time, Father Berger would transform the boring homily into a memorable harangue, replete with fire and brimstone. These heated lectures were usually delivered on the heels of credible rumors alleging small-town immoralities, the sins of his flock inciting his righteous anger. He'd admonish the congregation with a red face and vague parables while I watched his tight lips open and close in a grotesque display.

Everyone in town knew the names and addresses of the offenders. I was hoping to see a lightning bolt strike down the guilty parties in front of the whole congregation—that would have made an impressive statement and cured our boredom for all time.

It's not surprising that the stodgy atmosphere of Mass would tickle my funny bone. Once laughter had bubbled up to the surface, it was impossible to control. It took very little to begin an avalanche of uncontrolled snickers. A funny-sounding sneeze, a rude body noise—my sensitive ears could discern these sounds from a great distance—or an ugly hat poised on the head of a lady parishioner could all provoke irrepressible laughter. I'd hold my breath to temporarily quiet the silliness, but that usually made it worse; sooner or later, I'd expectorate a loud guffaw that turned heads in my direction.

One of these foolish episodes began with imaginary flies. There was a long metal cabinet at the front of the nave that was loaded down with religious candles. The edge of the cabinet had been painted silver and adorned with big black dots.

I was sitting next to Gérard Poulin, my school chum, when it all began. Our entire school was attending Mass to celebrate one of the many religious holidays.

"Pssst, look at the flies stuck to the candle holder," Gérard whispered.

The remark kindled my bored imagination. The longer I stared at the painted edge, the more I could discern the flies. The border soon became a gigantic flypaper strip, trapping unsuspecting flies onto the saintly furniture. The giggles had begun.

Flypaper strips were part of our lives, and there was nothing funny about them at home. But here they were hilarious. The sacrilegious idea of flies sticking to a religious artifact in the middle of a holy ceremony was more than I could tolerate.

"*Sanctus, Sanctus, Sanctus, Dominus Deus Sabaoth*," the priest said. As the words oozed from the anal-looking lips of the pious man, my brain visualized insect wings and tiny bug feet fluttering against the border of the candleholder. I giggled, my laughter accentuated by bouncing shoulders. I was spiraling out of control.

Gérard was snickering softly but managed to keep his composure. Predictably, our misbehavior had been witnessed by several nuns, who threw us threatening glances at every chance. But our funny bone had been acutely struck; we were helpless to stop.

The snickering ebbed and flowed throughout the Mass. As we were walking back to school after church, an angry nun caught up with us.

"I saw you laughing in church," she said with hands poised on hips. "Do you think your behavior was respectful of God?" she demanded.

We were mute.

"I'll report you to the principal if this ever happens again," she said, rushing back to school in a huff. *Phew*. Another potential disaster had been averted.

I had a huge blister on the end of my right index finger. It started as an innocent wood sliver that had gone untreated despite my parents' offers to lance it with a sewing needle. *No thanks*. I preferred natural pain over some manmade torture.

It was a beautiful Sunday morning in September 1961. We were at Mass, and I was fiddling with my bothersome finger. The blister was humongous, occupying a third of my finger. The skin over the pus bubble was white, revealing yellowish liquid on the inside. Although grotesque in appearance, the blister was far more annoying than painful.

But I was bored out of my mind, so I started caressing the ugly bubble, feeling its unnatural contour. I applied light pressure to the skin just to see what would happen; it bounced back. The more I played with it, the more painful it became.

Daring myself to go further, I gradually increased the pressure on the blister, squeezing it harder and harder between my thumb and index finger. Predictably, the pain grew more intense, eventually causing my finger to throb with every heartbeat.

I'd crossed the point of no return. Once the pulsating pain had exceeded my patience, I made the rash decision to rid myself of the blister once and for all. I shut my eyes, and squeezed the bubble as hard as I could. The pain was excruciating.

A few seconds later, I felt a popping sensation—like a tiny balloon bursting—and opened my eyes to inspect the damage. The bubble had lost significant girth, although it was still visible. The pain had subsided, but I was shocked to see a streak of pus and blood spread over the palm of my hand. *Oops*, I hadn't anticipated blood.

I tugged at my father's pants leg and extended my palm to show him the revolting blister guts. I tried to put on a pitiable face to ensure a sympathetic response.

"My blister burst," I whispered.

"Don't play with it," he answered while looking down at my hand.

He calmly reached for the soiled handkerchief lodged in his back pocket and handed me the wrinkled white cloth. His then turned his attention back to the Mass.

The startling sight of blood had already initiated a self-destruct sequence in my brain, the bloody mess continually flashing before my eyes. I was standing on the wooden kneeler when my legs turned into rubber stilts.

The dirty handkerchief was still wrapped around my finger when dizziness struck. Beads of sweat formed on my forehead and annoying dots floated before my eyes, obstructing my vision with a net of black balloons. The priest seemed to be talking through a tin can when the world started fading away. My eyeballs were pulling deeper into their sockets as I tumbled into a dark void.

My fainting episode then turned into a dramatic performance. The eyewitnesses watched me collapse onto the floor, my puny frame getting lodged under the wooden kneeler. My father had to struggle to untwine my spindly limbs from the church furniture before he could lift me in his arms to carry me down the aisle and out the main door.

I'm told that our exodus looked like a scene from *Bride of Frankenstein*. My head and limbs dangled with a theatrical flair, bouncing to my father's every step.

The next thing I remember, I was in the backseat of the car, lying flat on my back and dripping with sweat. My father was standing outside the vehicle with the rear door ajar, presumably to cool me off. The gentle breeze felt like a godsend.

"What happened?" I asked, with my head still in the fog. I noticed that my clothes were wet from perspiration and my limbs were the consistency of wet noodles.

"You fainted. Are you feeling better?" my father said in an impassive voice.

"How long have I been here?"

"Oh, about fifteen minutes," Papa replied.

I lay motionless as the haze began to lift from my brain. The commotion in the church parking lot soon told me that Mass had ended. Several rubberneckers stared at my supine form as they walked past our car; a few men stopped to talk with my father.

André Gagné, an older brother of my friend Jean-Marie, stuck his head in the car, radiating a sympathetic smile. He was chuckling with unseemly amusement.

"How goes it, my little man?" he asked.

I liked this guy; he was a good-natured soul with an infectious hyena laugh. But his chuckles struck me as downright annoying from where I was lying at the moment. Sweat trickled down my butt crack as I struggled to mobilize my limbs into a sitting position.

"A little," I replied to be polite. I just wanted to be left alone.

I spent the rest of the morning at home in my parents' bed. The hearty lunch did wonders to restore my stamina. By mid-afternoon, everything was back to normal.

But the accounts of my fainting spell and rescue troubled me. The embarrassing incident had taken place in public; I expected ruthless teasing from my schoolmates.

Luckily, my concerns about teasing turned out to be unfounded. The classmates who witnessed my sudden demise at Mass were left stunned. Seeing my lifeless body being carried down the aisle had apparently made a frightful impression. So, I ended up wallowing in the attention and sympathy of my school chums for a few days.

The aftermath of my public fainting episode lasted more than thirty years. Although the blister disappeared within a few days, I was branded with an emotional scar.

Church services became petrifying. In fact, I turned numb from fear in any public setting where my quiet escape seemed unlikely. At nine, I was already caught in the grips of *asthenophobia*, deathly afraid of reliving my fainting episode in a public setting.

The phobia invariably brought on full-blown panic attacks whenever three intimidating conditions existed in a room—first, if the setting involved a public gathering, second, if the room was closed off, preventing my premature departure, and third, if the mobility of the attendees was somehow restricted by an authority figure.

Asthenophobia became my private hell, and I chose to keep the irrational fear a secret. We visited doctors only under extreme circumstances, so the option of therapy didn't exist in those days. And the phobia threatened to expose a character weakness that I sought desperately to conceal, so I didn't dare tell anybody about my condition.

Church services turned into a series of panic attacks. I suffered all the classic symptoms: heart palpitations, sweating, dizziness, trembling, difficulty breathing, chills, and nausea. Sometimes, I'd also lose my eyesight.

The attacks would persist for the duration of Mass, mysteriously evaporating in the last fifteen minutes of the service. It seems that my impending escape from church was sufficient to subdue the phobia.

It was like standing on the edge of a precipice, waiting for the first symptom to push me headlong into the abyss. Public gatherings seemed to sensitize every nervous fiber in my body—even a minor discomfort or sensation was enough to start the panic sequence.

I anticipated panic attacks at every public gathering but forced them out of my mind as soon as I left the unpleasant scene. I'd learned to conceal the symptoms so well that few people took notice of my private hell. Yet I was quietly imploding.

Denial can lead to strange bedfellows. Two years after I'd started manifesting the symptoms of asthenophobia, I became an altar boy. That role would place me in the sanctuary for the duration of Mass, in full view of the congregation. On the surface, the decision seemed perilous and foolish, but I was determined to face the devil himself.

Serving as an altar boy did reduce the frequency of panic attacks, but it didn't end them. When they did come, they were more pronounced in the limelight of the sanctuary. In spite of the ongoing attacks, I still hung on to the role of altar boy.

One of my most troubling incidents happened during the holy communion. In those days, the faithful took the host kneeling at the communion rail, while an altar boy held a paten under his or her chin. (The paten is a gold or silver plate with a wooden handle, a safety net to catch particles of host that might dribble from the mouths of faithful.) The host was forever a source of Catholic paranoia.

We were warned *never* to touch it with our impure hands. Only a priest could retrieve it—no matter where it landed.

On this occasion, I'd been designated the paten holder. But when communion rolled around, I happened to be in the middle of a severe panic attack. Desperate to suppress the untimely symptoms, I rose from my kneeling position in time to join the priest at the communion rail. The all-too-familiar black dots were blotting my view.

When I reached the communion rail, my world turned completely black—I'd temporarily lost my eyesight. This had happened before, so I knew it would clear up, but I had no idea what to do in the meantime. There was no way to signal the other altar boy, and the priest was already moving along the communion line. So I decided to blindly follow the priest, trailing behind the mumbling beacon while striving to move the paten in step with the shifting voice that uttered, "The body of Christ."

I'll never forget that unfortunate collision with the man's throat, the paten recoiling on impact with his Adam's apple. Seconds later, my vision had returned. The priest was glaring at me in disbelief, and the kneeling man had a startled look on his face.

"I wasn't feeling well," I later told the priest. Nothing more was said.

I was assigned to be pallbearer at Grandfather Côté's funeral when I was sixteen. The wake had been miserable, as I fretted over getting panic attacks at the funeral the entire time.

The funeral ceremony was a trying event. I struggled with panic attacks as we carried the coffin up the church aisle, and I experienced symptoms throughout the Mass.

"You were strong. I never saw you cry," my cousin Sylvie said later. I didn't dare tell her that I was using every ounce of energy to fend off panic attacks.

Asthenophobia would plague me well into adulthood. My wedding day was no exception. The thought of standing in the front of the church under the glaring eyes of friends and relatives paralyzed me with fear. I felt light-headed and my heart was palpitating long before I joined my bride at the altar. I was sure to faint.

The entire wedding ceremony was uncomfortable, and the final walk down the church aisle was one long panic attack. Our maid of honor had noticed my discomfort and strange behavior.

"Are you all right? I saw you wiping your face," she said later.

"I'm fine," I said to conceal my condition, as usual.

It's a small miracle that my fear of fainting didn't do serious harm to my career. After college, I found myself rapidly promoted to higher levels of responsibility, eventually managing departments with large numbers of employees.

I constantly fretted over public meetings; the panic attacks regularly sapped my vigor and inhibited my contribution at these affairs. I especially dreaded closed meetings with corporate executives, terrified of fainting in full view of the bosses.

I avoided public speaking at all costs. Whenever I was requested to give a presentation, I'd first look to delegate the enviable opportunity to one of my employees. But that wasn't always possible, so I eventually had to face my demons on stage.

The anticipation of public speaking was terrifying. The same alarming questions tortured my brain before each presentation. *What if I faint on stage? What if my vision blacks out again? What if I'm forced to walk off the podium?*

I never did faint on stage in spite of the frequent panic attacks. I learned to compensate for my extreme jitteriness by interjecting a little humor into the presentation; laughter from the audience seemed to ease the crippling symptoms.

I gradually overcame the fainting phobia using simple techniques to reduce the symptoms. I'd practice deep-breathing exercises to ward off the early onset of panic, remind myself that I always had the option to leave, and acknowledge that it was no big deal even if I did faint. "So what," I'd tell myself.

I spent more than thirty years covering up and compensating for the emotional minefield that had been laid in my brain in 1961. The fainting episode had taught me a lesson: *Even minor childhood incidents can have a lasting impact.* That lesson would outlast the farm, St-Gérard, and my childhood, chasing me through my tumultuous teenage years, into my adult years, and across national borders.

11

Losing Doris

I was close to my eldest sister; she was like a second mother to me. She'd been a fixture in my life forever, at times playing the role of caregiver to relieve Maman. She'd been there to hear my first cries the night I was born. My sisters later took turns nurturing me with bottle feedings, diaper changes, carriage strolls, and caresses.

She had a quiet and gentle air about her, always understanding and rarely complaining. I argued with my other siblings—as competing children often do—but never with Doris. She was born with a charitable attitude, predisposed to making peace.

Doris underwent a profound transformation in 1961. That was the year she received her religious calling. She'd been marveling at the teaching nuns since fourth grade, but it was at the tender age of sixteen that her admiration would burst into bloom.

It began with an invitation to spend the winter pensioning with the nuns in St-Gérard. The call had been selective, extended only to young ladies deemed suitable for religious life. Doris begged my parents for permission, and after some hesitation they granted it.

She was never the same after that winter, her gentle character having been infused with purpose. The experience had increased her confidence too. She now walked with a more purposeful stride, smiled more freely, and spoke more fluently.

In May of that year, Doris attended an out-of-town religious retreat with fellow classmates. These weekend affairs were common events in the lives of Catholic teens.

"Have you thought about religious life?" a priest asked over the weekend.

"I think I'd like to be a nun someday," she confided shyly.

"I'll pray for your vocation."

But the priest did more than pray. News of her confidential affirmation had reached the little convent in St-Gérard at lightning speed. It was no secret that these religious retreats were for a means of identifying prospective servants of the faith.

Her intimation that she would *someday* like to be a nun was conveniently ignored, and the clerical wheels were set in motion immediately. The nuns were eager to begin Doris' religious transformation, so they convinced her to join the convent that same summer. She was seventeen.

My parents learned of her glorious ambition not long after the momentous retreat. They were startled and disenchanted with the rapid decision.

"I think you're too young," my father said.

"Why don't you wait till after eleventh grade?" my mother implored.

But neither Doris nor the nuns would consider their pleas. A delay would be too risky, inviting undue family pressure that might weaken her avocation.

So, plans were made for Doris to leave in August—only a few months away. We were stunned by the swiftness of her decision. Over the summer, Maman anguished over the upcoming separation, while my father harbored bitter feelings toward the nuns.

This would be our first family separation—that is, except for the summer my brother Jacques went to work in the tobacco fields of Ontario. He too had received a religious calling, intending to join the seminary at St-Victor-de-Beauce, eighty miles from town.

My parents were unable to finance his vocational training, so he elected to do the backbreaking work in the tobacco fields as a means to earn the funds necessary to enter seminary. Jacques had been sponsored by Father Berger, our intimidating pastor in St-Gérard.

After slaving in tobacco fields for a while, the sobered seventeen-year-old suddenly abandoned all religious ambition. By August 1960, he was back under our roof, working at the wood slat factory in town. We silently rejoiced over his disillusionment.

But we had little hope that Doris would ever change *her* mind; she was bubbling over with enthusiasm. So we started preparing for the inevitable day.

The most troubling part of her departure was the distance. She was headed for the big city of Winnipeg, where the Canadian branch of the Sisters of the Cross was based. We'd never heard of Winnipeg, but we were disheartened to find out she'd be living twelve hundred miles due west of our farm. It might as well have been China.

"When will she be back?" my mother asked Sister Superior.

"Her training will take a year, and then she'll be sent elsewhere."

"But when will we see her again?" Maman persisted.

"Her life is in God's hands now," she answered with a shrug.

Maman slowly relented to her daughter's decision, gradually accepting the painful outcome amidst tears. But my father resented the religious hogwash, convinced that the good sisters had manipulated Doris merely to propagate their own kind.

My memories of our last months with Doris are bittersweet. She appeared more contented and exhilarated than ever, as we struggled with our emotions. Her imminent departure overshadowed even minor interactions.

My parents decided to host a farewell celebration about a week before her departure. Friends and relatives crowded into the kitchen of our farmhouse to say goodbye. The evening was pleasant, but it heightened our separation anxiety. It meant the end was near.

Later that evening, a photographer arrived at the house to capture Doris on film. In an uncharacteristic decision, it seems that my father had hired the stranger to photograph Doris with her parents, siblings, and grandparents.

The man mounted an old-fashioned box camera on a tripod and ducked his head under the heavy black cloth to block out the ambient light. We stood there posing in the unlit living room, blinded by the explosive flash of his light bulbs.

Those pictures remain among my favorites, still stirring up nostalgia. They were all taken in our small living room and forever captured the humility of our abode: the wood slat ceiling, exposed light bulb, homemade curtains, and linoleum flooring.

Clockwise: Michel, Lucette, Jacques, Réal, Denise, Pierre, Laurette, Doris, Hervé. 1961.

My uncles imbibed respectable quantities of warm beer that day, which inspired them to sing traditional folk songs, belting out the verses with inebriated gusto.

"Has anybody seen Théodore?" my Uncle Léopold interrupted.

"Not me," the overlapping voices replied. Nobody had seen him for a while.

Théodore, my mother's brother, had a propensity for drinking himself senseless. The kitchen was still abuzz with speculation on his whereabouts when a team of men assembled outside to begin searching the grounds. But in the dark of night, scouring over acres of farmland would be like looking for the proverbial needle in the haystack.

It took hours for them to locate Uncle Théodore; he was lying face down in the ditch where he'd gone to pee. With the scare over, he was escorted home, safe but groggy.

A steady trickle of close friends and relatives had visited Doris over the past week to exchange final goodbyes. My heart sank a little lower with each passing day.

From the front yard, I watched my Aunt Fleurianne snap photos of Doris on the porch. I had one knee in my little wagon. As the gentle breeze rustled her new departure dress in a doleful sweep, I quickly wiped away tears with the back of my hand.

On the last day, Doris emptied her closet and donated all her clothes to my sisters. This was an emotional milestone, symbolizing her permanent detachment from our family. The house was filled with tender hearts as the reality of her leaving settled in like cement.

We were on our way to Sherbrooke Station. On the morning of August 13, 1961, we dressed up in our Sunday best and climbed into the family car for the fifty-mile ride. Doris was leaving on the train for Winnipeg.

I had just turned nine the previous Wednesday. I was wearing my only suit, a handsome double-breasted piece passed down from my well-dressed cousin, Réjean.

On the way to Sherbrooke, we engaged in lighthearted conversation to disguise our drooping spirits, painfully aware that she'd be gone in a few short hours. Butterflies were fluttering in my stomach by the time we arrived at the train station.

On her journey west, Doris would be escorted by Sister Jeanne-Rita, a teaching nun from St-Gérard. We joined the contingency of nuns on the train platform, watching in anguish as the noon Sherbrooke-to-Montréal train screeched into the station.

It was soon time to board the train. Some of us had been shedding quiet tears even before Sister Jeanne-Rita gathered the family for final photos, and we stared at the camera with puffy eyes. The resulting photos accurately depict a family in emotional distress.

Saying goodbye to Doris on the train platform. 1961.

Our last goodbyes were heart wrenching. Everyone was crying, except for Doris. She continued smiling with excitement, captivated by a glorious sense of adventure.

As for me, I had no composure at all. When it was my turn, I embraced Doris without saying a word. I was too choked to speak, trying to hold my breath to suppress the surge of emotions. I was afraid to whimper like a remorseful dog.

I quickly stepped away from the entourage to release the pressure inside my lungs. By the time I reached the far corner of the train platform, I was sobbing aloud. I hated to lose my grip on my emotions; it was embarrassing to cry in public.

As Doris waved from the train window, we caught our last glimpse of her through more tears. As the train pulled away from the station, I ran to the end of the platform and watched it careening down the tracks. I stood there until it had disappeared around a bend.

We were left emotionally drained and depressed, and the uncertainty made it even worse. None of us knew when we'd see Doris again. It was as though she'd just been erased from our family forever, and we were grieving her passing.

Aunt Noëlla Tessier—my father's cousin—lived in Sherbrooke. We liked this exceptionally short and energetic woman. She was kindhearted and funny, and her offbeat humor kept us in stitches. She'd joined us on the train platform just in time to see Doris board the train, shedding some tears of her own. The train had just pulled away from the station when Aunt Noëlla attempted to lift our doleful spirits.

"Come to my place for coffee," she said to my mother.

"Oh no, we should head back to the farm."

"Come for an hour. It'll do you some good to gab a little."

They bantered a little longer before my mother finally agreed to the offer. Aunt Noëlla served coffee to the adults and milk and cookies to the kids. She insisted I take a cookie, which I did, munching on it without tasting. This time, her comical stories did nothing to improve the morose atmosphere; we smiled just to be polite.

I wonder what Doris is doing now, I kept asking myself. I tried to picture the train, conjuring up her smiling face as she relished the passing scenery in blissful repose.

The drive home was quiet, our minds busy reliving her departure and nursing the open wound. As we drove past the little town of Ascot Corner, the cemetery appeared on a knoll to our immediate right, its dark metal cross standing tall.

My mother glanced over at the cross and burst into tears. I couldn't stand watching Maman cry, so I quietly contributed my own sympathetic tears.

"I can't believe she's gone", Maman blurted amidst long sobs.

I couldn't believe it either. This had been the worst day of my life. Her departure was further eroding the appeal of the farm.

The trip to Winnipeg took three days and two nights. Her roomette on the train contained only a single bed, so Doris had no choice but to bunk down with Sister Jeanne-Rita. She didn't sleep at all, embarrassed to be sharing a bed with a professed nun. But despite her insomnia, the journey remained an exciting adventure to the great unknown.

As soon as Doris arrived in Winnipeg, she began her postulant training, throwing herself into the studies while the rest of us back home slowly adapted to her absence. As was the custom at the time, she also changed her name, taking on the religious name of Sister Marie-Lorette. Doris Blanchette no longer existed.

She was granted permission to write one letter a week on Sunday. This was our only means of communication, so we looked forward to each letter with anticipation. Maman was always the first to read it—usually several times. Then, she'd leave it on the kitchen table or the counter for the rest of us to savor.

Her letters were filled with well-crafted religious prose, the lofty words sounding divinely inspired. It was comforting to know that she seemed happy, but we knew that she could never admit to feeling lonely. Religious orders were like armies: the good of the whole took precedence over that of the one. Maman studied each letter with great interest and invariably broke down after reading the affectionate words. Most of us did the same.

A few months after Doris left for the convent, the nuns in St-Gérard gave my mother a photo album entitled *Souvenirs of Our Dear Doris*. It contained an artistic collage of family photographs and quotations portraying my sister from birth to the present. The monochrome photos had been mounted on black pages using sticky corners, and the cursive narrations beneath the pictures had been handwritten in white crayon.

The album was a sentimental treasure, and it broke our hearts all over again. There were pictures of Doris as a baby, toddler, teenager, and postulant. The handwritten passages under the pictures were at times lighthearted and at others melancholic.

"I take my leave, life carries me away toward distant unknowns," one picture read. "I hold in my soul a living memory," said another, hinting at her past family life.

My mother cried every time she looked at the album, as did I. The photos showing her departure bore inscriptions that sent chills up my spine and tears to my eyes.

As with all things, time diminished the poignancy of our loss. Daily chores again occupied our time and energy, leaving only enough time for periodic bouts of nostalgia.

Six months into her religious formation, Doris graduated from postulant to novitiate status. This happened at a private investiture ceremony in Winnipeg.

A month before the graduation, Sister Superior extended my parents a generous offer: the Sisters of the Cross would cover their expenses to attend the graduation ceremony in Winnipeg. The kind offer moved my mother to tears.

They were soon on their way to Winnipeg, riding on an airplane for the first time in their lives. My father was thrilled to be flying, but my mother remained in a state of nervous agitation for the duration of the trip. As the jet approached the runway for a landing, the rapid descent threw Maman into a severe panic attack.

My parents' attendance had been kept a secret. The nuns were worried that advance news of their visit might distract Doris from her religious preparations. As the white-gowned postulants walked down the aisle holding candles, Doris noticed my parents in the crowd. It was a touching moment filled with strong emotion and happy tears.

The trip had been a kind and wise gesture on the part of the nuns; it helped my mother overcome her loneliness and eradicated my father's bitter feelings.

We didn't see Doris for two years. Then, one day, the nuns informed us that she would return to the little convent in St-Gérard to finish high school. She was nineteen.

But the closer proximity did little to improve our access to Doris. Sister Marie-Lorette now belonged to a religious order, which meant that all interactions with outsiders had to be approved by Sister Superior. Permission to meet with family had to be requested in advance, after which we could visit the convent for two hours on Sunday afternoon. The carefree chats with our gentle sister had turned into regimented visits with a clergywoman.

By now, Doris had professed her vows, so she wore the full habit of the Sisters of the Cross. That included a black dress, a black overlay, draped sleeves, a black veil, a white collar, a rosary down to her ankles, and a large wooden crucifix around her neck.

Although very little flesh remained exposed, I nevertheless found her prettier than ever. The black veil accentuated the gentle contours of her face, her exuberant smile enlivening the stark costume like sunshine through storm clouds.

It seemed strange that Doris was forbidden to enter the homes of family members. My Côté grandparents had an apartment a few hundred feet from the convent. Still, she was not permitted to walk the short distance to visit my aging grandparents.

My brother Jacques married Thérèse Gagné in 1963. Thérèse was the sister of my friend Jean-Marie. The wedding was held at the church in St-Gérard, right next to the convent, yet Doris was denied permission to attend the wedding and reception.

Doris with Jacques and Thérèse on their wedding day. 1963.

We never understood these silly prohibitions. *Why can't she attend the wedding Mass?* The only conclusion we could reach was that the nuns spurned all secular exposure; it could corrupt her moral values and weaken her religious resolve.

Sister Superior granted Doris permission for a rare visit with family in 1964. I was twelve years old when my parents rented a cottage on Lake Aylmer for two weeks. My Aunt Juliette and her family rented the cottage right next to ours. We had a blast.

We were surprised that Sister Superior had accepted my mother's invitation to lunch. Naturally, Doris wouldn't be alone; her escorts would include Sister Joseph-Saint-Paul, Sister Jeanne-Rita, and Sister Saint-Joseph. But at least she'd be away from the convent.

Our little cottage lacked most cooking appliances, so my mother decided to serve our illustrious guests a humble fare of beans and salmon pie. That lunch menu seemed risky considering the potential gastrointestinal aftereffects, but these beans were homemade.

"I want you to be quiet in the presence of the nuns," Maman said. She was determined to make a good impression, hoping that the luncheon might loosen the regulations on future visits. I promised to be a charming boy.

By the time our black and white guests arrived at the modest cottage, my mother was already a nervous wreck. Priests and nuns topped her list of intimidating figures. She'd fret over every word, paranoid over doing or saying something inappropriate.

When it was time for lunch, our prominent guests sat at the rectangular table while the rest of us waited nearby for a second seating. Ignorant of etiquette, we stood near the kitchen counter and watched our honorable guests munching ten feet away.

It happened as she approached the table. We heard it clearly and distinctly, like a wind chime ringing above the clamor of human voices. It was the unmistakable noise of passing gas, a flatulent expression of her anxiety. My mother had farted aloud.

The body noise recoiled against the large window facing the lake, playfully bouncing against the ceiling and walls before leaving its exaggerated imprint on our brains. Our only consolation was that my mother's timing could have actually been worse: it could have interrupted the prayer given before the meal.

Lucette, Pierre, Christian, and I were dumbfounded and embarrassed for my mother. Surely, she'd have to admit the intestinal indiscretion, I thought. But Maman pretended that nothing happened, her mind too agitated to ponder corrective action and her body too busy repressing a recurrence of the abdominal turbulence. She was living her most embarrassing nightmare, yet she never slowed her pace.

For their part, the good nuns simply chose to ignore the crude noise, continuing to beam white-tooth smiles amidst the pleasant small talk. But the ambiance of the room had definitely changed: locker-room humor had sullied the blessed occasion.

It took very little time for the scene to rouse my funny bone. I glanced over at Lucette and saw that she too was losing the fight to control her widening smile. I gave out a loud guffaw; Lucette nudged me with her elbow and tried to hush me.

My shoulders were soon jumping up and down in violent spasms. There was nothing else to do but leave; my behavior would only add salt to my mother's wounds.

I opened the screen door onto the porch and rushed to the side of the cottage, where our important guests couldn't hear. Desperate to release the pent-up hysteria, I was soon bent over in half with crazed laughter.

A few minutes later, Lucette stepped out of the cottage to release her own snickers. She then addressed me with words that threatened to obliterate my charm.

"They think it was you," she said through giggles.

"What do you mean?" I retorted, no longer amused.

"You ran out so fast that they think you did it."

"No!" I screamed a little too loud.

"Yes, I think so," she said with a smirk.

With the finger now pointing at me, I was in great distress. The incident had taken a most serious turn, and my boyhood honor was at stake.

After thinking over my meager choices, I decided to reenter the scene of the crime in the hope of somehow exonerating myself in front our honored guests. Humiliation had replaced humor, so the risk of further giggles was no longer a practical danger.

I reentered the cottage and retook my place, standing with Pierre, Christian, and Lucette. I made small contributions to the conversation whenever it seemed appropriate, trying hard to uphold a responsible and charming demeanor. The response from the pious women seemed positive, which slightly improved my shattered outlook on life.

After everybody had eaten, someone suggested that we take a rowboat ride on the lake. Our cottage came equipped with two large wooden rowboats painted in vivid colors. It seemed like a good opportunity for me to ooze my charm, so I hurriedly jumped into one of the boats, offering to pilot the good nuns around the lake.

Michel in the rowboat at Lake Aylmer. 1964.

My mother and our religious guests were soon divided between two rowboats. Lake Aylmer echoed with the sound of hearty laughter as the nuns in black habits leaned over the side of the boats and splashed each other with childish abandon.

The rowboat ride lasted about an hour, and then it was time to return our holy cargo to the wooden quay. As my mother strained hard to disembark the unsteady rowboat, she disgorged another gaseous wind, one that might have scattered waterfowl for miles.

The flatulent sound cascaded over the water like a rifle shot during hunting season, exaggerated by the low overcast skies above the lake. Maman bashfully apologized for the vulgar ejection, her nervous intestine struggling to digest the homemade beans.

This time it was impossible for my mother to deny her guilt, given that she'd dropped the bomb inches from the ears of our guests. The diplomatic nuns continued flashing their generous smiles.

By now, Doris had given up all hope for a graceful visit with family. Her face was flushed with embarrassment when she decided to offer an explanation.

"When my mother's nervous, she farts," Doris asserted humbly.

I felt bad for my mother, but a selfish part of me rejoiced. This latest accident exonerated me of prior charges. And I'd learned the lesson: *Nuns and beans don't mix.*

Not surprisingly, the luncheon did little to pave the way for unsupervised visits; Sister Superior had simply made an exception to the rule. But the day was still memorable: Maman had welcomed Doris home with a resounding two-gun salute.

12

Lesson of the Bicycle

I was lonely. In September 1962, my Aunt Juliette and her family abandoned the little town of St-Gérard, moving a few hundred miles south to New Hampshire. My uncle's search for a steady job had resulted in a permanent move to the United States. Prompted by a destitute economy, the exodus of families was sapping the vitality of our town.

The aura of the farm had deteriorated with the departure of my aunt. Sylvie, Christian, and Guy had always been privileged members of our extended family; the close bond had implicitly raised their status from mere cousins to virtual siblings.

Their departure created in me a feeling of emptiness that I found impossible to shake. My lonesome reflections were also filled with envy: I longed to share their newfound life elsewhere. Weary of the farm, I became a ten-year-old in search of greener pastures.

My bleak mood was made worse by the circumstances facing the family. My father had taken a job eighty miles away, and commuted home only on weekends. This left my mother alone to manage the farm and tend to our large family, as Papa tried to keep us financially afloat with his job in distant Beebe. And we still bore the scar from Doris' departure.

The new school year began a few days after my cousins left town. The hours I spent at Mater Domini kept me out of the doldrums, but the dark sentiments would reemerge on the long walk home. The farm had become a desolate place.

The arrival of autumn made these feelings even worse. The leaves were changing color, providing a vibrant reminder of their impending death, the birds were flying south to avert the hellish winter that would soon invade the landscape, and the days were getting shorter as the sun prepared to abandon Québec in favor of foreign lands across the globe.

My disquieted brain was longing for hope and appeasement. The solution dawned on me one day as I walked past our old unpainted garage. The slim black and white bicycle was leaning against the side of the garage like a horse waiting for its rider.

I didn't have a bicycle. My parents couldn't afford them, but we did have a fleet of Frankenstein contraptions that had been assembled from spare parts. These old bikes were always in disrepair, hobbled by flat tires or broken chains.

The problem wasn't just the equipment; it was my size. At ten, I was stuck in the body of a seven- or eight-year-old, weighing in at fifty pounds. My pint-size frame made it nearly impossible to lift and mount these heavy bikes with their balloon tires.

I'd outgrown all my means of transportation. That included the red tricycle that my father had bought me when I was four or five years old. Its seat floated about twelve inches off the ground, and I looked asinine pedaling that thing, my knees high up in the air. And I'd lost interest in my little wagon, tired of pushing myself around on one knee.

Nobody had taught me to ride a bicycle either. It would have been senseless to learn without the proper equipment, sort of like learning to catch trout without fishing gear.

But that black and white bicycle was calling me. Unlike the damaged dinosaurs reclining in the garage, this beauty had thin tires and a sleek metal frame. It was also light enough for me to lift and maneuver. I was left now with only two problems. The first was its height: it stood at twenty-six inches, which would make mounting and dismounting tricky. The second was the gears, as the three speeds would complicate my training.

The dream bicycle belonged to my older brother Jacques. He'd bought it secondhand with his own money for the exorbitant sum of five dollars. This was *his* mode of transportation when he wasn't at work. But he worked at the slat factory all day, so I figured it could become *my* mode of transportation without his knowledge.

I was sure that Jacques would never agree to lend me his bike, so I never bothered to ask him. It would have been useless banter with a predictable outcome:

"Can I borrow your bike?"

"No."

"Why not?"

"Because I paid for it, that's why."

"I won't break it."

"You're too small to ride. You'll fall and dent it."

"I'll be careful."

"I still don't want you to use it."

Not only would I be denied permission, but my bold request would probably make Jacques suspicious of my intentions, encouraging him to hide the bike someplace else. No, it was better not to ask in the first place. Anyway, he'd never notice as long as I restored the bike to its normal location in its original condition.

There was always the risk that Jacques would learn the truth from a sibling; my occasional naughtiness gave Pierre and Lucette darn good reasons to report any acts of theft on my part. But I'd just have to take my chances.

"Does Jacques know you're using his bike?" my mother asked me one day.

"I don't think so, but I'm real careful," I said. It was the only time Maman brought up the topic. I interpreted her subsequent silence in my favor, sensing implicit support for my self-improvement program. I knew she'd defend me if necessary.

Invigorated by the daring plan, I began training after school. This would last for weeks. The moment I finished my homework, I'd dart out of the house and head for the trusty black and white bicycle parked in the old garage. I was hell-bent on riding.

The training was exhilarating. I was determined to overcome the obstacles one at a time. Distrustful of my siblings, I insisted on practicing alone despite the fact that riding solo added complications.

My brother Pierre, a mischievous fourteen-year-old at the time, had been present on a few occasions, usually with troubling results. He was prone to yanking on my bicycle seat at the least auspicious moments. The sudden lunge would crush my jewels against the handlebar post, throwing off my sensitive balance and dropping me like a rock on the gravel road. Every new scratch on the bike increased the likelihood that my illicit adventure would be discovered.

"Do you want me to help you?" Pierre asked.

"No, leave me alone!" I yelled back, painfully familiar with his pranks.

Training alone required me to overcome the hurdles of mounting, dismounting, and accelerating the three-speed bike on my own. It was like riding bareback on an Italian steed, the high-strung animal attempting to throw me off at every turn.

Mounting the staggering bike was a significant problem. John Wayne would have placed one foot in the stirrup, swung his generous butt over the saddle, slipped his other foot into the second stirrup, and kicked his spurs to start the horse moving.

But I was too short, and thus I'd need a boost to mount the steed. I settled on a tree stump. The leftover log pile behind the house provided an array of options. I rolled a stump toward the front yard; this would become my departure point.

I stood on the makeshift ladder while holding the handlebar, extended my leg over the center bar to reach the pedal, and shoved off the stump with my other foot.

It was a fussy move; one small error and I'd topple onto the gravel surface with my limbs entangled in the wheels. To stay mounted, I had to plant both feet securely on the pedals and apply steady pressure to gain momentum. But the pedals were made of metal, so my feet would often slip off, precipitating a swift tumble to the ground. Relentless practice gradually paid off, but success begged for perfection.

After mounting the stallion, I faced the challenge of riding. I was too short to reach the pedals from the adult saddle, so I had to stand up on them to ride. With all my weight resting on the slippery pedals, each turn threatened my demise.

Having succeeded with the departure, the road itself presented my next challenge, its gravel surface filled with potholes and rocks. The holes were most treacherous after a rainstorm, as the pools within made it difficult to gauge depth from afar. Unlike the wide balloon tires on those mongrel bikes in the garage, the narrow tires on my brother's three-speed bike were intolerant of obstacles large and small.

Every rock and pothole posed a potential hazard, requiring me to scan the ground ahead while pedaling the training course between our house and Grandpapa's farm. My eyes were like radar antennas sweeping the landscape for menacing depressions and stones, my legs were locomotive pistons constantly adjusting the traction under my feet, and my torso was the human gyroscope sustaining my balance over the obstacle course.

Shifting gears was a touchy move, as it required pedaling in reverse. The maneuver is easy when your butt is anchored to a saddle, but my standing position denied me any such leverage. Manipulating the gear was simple enough, involving a mere flick of the thumb against the little chrome lever attached to the handlebar. But reversing the rotation of the pedals—which was attended by loud clicking noises from the crank axle—was like reentering earth's atmosphere from outer space. One false move and all was lost.

The momentary reduction in speed combined with the loss of traction under my feet often resulted in an ungraceful dismount. Every pathetic fall was the same; my balls would slam down on the support bar, the sharp pain throwing off my equilibrium. The dull thud was barely audible above the clinking of metal parts.

Every fall postponed my training for a few tedious minutes as I impatiently headed back to the stump to remount my delicate steed. Then I'd start all over again.

"*Maudit!*" I swore, often frustrated with the grueling regimen.

The narrow dirt road to my grandfather's house also made it hard to reverse direction without stopping. To turn around, I had to slow down to a dangerous crawl and make a hairpin turn while the tip of the handlebar threatened to impale my crotch.

I decided to deploy a second stump to solve the turnaround problem, strategically placed on the road near my grandfather's house. I had calculated the rough distance between stumps to account for endurance and fatigue. (Riding in a standing position was sapping my energy more rapidly than normal.)

However, my approach to the pit stops was difficult; it was like landing an airplane on a tennis court. Gliding toward the stump, I'd slow down the bicycle and extend my foot to land it on the small target. There was no backup plan; overshooting meant falling.

After making a precision stop, I'd dismount the bike for a minute to rest my legs, turn my steed around, and remount again to face the training course.

My mother later told me that I had an audience: my grandparents often watched me maneuvering the bicycle from their kitchen window. It seems that Grandpapa was greatly amused with my logistics and tenacity in the face of challenge.

The regimen lasted for weeks, becoming entrenched in my daily routine. It occupied at least two hours of every afternoon, between homework and dinner time. I persisted through all kinds of weather, including strong winds and light rain. Only hard rain could foil my practice. I sometimes struggled to control my fragile balance against blustery autumn winds—nature was merely another obstacle for me to surmount.

The relentless practice yielded tangible results, and I soon mastered every move with precision handling. The mounts, dismounts, gear shifts, and turns soon became second nature. I had counteracted my vertical handicap with discipline, much like our dog Puppé had adapted his stride to compensate for a severed leg.

A wonderful thing started happening after I'd perfected the cycling routine: my automatic pilot would engage at will to free my mind from the rigors of riding. Trusting my reflex to handle most contingencies, I found myself flowing gracefully.

The experience of gliding through air was exhilarating. The wind gently tousled my hair, muffled my ears, and moistened my eyes, causing me to lose track of time. My body became one with the bicycle, my soul soothed by the intoxicating motion.

The blissful state excited my imagination. I'd steer my sailplane through the puffy clouds, above the green forests, over the blue oceans, and into foreign lands. The exhilaration of riding had become my escape from the doldrums of 1962.

Riding was my first competence, the only skill I'd mastered on my own, and it paved the way for yet more ambitious dreams. The experience had increased my confidence, restoring my hope in the world.

I'd gleaned valuable knowledge from that bicycle, the seeds of which germinated in my brain like tulip bulbs. It had taught me firsthand that *hard work leads to satisfaction, perseverance is the key to mastery*, and *perfection begs attention to details*. These old adages may be self-evident truths, but they were awe-inspiring revelations to a sensitive ten-year-old child. And unlike the nagging diatribes recited by parents everywhere, these facts had been self-taught. I was now an independent boy.

Riding had inspired my new modus operandi: I started applying the biking formula to every new endeavor. I'd persevere through the initial feelings of incompetence, conquer one detail at a time, and finally polish the results to perfection.

I applied the same formula to each school year, starting off at a sluggish pace but always finishing at the top of my class. I never attributed these little triumphs to ability; the results were solely due to methodology. Many kids were smarter, but I compensated by working more diligently. These habits are forever etched in my brain.

Over time, these tactics would benefit my career in a similar manner. It turns out that the corporate world loves workaholics and perfectionists, rewarding their demanding nature with generous pay and stature. The three-speed bicycle had taught me well.

13

Farewell to the Farm

It was a bad year. By 1962, the province of Québec was having a tough time competing in growing world markets. Unemployment had risen to ten percent, and it was even higher in our isolated little corner of the province. Those who'd lived through the Great Depression talked about a recurrence of those terrible years.

Farmers were at the bottom of the economic ladder, financially ravaged by a lower demand for their agricultural products. The cost of production often exceeded the market price, resulting in frequent bankruptcies and desertions. Small farms were dying.

Those who tried to sell out faced an overabundant supply, which lowered the price of their land to ridiculous depths. A one-hundred acre farm could be purchased for as little as five thousand dollars, including buildings and farming equipment.

Jean Lesage, the premier governing the province in 1962, along with his Liberal Party, were working hard to modernize Québec with their "Quiet Revolution." Lesage was pushing for economic, political, and social reformation. But his efforts would be too little and too late for many farmers; their poverty couldn't wait for long-term reform.

This was our reality in 1962. At the age of ten, I would soon learn that poor economic times draw out the worst in people. High unemployment had turned friends and relatives into backstabbing competitors; every man was out for himself.

My father, brother Réal, and Uncle Gérard had all been affected by the system that pitted brother against brother—they had lost their jobs at the granite quarry. It usually started with a treacherous report to the boss, alleging poor workmanship or disloyalty.

The result of these self-serving and dubious allegations was always the same: the victim would be left unemployed, mysteriously replaced by the plaintiff or one of his kin. Threatened by a dissolving economy, integrity lost out to jungle survival.

My father had lost his job at the granite quarry where he'd worked for twenty years. His troubles had begun after he was elected union chief, his calm and unpretentious nature most likely responsible for his nomination by peers.

Papa got along well with the man who managed the quarry, but not with his nephew. Once the nephew had gained power, he sought to purge the union, viewing it as a serious drain on productivity and profits. This declaration of war placed my father in direct conflict with company management. He fought and lost the battle, thus joining the growing ranks of the unemployed.

There were very few opportunities for work in our neck of the woods. The only industries within a twenty-mile radius of our town were granite quarries, mines, and logging companies. St-Gérard hosted only one granite quarry and one wood slat factory. The other enterprises were all small family-owned stores.

At fifty years old, my father was unemployed with little hope of finding another job. Fifty was also the age of silent discrimination, with many companies discreetly favoring younger, cheaper, and less demanding labor. Papa was left bitter.

My father's job at the quarry had been essential, as it supplemented the dismal revenue we derived from our farm products. Our little dairy farm had never been profitable, requiring Réal, Jacques, and Denise to pool their earnings in order to survive. In 1962, my father was earning a measly eleven dollars a week selling milk products.

Without my father's job, we'd suddenly entered a financial danger zone—we had no reserves or savings to draw upon. While we waited for a miracle, my father slowly depleted our supply of chickens and cows, necessary measures to feed the family.

My parents rarely spoke about these problems in front of the children. But we knew. I'd caught Maman crying over unpaid bills on several occasions, and there were signs of despair in Papa's eyes. Although I didn't fully grasp the severity of the situation, I knew there was trouble. Our months on the farm were numbered.

There was a sudden break in the clouds. Uncle George-Émile, who lived in Beebe Plain near the United States border, had brought some fresh encouragement.

"Why don't you come to Beebe?" my uncle said to Papa.

"What will I do there?" my father replied, cynical about the future.

"At least there's work in Beebe. I can help you find something."

"And leave my family here?"

"They can come later, once you've settled in a job."

But Papa wasn't convinced. Working in Beebe would mean living eighty miles from his family and commuting home only on weekends. He'd spent most of his life on this farm, the nostalgic black-and-white family photos a testament to his childhood presence. Abandoning the paternal farm was a disheartening thought; he loved this place.

"Maybe we can tough it out," Papa told my mother.

"But what will the children do here when they grow up?" she asked, feeling that the oppressive economy bode poorly for our future as well.

"They'll find a way," he said, desperate to preserve hope.

There were no easy answers, so my defeated father begrudgingly accepted a lowly job at a gas station in Beebe. He'd temporarily board with my Uncle George-Émile.

My parents never brought up the option of moving, so I never thought it a possibility. Several of my uncles were also working out of town, coming home to their families every weekend or two; I assumed that my father would do the same thing indefinitely.

But Papa couldn't tolerate living without his wife and family, and he was terribly lonely. So, my parents began secretly planning our relocation. Not even my grandparents and siblings knew the shameful secret: we were abandoning the farm.

My father went out scouting for apartments in Beebe Plain and nearby towns, not an easy task considering the size of our family. He'd draw sketches of the apartments he visited and mail them home for my mother to review. This is how they picked our apartment—my mother didn't see the place until the day we moved.

Maman told us about the move two weeks before the fateful day. My father had insisted on keeping our departure a secret until the end; his confidence had been eroded by the recent unemployment and he was afraid of losing this job too.

There were other reasons for keeping quiet about the move. Leaving town was a controversial choice. While some folks might offer sympathetic encouragement, others would bemoan your spineless lack of resolve for running away from temporary difficulties. So, it was best to minimize this period of controversy.

And there were the creditors. We were in debt with merchants who would have descended on us like a swarm of locust had they learned of our intentions.

"I have something to tell you," Maman said to Pierre and me one evening.

I could already sense important news was coming by her tone of voice.

"Your father rented an apartment. We're moving in two weeks."

To say that I was pleased with the news would be understating my emotional response. I jumped up and down like a puppy rejoining his master after an extended absence. There were happy tears in my eyes. I cried, giggled, and ran around like some crazy kid.

"But you can't tell anybody," Maman said.

After we promised to protect the secret, my mother proceeded to fill us in on some of the details. We were moving to a second-floor apartment in a small city called Rock Island. The place abutted the United States border, Derby Line being the nearest town on the opposite side. I had no idea where this was.

There were seven of us going on to Rock Island. My brother Jacques, now in love with the sister of my friend Jean-Marie, was staying behind with my Uncle Roland.

I would have preferred to move where my Aunt Juliette and her family had gone. But this English-sounding place called Rock Island was at least a ticket out of town. My respect for the community of St-Gérard had reached an all-time low.

"Can we bring Puppé?" I asked.

"No, dogs aren't allowed in the apartment. He has to stay here."

"But where will he go?"

"Mister Gagné agreed to take him. He'll be in good hands."

I had no trouble keeping the secret. I didn't say a word to anybody, worried that spilling the news might somehow jinx our relocation plans.

My parents announced our intentions to neighbors and relatives one week before the departure. As expected, the public response included a mixture of disbelief, sympathy, sadness, and bitterness. My Côté grandparents were devastated. They'd been our closest neighbors for ten years, enjoying an enviable intimacy with my family.

My friend Jean-Marie came to our house—now in packing disarray—with his mother one evening during the last week. I could finally tell him the news.

"We're leaving the farm," I blurted out.

"No, that's not true," he said, suspecting a prank.

"Yes, we leave on Saturday."

He seemed both baffled and skeptical; he ran out to ask his mother.

"Yes, it's true," she confirmed with a serious face.

Ever since Maman had told me about the move, I had worried that the relocation plan might be aborted at the last minute. So, I was unsettled until the news had been made public knowledge. But now it was official: we were leaving St-Gérard.

We were forced to leave a lot of stuff behind. In order to fit the family in an apartment, we were bringing our clothes, furniture, kitchen accessories—and little else. My parents prepared to evacuate the farm as we attended our last days of school.

I found it difficult to concentrate. Everything would become irrelevant in a few days—the teachers, lectures, books, and homework would be different in Rock Island, making these last days at Mater Domini inconsequential. It seemed futile to apply myself.

I saw a truck with an attached trailer parked in the front yard while walking home from school one afternoon. My father had sold our cows to Albert Houde, an old friend who lived in town. The dozen cows were being loaded into the open trailer.

I approached slowly, alarmed by the commotion. My father, his friend, and a hired hand were busy fetching one cow at a time from the stable, coercing each animal into the open trailer. The brutal scene raised the hair on the back of my neck.

Each cow was pulled by a rope tied around its throat. The animals gasped for air, white foam drooling from the corners of their mouths. To speed up the pace, another person twisted their tails mercilessly. The cows mooed in a feverish pitch, wild-eyed with fear.

Predictably, the panicked cows resisted the forced march to the trailer ramp, veering left and right in desperate attempts to flee their captors. An attendant swiftly punished the bovine disobedience by slamming a two-by-four plank on their bony rumps.

We'd always been gentle with our animals, periodically brushing their hides and patting their backs with affection. This scene was an abomination, something my father would have never tolerated in the past. The men's behavior was downright repulsive.

It gave me the chills to watch Brunette, Blondine, Caillette, and la Grande Blanche being mishandled. These gentle animals had served us for years. I was ashamed to watch our faithful cows being abused at the hands of ruthless strangers.

I ran up the steps to the porch and entered the kitchen. Maman was standing inside the screen door, staring out at the pathetic scene unfolding in the front yard. She barely noticed my arrival, her moist eyes transfixed on the trailer. She was vigorously biting her nails, occasionally stopping to wipe away tears. I stood by her side.

"Where are they bringing them?" I asked.

"I don't know. Ask your father," she said with eyes riveted to the window.

"Will they be slaughtered?"

"You'll have to talk to your father."

We glared at the mass of confusion in a stupor. The frantic shuffle of animal feet kicked up dust above the dirt road, the callous men hollered brisk orders, the cows emitted terrifying moos, and the plank man whacked their rumps mercilessly.

I soon joined Maman with silent tears of my own, holding my breath for stretches to avoid alerting her with sobs. My mother was struggling with her own emotions; the last thing she needed was to see her ten-year-old son blubbering nearby.

The men finished loading the trailer. My father shook hands with Albert to finalize the deal as the truck pulled away with depressing finality. The departure of the cows signified the death of our farm; it was a devastating end to a memorable family era.

Realizing that this was the last time I would see our cows, I rushed outside just as the truck started moving down the road, bidding them farewell with sympathetic eyes. Thick dust kicked up from the vehicle tires while the cows continued mooing in panic.

I stood in the middle of the dirt road, trailing them with my eyes as they passed my grandfather's farm and negotiated the sharp left turn toward town. The mooing sounds grew faint, although I could still see the agitated sweep of their tails.

Eager to distance myself from the dreadful scene, I walked down to the stable and entered the low building. The place was an eerie cemetery, unnaturally void of all sound. I paced the aisle while clearing my eyes and then walked out for the last time. There was no reason to ever return there; the place had ceased harboring life.

"What will he do with our cows?" I asked Papa later.

"Albert will probably sell them," he said. My father didn't want to know their fate anymore than we did; he too was emotionally attached to them.

"He won't butcher them, will he?"

"I don't think so. Well, maybe the older ones, but not all."

My heart tumbled to the bottom of my chest.

Our farm died that day. Without chickens and cows, the place ceased to be a home. All that remained was a sundry of tired old buildings that struck me as ugly. Even the birds seemed to have abandoned the place, leaving an unsettling quietude in the air. The time had come to leave; my emotional attachment had been irreversibly severed.

The Friday before the move was an exciting day. My teacher announced our departure to the class, which precipitated heartfelt applause from peers. After school, I shook hands with my school chums, joking around to suppress any display of emotion. Gérard Poulin seemed more affected than other classmates, remaining by my side till the end.

"I'll see you around," Gérard said, his face flushed with emotion.

"Yeah, we'll be back to visit relatives."

"Maybe I'll see you at church," he said, waving a last goodbye.

My final walk from school was exhilarating. I strolled alone, noticing little things along the way like never before. The texture of pebbles on the gravel road, the sway of the changing maple leaves, the fresh smell of autumn air, the gentle contour of the land, and the profile of farm buildings had cast their last childhood impression.

Puppé greeted my arrival; he was the only animal left on the farm.

"We leave tomorrow," I said to Puppé. He wagged his tail and barked approval, unaware that he would soon be living the life of a refugee.

By the time I got back to the house, our belongings had been packed in boxes and the beds had been disassembled into moveable parts. My parents and I would sleep at my grandparents' house that night, while my siblings stayed in town with uncles.

We ate dinner with my grandparents that evening. I was in a dreamy mood, living in anticipation of our promising new life. It was *my* turn to be swept away by a great sense of adventure, not unlike the one Doris had experienced the year prior.

"Are you glad to be moving?" Grandpapa asked me.

"Yes, but I'll miss my friends a lot." I was trying hard not to sound overzealous, knowing that our departure was particularly tough on my grandparents.

"I'm sure you'll make new friends in Rock Island."

I slept upstairs with my parents that night, in the only spare bedroom. This was the same room my mother had shared with her siblings as a young girl, the boys and girls piled into one room without privacy.

My grandfather's farmhouse had changed little over the years, looking like it belonged in the prior century. Grandpapa had never been much of a handyman, avoiding all unnecessary renovations to his buildings. The dilapidated old barn near the house had been abandoned years ago, and all that remained was an empty shell for the kids to explore at every chance in spite of parental warnings to do otherwise.

The old hand pump on the kitchen counter was the only source of water in the house. In the daytime, the unpainted outhouse in the back was adequate for bathroom duty, the old newspapers substituting for bathroom tissue. Wiping was never a pleasant task, the coarse paper threatening to imprint the daily news on your butt. Nighttime urgencies were relieved using the disgusting chamber pot stowed under the bed.

I woke up earlier than usual the next morning, filled with unbounded excitement. After munching on the usual toasts, we headed back to the farm to supervise the loading of our modest belongings onto the truck.

Our moving transport was a small cattle truck owned by Albert Houde, the same man who'd purchased and brutalized our cows a few days earlier. The cargo box had been swept clean for the grand occasion but continued stinking of animal dung.

With nothing else to do, I loafed on the porch with my dog Puppé, watching the hired hands loading our belongings. I was getting impatient to get on with our new life.

"How much longer will it take?" I asked once too often.

"It won't be long now," my father said.

"But that's what you said last time."

"Well, stop asking the same question."

As soon as the men were finished loading the truck, Puppé and I entered the house one last time to take in the empty surroundings. This was the only place I'd ever known, and I was curious to see how it looked devoid of furniture and life.

We walked the length of the upstairs and downstairs as the sound of little feet and dog claws echoed against the linoleum floor and wooden ceilings. I climbed up the steep staircase that had witnessed my early falls, glanced at the wall where my baby crib had stood during my toddler years, noticed the permanent scars in the linoleum imprinted by my grownup bed, looked into the bedroom where my sisters had slept all those years, and paced the kitchen where I'd taken my meals since the age of eight months.

Despite pangs of nostalgia, I was still glad to leave this place. My childhood memories had been pleasant, full of carefree days and blissful adventures. But the appeal of the farm had quickly disintegrated with the departure of loved ones, and it would never be the same. The paternal land had ceased to play a pivotal role in our lives; it was now merely a memorable chapter in our family's history.

Maman's voice suddenly shook me out of my dream state. It was finally time to leave. The cattle truck had just pulled away to begin its eighty-mile journey to Rock Island.

But I still had one unpleasant task to perform before leaving: I had to say goodbye to my dog, Puppé. I'd been dreading this moment for days. I settled on the edge of the porch with Puppé by my side, patting his fur while my parents waited at the car.

"You've been a good dog. I'm sorry you can't come with us but you'll like the Gagné family," I said with heavy heart. I felt rotten to be leaving him there.

I didn't tell him that the day before, Mister Gagné had stubbornly refused to see us. When we went over to say goodbye, the man had stayed upstairs pretending to be asleep. But we knew better—he was upset over our sudden departure.

Puppé was happy to receive the attention, shimmying on his tummy, licking my hands, and shuffling his tail in rapid movements. I wrapped my arm around his back one last time and stood up to leave. Puppé followed me off the porch, panting enthusiastically.

"Puppé, you have to stay here," I said, retracing my steps to the porch in an effort to lure him back. "Mister Gagné will come and get you soon."

My father fired up the engine as I knelt on the back seat to look out the rear window. Puppé was standing on the vacant porch watching our exodus; his tail wagged vigorously and his snout moved to silent barks. I stared at the receding animal, forcing back tears until we pulled up to my grandfather's farm. I had just abandoned my best friend.

We could hear my grandmother's loud sobs the moment we stepped out of the car, the screen door to the house allowing her grief to spill out into the morning air. My grandfather was making futile attempts to hush her emotional outburst with mild reprimands.

"Stop that, Diana! They'll hear you," he warned.

"My goodness, listen to her," my mother said. She heaved a long sigh as if to summon courage and then climbed the steps onto the unpainted porch.

My stomach was tied up in knots. My grandmother's emotional state had seemed fine at breakfast; I was shocked by the dramatic shift in her composure.

"She's been like this since you left this morning," Grandpapa said.

"We'll *never* see you again," my grandmother muttered between her sobs.

"Maman, of course you'll see us again."

"We're only two hours away," my father added.

"But it will never be the same."

My grandmother's tears gradually subsided as Maman addressed her with soothing words. I watched the emotionally-charged scene, in awe of my mother. I knew her to be nervous, emotionally volatile, and prone to tears. But now, she was playing the comforting daughter, with an emotional strength I never knew she had.

We stood in the kitchen engaging in chit-chat until the mood had lightened and Grandmaman's emotional condition had stabilized. My father looked at his watch.

"We should go soon," he said.

Maman embraced her mother as they both promised to write. Fearing a repetition of the earlier scene, my father interjected a little humor to improve the emotional climate. My grandparents responded with nervous smiles and feigned laughter.

When it was my turn to say goodbye, Grandmaman hugged me so hard that I was pinned against her chest. She kissed my cheeks several times, blending her tears with mine while mumbling good wishes about my new school.

Grandpapa was an old-fashioned kind of guy who shunned sentimentality. But on this occasion, his red-rimmed eyes belied his smile. He reached for my hand, shaking it firmly while uttering encouraging words. He didn't let go my hand for several minutes, shaking it with vigor as my arm turned numb from the incessant motion.

But I didn't mind. I knew this was my grandfather's way of telling me he cared. We'd been closest neighbors for nearly my entire life; they'd watched me take my first steps, and years later they'd cheered my attempts at riding the demanding three-speed bicycle. When I was still a toddler, it was to their house that I regularly eloped, dragging a dusty old broom behind me for comfort. Now we were leaving for good.

"Send us news often," Grandmaman said.

We finally made our way down the porch stairs and got into the car. With the car windows lowered, my father backed out of the dusty driveway and we waved a last goodbye. My grandmother was crying quietly. The watery reflection in Grandpapa's eyes revealed that he too was shedding tears under the dark-rimmed glasses.

My grandparents were standing on the porch side by side, waving sadly at the retreating automobile. That heartbreaking image would haunt me for a long time.

The moment we were out of sight of the old farm, my mother broke down in tears, releasing the pent-up emotions she'd been suppressing. It was more than I could tolerate; I knelt on the car seat to look out the rear window, watching the air fill with dust thrown up from the tires. And like Maman, I too mourned the traumatic separation.

My head was full of nostalgic recollections during the short ride to town. The cow pasture where I'd hidden on the fateful day Maman caught me playing doctor with Danielle was on my right. The field that we'd strolled to reach Lake Aylmer was a little further. The rolling hills where we went sledding every winter were to my left, as was the brook that we frequently fished with hushed-over voices during the summer months.

My parents had to pay bills and pick up the mail before leaving town. Our first stop was at the furniture store owned by the Marcou family. We had debt there, and my father was using the proceeds from the sale of his animals to pay off the loan.

I begrudgingly entered the store with my parents, hating every minute. I'd become distrustful of local merchants, convinced that they were all cheaters and backstabbers. The pleasant wife of the owner greeted us at the door. I stared back in disdain.

Next, we stopped at the Brière store. This was the same place where I'd once absconded with a miniature bag of salted peanuts. My mother and I stayed in the car while my father went inside to clear our debt and pick up the last bit of mail. Father Berger suddenly knocked on the passenger window, stopping to exchange some parting words with my mother. Maman's eyes were red and puffed out from the fresh tears.

"It's a pity that families have to leave the land to find work," he said.

Our last stop was the house of Uncle Roland, my father's youngest brother. My siblings were already there waiting for us. The adults exchanged tearful goodbyes while I shook hands with my cousin Ghyslain, a regular playmate since my toddler years.

My parents and five of their children piled into the family car, a little Hilman that could only seat four adults comfortably. Being the smallest member of the family, I alternated between standing on the transmission hump and sitting on a big sister.

Uncle Roland's family stood in their front yard as we pulled out onto Route 1 south, waving and brandishing weak smiles that concealed their tears. Our new life had just begun.

14

Lonely Hearts

My Côté grandparents abandoned their farm a few weeks after us, leaving the Gagné family as sole inhabitants of Rural Route Number Seven. Depressed over the departure of her eldest daughter, my grandmother refused to continue living in the countryside.

They first moved in with my Uncle Léopold and later rented a small apartment in the center of St-Gérard. They would spend the next seven years living happily on the second floor of an old apartment building, until my grandfather's sudden death in 1969.

My family would not be the last to leave town; grandparents on both sides would endure the departures of several more children before the Québec economy stabilized. Within two years, the Côté and Blanchette clans had dispersed to cities like Sherbrooke, while others had relocated to the United States in a desperate search for jobs.

"If you ever move back to the farm, so will we," Grandpapa Côté had said. They held onto their farm for years, secretly praying for our return. But their prayers were never answered. Their farm gradually fell into disrepair, the old barn finally collapsing and the unpainted house burning to the ground. The place had hosted its last boisterous celebration on January 1, 1962. Within nine months, everything had changed.

I have vivid memories of that place: the aromas of cooking mixing nicely with the festive music of my uncles. The old house may be gone, but part of me is still there sitting on the narrow staircase with naughty cousins, listening to the merriment with glee.

We reached Rock Island in the afternoon of September 22, 1962.

This place was quite different from St-Gérard. Most towns along the St-Lawrence River were founded during the seventeenth century by French immigrants, who stubbornly clung to their French culture and language long after the

British occupation. Both sides of my family descended directly from these French immigrants.

But Stanstead County was more recently settled, having served as an Indian hunting and fishing ground until it was surveyed by the English in 1792. Everything about this place was Anglo-Saxon. Even the towns around Rock Island had proper English names like Beebe Plain, Lineboro, Cedarville, Griffin, and Barnston.

The county included a mix of French- and English-speaking families by the time we arrived. But to say that the towns were bilingual would be incorrect. People either spoke French or English; few families were able to converse in both languages.

The reasons for this unilingual tradition were deeply rooted in culture and religion. The French had resented the English even before King Louis XV ceded Québec to England two hundred years earlier. Although time had mitigated the overt animosity, polite avoidance remained as a subtle sign of resentment.

Religious differences drove a deep wedge between the French and the English. The French were staunch Roman Catholics, whereas the British were devoted Protestants. Their churches often competed for the best land in town, each believing that eternal salvation was an exclusive privilege bestowed by God upon their members. The French prayed for the lost souls of the English, and the English reciprocated in kind.

My childhood experiences exemplified these religious differences. Our Catholic teachers often warned that there were two great evils in the world.

"Communists are the devil incarnate," they told us.

Communism sought to destroy the free world with weapons of mass destruction and then torture the unfortunate few who survived the nuclear holocaust. Torture at the hands of communists sounded despicable; these people were ruthless pagans. Our teachers would occasionally shock us with gory reports of torture in some godforsaken place.

"Our Catholic nuns in Africa have been captured by communists," the teacher said. "Armed men entered the convent, shot one nun, and demanded that the rest renounce their faith. When the nuns refused, they punctured their eardrums with metal spikes and severed their tongues with a machete." We cringed at these horrifying stories.

Pounding metal spikes through the ears was apparently a common form of torture, along with severing the tongue to prevent saintly people from voicing their faith. Later, these reports were embellished in the schoolyard, with accounts of glass tubes broken inside their penises and the amputated testicles they were forced to swallow. The heathen communists seemed to have molded into a hybrid form, adopting the worst traits of the Gestapo, ancient Romans, New York mafia, and Ming Dynasty.

The second danger facing our society, we were told, was the Protestant religion. Protestants were heretics who had the audacity to reject the authority of the holy pope, God's unequivocal representative here on earth. Adherents to the Protestant faith were not only misguided, but they also threatened the very soul of the Catholics.

"You shouldn't befriend a Protestant," they told us.

I never completely understood how some Protestant kid could harm my soul. The warning hinted that Protestants had all been trained to entice, seduce, and deceive. This would somehow lead to our God-defying conversion and spiritual corruption.

"You should always cross the street when you pass in front of a Protestant church," our teacher had advised. There was an old Protestant church near our school in Stanstead. Unsure about the validity of the warning, I did as she suggested, tacking to the opposite side of the street whenever I approached the intimidating stone building.

They never told us what would happen if we failed to heed the warning, so I made up my own frightening scenario. The large doors in front of the Protestant church would be thrown open just as I reached the stone structure. Black shadows would quickly descend the stairs to ambush my frozen form and carry me inside the heretics' building.

There, I'd be forced to drink mind-bending liquid and obliged to listen to their version of the Bible until my brain had given up all resolve. The ceremony would end with their form of baptism, involving full-body immersion—probably stark naked. This ordeal would turn me into a Protestant, a heretic who hated the pope in Rome.

Although French and English folks peacefully cohabitated Stanstead County, I had the impression that most good things were English. The only newspaper covering our region was the *Stanstead Journal*, an English newspaper that had managed to ignore the French since its inception. And Stanstead College, the prestigious college prep school founded in 1872, boasted the tradition of a fine English education.

Stanstead gave off the aura of an English town, whereas Rock Island exuded the atmosphere of a French-Canadian town. It may not have been entirely accidental that Stanstead stood on the crest of the hill, while most of Rock Island was mired in the depths of a gorge. I had the impression that only the poorer English-speaking families dared take up residency in the lower extremities of Rock Island. And there we were.

Our red brick apartment building stood half a mile from the center of town, at the base of a long and curvy hill that ended at the lowest point in Rock Island. The simple three-story building sat on a paved street—a heavenly blessing in my youthful mind. The tenement house was in the middle of a steep hill, and as such it was visible from a distance.

Our Rock Island apartment house. We lived on the 2nd floor.

I was standing on the transmission bump when my father pointed out the house, steering the little Hilman with its crowded human cargo down the long hill. The big square building with the flat roof met the hill at a steep angle—not pretty, but most definitely intriguing. As red brick houses were rare in St-Gérard, I felt that maybe we were privileged to have found this place.

"Which one is it?" I asked, above the voices of siblings.

"The red one on top of the hill," Papa said.

"Wow, it's really big."

"It's got four floors if you count the basement apartments."

"It's on a steep hill, too," I said. I figured that these hills would be fun on bicycle.

Our apartment building was only a half-mile from the United States border. In fact, the ironworks factory situated a block from our house was actually in the United States; the Canadian employees living across the street needed visas to work there.

The brick color of our apartment building provided a sharp contrast to the white porches on the main floors. There were also verandas in the back, the hill exaggerating their height above the gravel surface. Our apartment was on the second floor in the front of the house, but on the third floor in the back. Leaning over the edge always gave me the creeps.

The inside of our apartment looked a lot like a bowling alley, consisting of a long and narrow corridor with small rooms to the left and right. The only rooms that violated the alley layout were the small parlor at the entrance—we rarely used this room—and the kitchen at the rear of the house, its door spilling out onto the high-perched veranda.

We soon discovered that our kitchen was infested with cockroaches. Their nighttime frolicking was revealed by the pitter-patter of tiny feet dancing across the kitchen floor. My mother, a cleanliness fanatic, was horrified that vermin were living in our house, and she embarked on nighttime missions that resembled well-planned police stings.

"We'll get up at eleven o'clock," my mother said. "They should be out by then."

We'd turn out the lights and pretend to go to bed—this was meant to fool the dumb vermin. Then we'd lie awake, waiting for the incriminating sound of insect feet.

When it was time, we'd enter the kitchen on tiptoe to avoid tipping off the skittish cockroaches, bending on our knees in front of the refrigerator with our noses practically touching the floor. Our raid tools included a flashlight, yardstick, and blunt instrument. Once in position, we would quickly shine the flashlight under the refrigerator, causing the numerous little criminals to scatter in all directions. We would then use the yardstick to sweep the underbelly of the fridge to foil their escape. Once exposed, the fleeing vermin were pounced by the blunt instrument with gusto.

"Don't let them escape! Watch the side!" Maman would yell. "There, take *that*!" We were like cowboys herding cattle into a death corral.

The sound of crushed cockroaches was truly disgusting; these bugs were huge, seeming well fed in the surroundings of our apartment house. Once the raid was over, we'd clean up the kitchen floor and return to the safety of our beds—until another night.

The landlord finally sprayed the kitchen with pesticide, ending our nighttime prowls. But my mother remained forever vigilant of the creatures that had invaded our abode, emphatic that no crumb be left on the kitchen counter or floor to invite their return.

"Who left crumbs on the kitchen counter?" she'd often rebuke.

I shared a bed with my brother Pierre in a small bedroom near the only bathroom, about midway up the bowling alley on the right. Our room had a window without a view, its glass facing a mysterious five-foot gap in the middle of the house.

I never understood the reason for this covered gap, an inaccessible three-story wedge surrounded by unpainted walls and trick windows that peered out into darkness. Undaunted, my mother nevertheless covered the make-believe windows with nice homemade curtains, framing the void with a pretty border.

Opening the window discharged a dusty and moldy smell, as though breaching the walls of an ancient Egyptian tomb. For months, I dreamed of descending to the bottom of that gap for a closer examination. The idea of walking the odd separation had teased my imagination, as though it were an ancient cave allegedly filled with rare artifacts.

I eventually succumbed to the calling, tying a rope to the foot of my bed—I weighed less than sixty pounds—and lowering myself down to the filthy ground below. But there were no artifacts; I found broken bottles, candy wrappers, and little else. The place was stiflingly hot and dusty, prompting me to scale back up to the surface in a hurry.

Even before my disappointing archeological excavation, the gap had already rewarded me with my first English words. Just a few hours after our arrival, I was in my room when I heard a boy's voice. Curious about its origin, I opened the window to listen; the voice was coming from a third-floor window I couldn't see.

"I'm Robby. What's *your* name?" the faceless voice said.

"No Inglish," I replied, feeling my face blush.

"Your name? Me Robby. What's yours?" he repeated. I got the gist.

"Michel," I answered meekly.

"How old are you?" he asked. I didn't understand. "What is your age?" he tried again, speaking slowly and loudly as though addressing a deaf person.

The word "age" is the same in French, so I latched onto the meaning despite the pronunciation difference. But I didn't know how to say "ten" in English.

"Where do you go to school?" he continued. I failed to get his meaning at first, but he persisted, using different words, and I eventually understood.

"Sacré-Coeur," I answered with few words to avoid embarrassment.

The conversation went on for an hour, becoming easier and gradually turning silly as I grew bolder with my responses. In the process, Robby had taught me my first English words. The list included terms like "funny," "clown," "crazy," "name," "play," and "school." Nothing too impressive, but the experience had nevertheless left me exhilarated and longing for more. I now spoke English.

Unlike St-Gérard, which contained a small and homogeneous population of farmers, Rock Island hosted a mixture of French and English people with a variety of histories, occupations, interests, and habits. I'd never seen such diversity in my life; it was confusing, unnerving, and exciting at the same time. School would prove no exception.

The Sunday after we arrived, my parents enrolled Pierre and me at a Catholic school for boys in the nearby town of Stanstead. The formality was completed over a brief meeting with the principal, held at his pristine white house adjacent to the school grounds. He looked to be in his early thirties and had young children of his own.

"Do you like school?" he asked us.

"Yes, sir."

"Are you quiet in class?"

"Yes, sir."

"Good, then you should do fine here."

We were now members of the illustrious Académie du Sacré-Coeur (Academy of the Sacred Heart). Unlike Mater Domini, this school was large and modern, sprawling over several acres of land that were surrounded by attractive homes. The L-shaped orange brick building stood one-story high and included a big playground in the back that had instantly grabbed my attention. I had high hopes for this place.

I was surprised to hear the principal say that there were no nuns here; the entire staff was comprised of lay personnel. It seemed strange that a Catholic institution would be void of religious authorities, but I interpreted their absence as a positive sign that suggested a more relaxed level of discipline. I was dead wrong.

Sacré-Coeur turned out to be like a military school for boys with a Catholic twist. It served several towns in the region, and its student body was large and varied, including ruffians who roamed the playground and halls in the devious hope of causing bodily harm.

In order to keep the tough students in line, the principal created and steadfastly enforced rules of behavior that were inviolate, many of which were downright ridiculous. Adherence to all the silly edicts became a constant source of tension. There were no gentle warnings here; all violations were ardently punished upon discovery.

My parents had also enrolled Lucette in a well-respected Catholic school in Stanstead, founded by Ursuline nuns in 1884. It was an Ursuline nun who had sailed from France in 1639 to found the first school for girls in Québec and North America.

The Ursuline school for girls was a large and intimidating brick building with a silver cupola on its roof; it was located across the street from Sacré-Coeur. The rear of the building was adorned with a lush garden and a lazy park lined with enchanting trees. But Lucette would quickly learn that the casual atmosphere of the grounds contrasted sharply with the police state that existed inside the brick walls.

The Ursuline sisters were a cloistered order who shunned unnecessary contact with the secular world. This predisposition was not exactly conducive to progressive change. The nuns still taught their impressionable young subjects with methods dating back to the illiterate world of the seventeenth century. These young girls had simply replaced the Algonquin Indians they'd sought to convert in the early days of New France.

The Ursuline nuns were hell-bent on driving three virtues into the teenage skull of every young girl in their custody: humility, obedience, and respect. The humility lessons took the form of verbal abuse, in which they debased their self-esteem at every opportunity so as to strip away the core of irreverent arrogance in every uncivilized child. Humiliation was a powerful weapon against a fifteen-year-old girl.

"You must have exaggerated your grades in St-Gérard," the nun accused.

"No, sister," Lucette replied.

"Well, you'll never be a good student here."

Obedience was taught using strict rules and rigid enforcement. There were God's laws and the Ursuline's laws, the latter far more imposing. You were a non-entity, expected to blindly follow the orders of your overseers with a saintly demeanor.

One of the nuns' intentions was to instill a sense of reverence for religious persons. These nuns were holy women who'd dedicated their lives to solitude and contemplation. They were closer to God than the lay population, a fact that entitled them to honor.

The girls were not allowed to look at an Ursuline nun in the face unless spoken to. And they were never allowed to obstruct their hallowed path either. Whenever a nun appeared in the hallway, the girls were expected to back up against the wall and bow their heads in homage as the distinguished figure in black blessed them with her fleeting presence. If the girl happened to be walking up or down the stairs when a nun approached, she had to reverse direction without disrespectfully turning her back. The girl would back up or down the stairs until she'd reached the landing.

Not surprisingly, the more indignant girls hated the nuns, releasing stress through humor that included exaggerated grimaces behind the nun's back. Several nuns were also assigned unflattering nicknames that the girls used among themselves. One notorious sister was named *Soeur Petit Cul Doré*, meaning Sister Little Golden Ass.

Lucette was a strong-willed and independently-minded girl even at fifteen. She'd been a tomboy through puberty, so this oppressive institution didn't bode well for her.

Since both schools were situated about two miles from our apartment, we traveled by bus, waiting at Notre-Dame down the street each morning. The building had once been an elementary school but now served as the residence for a gentle order of nuns.

When weather permitted, we waited outside at the old Notre-Dame school. The rest of the time, we waited inside a little cement bunker in the basement of the building. English and French kids alike waited here to be shipped off to various institutions.

Our first day waiting at the bus stop would forebode our later experience at school. School had already been in session for a few weeks, so the kids looked at us suspiciously, at times mocking us. These strange kids scared the hell out of me. I stayed close to my sister Lucette, who'd magically transformed from pesky sister into loyal protector.

A disheveled girl with a spiteful look on her face was brandishing a pen knife at me while making verbal threats. The knife looked tiny, but I still envisioned being sliced from neck to bellybutton, disemboweled by the insane surgeon with her sharp scalpel.

"Leave my brother alone," Lucette said in a menacing tone. When the crazy girl persisted, Lucette raised the stakes. "Stop that! I'm not afraid of hitting." The others may have thought that Lucette was bluffing, but not me.

We were pleasantly surprised to see our transport finally pull up to Notre-Dame. My attention was instantly drawn to the sound of air brakes. This wasn't a yellow school bus; it was a retired touring bus. This would be my first time on a bus.

"Wow, this is a real bus," I said to Pierre, impressed with the shiny chrome.

We sat on bouncy seats made of soft fabric, perched high above the world passing below our large tinted windows. In hot weather, we even traveled to and from Stanstead cooled by the invention of air conditioning. Now, *that* was something.

I watched Lucette get off the bus at her school with grave trepidation; Pierre and I were left at the mercy of ruthless kids. But we managed to reach the school without incident, joining the throng of noisy boys in the playground while waiting for the bell.

The start of the school day was signaled by the obnoxious sound of a mechanized bell. This caused the entire playground to freeze in motion, reminding me of the biblical story of Lot's wife, who turned into a pillar of salt upon leaving Sodom and Gomorrah. The kids remained motionless like mimes as long minutes passed, silent in the morning breeze. This was our first exposure to the quirky edicts of the principal.

The loud bell would ring twice in succession to sound the beginning of the school day and the end of recess. The first bell mandated that all talk, laughter, and movement cease at once, regardless of our physical location and posture.

One time, I was sitting on a fast-moving swing when the bell rang. I tried to halt all body motion, but the swing continued its pendulous trajectory through the air. On another occasion, the bell rang as I hung upside down with my feet inserted in trapeze rings. I was forced to remain suspended until the second bell.

After ringing the first bell, the principal would stand at his office window and scan the playground with binoculars to catch disobedient boys, calling out the names over the intercom of any students who'd violated his law of silence and immobility.

"Jean Gosselin, René Boutin, and Denis Simard, come to my office please." The violators walked with hesitant steps to the rear entrance, mentally preparing themselves to receive a strap deemed suitable for their age and physical dimensions.

The second and last bell would announce the start of classes, prompting a mad rush for the safety of our respective classrooms. Unlike Mater Domini, we didn't form lines in the schoolyard here; the crowd simply hastened toward the student entrance.

Once inside the doors, every boy was required to show his completed homework assignments before he was permitted entry. Student assistants, sitting in desks that lined the entrance hall, performed the morning check. The students who could not provide proof of their homework were barred from class and directed to the principal's office.

The principal would punish most offenses with lashes. Hooks on his office wall proudly supported straps of all sizes to serve the various age groups. The smallest strap was reserved for the first and second graders, the largest for the upperclassmen.

The boy with the audacity to smuggle in binoculars to scout for girls at the Ursuline school across the street got the strap. The two first graders who gave each other playful piggyback rides also got lashes; they'd violated the school rule that prohibited all physical contact between students. And every kid who was ever involved in a playground fight or showed disrespect to a teacher received the strap. Leather cured all problems.

Loose coins had once been stolen from the office, the theft totaling less than a dollar. The principal's faceless voice announced the violation over the intercom system, giving the petty thief an hour to turn himself in for rightful punishment. Students were encouraged to report and implicate suspicious peers to speed up the investigation.

"If the thief doesn't come forward to confess, you all lose privileges," he threatened. "I won't tolerate stealing. Nobody goes home until I find the guilty boy."

When the little thief had failed to turn up within the allotted time, the voice over the intercom ordered us all to step out into the hallway, one class at a time.

"I'll be frisking every one of you myself," he said.

We formed a single line, nervous with anticipation. He ordered each boy to approach him with our palms turned up, as he searched our shirt and pant pockets.

To deter repeat offenses, the principal would sometimes turn a boy's punishment into a public execution. This was the case in the matter of the stolen change. Classes were interrupted once more as his voice sounded yet another announcement. He read out the name of the boy who'd been accused of stealing the loose change from the school office and proceeded to administer his punishment over the airwaves. We sat frozen to our chairs, listening to the snapping sound of the strap and the ensuing cries that arose from the naughty boy.

"Let this be a lesson for the rest of you," he said before turning off the microphone.

As I glanced over at the teacher, I saw her quickly brush a tear from her eye, her sympathetic reaction earning my admiration. The onerous rules were rarely enforced by the teachers; it was always the dreaded principal who played the part of the aggressor.

From time to time, the principal would visit classrooms to observe student progress. One day, he decided to inspect our class while we were taking a grammar test. As we scribbled the answers to the questions on our papers, he paced the class authoritatively, clicking his heels, holding a pointer with a metal tip that resembled a bullet casing.

I never performed well under threat, the fear often overpowering my thinking ability. This would be no exception. As I struggled to conjure up the answers to the grammar questions, my brain was incapacitated by the sound of approaching footsteps.

The ominous footsteps advanced slowly from the back of the class and then turned up the aisle to my immediate left. They stopped abruptly at my desk. *Oh shit.*

"That's not correct!" the principal said in a booming voice above the hush, slapping the metal tip against my fingernails three times. I had apparently misspelled a word, and he was waiting for me to correct the error under his threatening glare.

"NO!" he shouted after witnessing my first attempt at repairing the spelling, banging the pointer on top of my desk. Holding back tears, I finally coerced my frightened brain to produce the correct spelling. He walked away without another word.

Despite the disquieting setting, I managed to blossom under the tutelage of my lady teachers, and I was enjoying school more than ever. By the end of fifth grade, I ranked at the top of my class, competing with only one or two other students for first place.

While the teachers liberated my mind from the burdensome rules, the wellstocked playground behind the school emancipated my body. This was my first experience with real sports equipment. This place even had an indoor gymnasium.

In addition to the ball field and basketball hoops, there were tether balls, heavy-duty swings, and outdoor trapeze equipment. I especially liked the trapeze bars and rings, and I'd spend many lunch breaks and recesses performing simple acrobatics moves.

In the winter, the playground would be transformed into a glorious skating rink, its glassy sheen maintained by the upperclassmen. We kept a pair of old skates in our lockers, eager to enter the rink at noon after gulping down our sandwich.

The older students also built an awesome slide in the schoolyard. The ice chute was tall and long, providing a high-speed thrill like none I'd ever experienced before. The icy surface was hosed down every few days to guarantee the students an eye-misting and hair-raising ride.

I quickly adjusted to the new school, growing fond of my teachers and the extracurricular activities, despite an all-consuming fear of the principal. But stepping out of the classroom would place me in the immediate line of danger. Emergency visits to the bathroom during class were hazardous affairs, exposing me to the hoodlums who'd somehow escaped from their cells to terrorize younger kids in the central toilet.

"What are you looking at, punk?" the tall boy said.

"Nothing," I replied.

"Hey, don't talk back to me like that, kid."

"I didn't say anything."

"So, you want a beating, you little shit?"

"No."

"What if I push you around like this?" he said, shoving my shoulder.

"Leave me alone. I just want to use the bathroom."

"Why? Did you piss your pants again, wimp?"

"No."

"Next time, stay out of my bathroom."

These stressful incidents rarely progressed beyond swears, threats, and shoves. But they were enough to make any trip to the bathroom regrettable. You never reported them either, fearing a backlash from the vindictive hoodlums. It was best to ignore them.

I did make new friends at school. But in spite of my high grades, I chose to befriend few intellectual boys, preferring to hang out with the simpler kids. For a while, I'd been friends with Donald, one of the boys who competed with me for first place in fifth grade. He was smart, even tempered, and handsome. He was also a Boy Scout, altar boy, and paperboy in Stanstead, standing tall on the community pedestal.

He'd invited me to his house one Saturday morning. We were planning on spending the morning together, but by noon I was bored to death. This responsible boy seemed like a forty-year-old man wrapped in the body of an eleven-year-old.

In spite of peer pressure to do otherwise, I ended up befriending a boy who was struggling to maintain passing grades in all subjects. His name was Mario Poirier. He'd remain a good friend for the remainder of our stay in Rock Island.

Mario was a skinny kid with buckteeth. Despite his goofy appearance, he consistently redeemed himself with slapstick humor. He was one of the silliest kids I'd ever met, and his absurd interludes temporarily lifted my brain above the fear.

"Why do you hang out with that moron?" a classmate asked.

"Because he's funny," I answered. His unorthodox conduct and brainless games fulfilled my need for emotional respite during our time in Rock Island.

In 1963, Rock Island was a lonely place, mainly the result of my isolation from close relatives. The language barrier worsened our feeling of seclusion. So, we mostly kept to ourselves, suffering recurring bouts of loneliness. It would only get worse.

Although my Uncle George-Émile and his family lived nearby in Beebe, we rarely saw them. They were a private family, preferring to live in quiet isolation.

In our apartment building, only the Caron family spoke French. The rest were English-speaking folks with whom we exchanged greetings and little else. The Carons consisted of a grim father, spirited mother, nitwit son, and three young daughters.

I'd seen Mister Caron a few times but knew little about him except that he was never around. The man seemed especially susceptible to "indigestion," as Mrs. Caron called his condition. Late at night, we'd sometimes hear him struggle with his indigestion, heaving the content of his stomach on the front sidewalk—surprisingly like a drunk.

Micheline Caron was a tomboy my age, and we immediately bonded. Everybody called her Mimi, and so I took to doing the same. The afternoon we moved in, she was already standing on the porch, her face smudged from dirty fingers, eager to engage me in conversation. Her outgoing personality drew me out of my shell.

Mimi's little brother was about five years old. He was an idiot kid whose entire vocabulary consisted of nonsense words strung together to shock his listeners. Lucette started calling him the "*petteu-pipi-caca-alloon*" kid, because the label contained all his favorite syllables. The "alloon" part referred to his nincompoop mispronunciation of the word "balloon," the first letter of the word was apparently omitted in his imbecile dialect.

My parents and older siblings were working, so Lucette, Pierre, and I had to fend for ourselves during the days of summer. The Caron family became a respite from the loneliness that often gripped my spirit. I spent much time playing with Mimi, often joining her family in pleasant games. On rainy days, we'd gather in the Caron apartment, cozily shielded from the raging storm, surrounded by friends who shared our language.

Although our apartment building was mainly occupied by families, there were exceptions. The apartments on the lower level were too small to house families. An old couple rented one, the arthritic husband confined to a wheelchair, his hands, fingers, and feet deformed by the debilitating disease that would eventually take his life.

Another small apartment—this one was accessible only from the rear—housed an eccentric old man with a scruffy white beard and countless cats. Neither he nor his disgusted neighbors knew the number of cats that shared his tiny apartment.

"Come with me. We'll go feed the cats," Mimi said one day. She knew the cat man.

He answered the door, inviting us to assist him in replenishing the cat food dishes spread out on the kitchen floor. At the sound of the can opener, a multitude of cats immediately descended on our location. There must have been thirty cats.

The smell and look of the place turned my stomach, activating my gag reflex. The stench of cat pee hung in the air, bits of cat fur clung to the upholstered surfaces, and cat poop littered the filthy linoleum flooring. Maman would have gone into cardiac arrest; the repulsive apartment was a virtual ballroom hall for cockroaches.

Our dog, Puppé, adapted poorly to his new family, refusing to stay on the Gagné farm. They'd go to retrieve him from our deserted farm only to find him returned to his post on the empty porch, awaiting our return. Every attempt yielded the same futile result.

A month after relocating to Rock Island, we received a letter from Uncle Roland with news of St-Gérard. His letter spoke of Puppé. My mother read that part aloud.

"I had to go get Puppé. He was starving to death. He was still sitting on the porch when I arrived, waiting for you to come back. He's already put on some weight..."

I ran to my room and cried my eyes out. His loyalty had nearly cost him his life.

After several weeks of starvation, the emaciated animal had been nursed back to good health, and my uncle adopted him as one of his own animals. There, he adjusted to his new family, the distance to his prior home averting all further attempts at desertion.

We visited St-Gérard a few weekends later. Seeing Puppé again would be one of the highlights of our sojourn. *But will he remember me?*

Puppé recognized the car as soon as we turned into Uncle Roland's yard. He was barking excitedly, running at top speed in large circles around the car. He rushed to my side before I'd even climbed out of the car, jumping up and down like a furry rubber ball, panting and barking approvingly. His friend had returned.

I spent the weekend with my cousin Ghyslain, paying as much attention as possible to Puppé without ignoring my other playmate. It was comforting to see him prancing around my uncle's farm, now adjusted to his environment. But he was no longer *my* dog.

It turned out to be the last time I saw Puppé alive. He didn't survive the next winter. Once again, the unhappy news arrived by mail from Uncle Roland.

"Puppé was hit by a car last week. He died on the road in front of the house."

It all seemed unfair. He'd barely recovered from the starvation when he met a tragic ending in his new habitat. The news made me feel melancholic.

Later that winter, we paid another weekend visit to St-Gérard, staying with my Uncle Roland as usual. I decided to ask Ghyslain about Puppé.

"Where was he killed?" I said.

"Just across the street," Ghyslain replied. "He's still there. Do you want to see him?" he said, as though daring me. The frozen ground prevented burials over the winter months, so the dead animal had simply been left near the scene of the fatal accident.

We crossed the busy road and stood over the carcass of my pet dog. The coldness of winter had kept the body mostly intact, his soft fur gently caressed by the winter breeze. His fatal injuries were clearly visible, the frozen blood matting his fur as a poignant reminder of the tragedy that had abruptly ended his life.

The worst part of the grisly scene was the frozen expression on his face. His teeth were bared in anger, and his jaw was clenched in pain. The death mask spoke of anguish. But I shed no tears. Puppé had finally found his way home.

That happy-go-lucky dog long remained in my thoughts. Puppé had taught me lessons that I'd never forget. His life had made a difference in mine, helping a timid little boy through his formative years. After all, true friends are forever.

Our financial woes trailed us to Rock Island. The week before we arrived, the gas station where my father was working went out of business. Worried about frying my mother's nerves, Papa decided to delay the bad news until we'd finished unpacking.

"Don't worry, I'm already looking at other jobs," my father said.

Armed with a good recommendation, he soon found a job at the granite quarry in Beebe, the same place where my Uncle George-Émile was working. But this didn't last either, as the granite company declared bankruptcy a few months later.

Papa was living his worst nightmare: unemployed in a strange place. His mind became infected with regret and self-doubt. Stuck in a downward spiral, he felt powerless to alter our trajectory toward poverty. Before long, Papa was collecting unemployment compensation, and his pride shrank a little with every check.

The winter of 1963 was miserable, with my father in a bad mood most of the time. He stopped shaving, and the dark growth gave him an indigent appearance. I now feared the strange man who grumbled and barked at us with intolerance.

"What's wrong with Papa? He's always in a bad mood," I said to my mother. He was passing the days alone in the small living room, rocking in silence.

"Just leave him alone," Maman replied. Her message didn't fall on deaf ears; I avoided him at all costs. This was not the even-tempered father I'd known.

For her part, my mother had taken a full-time job at a local clothing factory, sewing blue jeans. She was paid twenty-two dollars a week on piece work, using the hard-earned cash to feed her family and repay the creditors who still threatened legal action.

"People will think I'm lazy," Papa said. While Maman held a stressful job, he idled at home in a state of depression.

In spring of 1963, my father ended up returning to St-Gérard, getting a job at the same wood slat factory where my brother Jacques was employed. It was now Papa's turn to board with my Uncle Roland while the rest of us waited in Rock Island.

Maman paid an emotional price for my father's absence. She hadn't worked outside the home in over twenty years, and now she was the breadwinner. The stress wreaked havoc on her nerves, but my father was too lost in his own shame to offer consolation.

Pierre and I were playing in the backyard with neighborhood kids one Saturday morning when two men dressed in dark suits approached us.

"Can you tell us where Hervé Blanchette lives?" they asked. We informed them that we were his sons and innocently directed them to our second-floor apartment. My father was working out of town by then, so my mother was the only parent at home.

The two strange men immediately made their way up the rear staircase to our apartment. After fifteen minutes, our unsettled brains turned suspicious of the dark characters. Pierre and I barreled up the stairs to check on Maman.

She was crying when we entered the kitchen. The two men had exited the front door after threatening to repossess our kitchen appliances and furniture.

They'd come to deliver a warning, promising to come back with movers if the debt remained unpaid.

Pierre and I were furious, promising to protect her from future threats and beat the men in the dark suits if necessary. We'd kick, punch, and pinch until they desisted—two naïve little boys whose anger had been roused by their mother's tears.

Their threats were no doubt a standard ploy to frighten susceptible house-wives, and it certainly worked on my mother. Afraid of losing our meager posses-sions, she doubled up her efforts to pay down the debt out of her small paycheck.

Before long, a rumor was floating around the house that we were returning to the farm, which I first heard from my sister Lucette. The news didn't settle well with me. The thought of going back to St-Gérard was troubling—nothing would have changed. Despite our problems, I still felt that Rock Island held more prom-ise for our future.

My father was leading the charge, making plans for our return; it seemed that we were going back to the boring place after all. Naturally, my Côté grandparents were thrilled, ready to move back into their old house as soon as our plans jelled.

But before the plans had solidified, my father lost his job again. This time, he was replaced by a cousin's teenage son. Depressed more than ever, Papa came back to Rock Island, abandoning all aspirations for the paternal farm. I quietly rejoiced.

Once again, he found himself unemployed, accepting short-term work when it was available. Papa was nearly despondent, his dark moods causing us to fret over his emotional stability. The family was in trouble, and our future was look-ing bleak.

Distressed over our financial struggles, Papa had no choice but to sell the paternal farm a short time later. He sold the farm with its seventy-five acres for the measly sum of four thousand dollars. The lot abutting Lake Aylmer was sold separately for one thousand dollars. Most of the money was used to pay off the family debt.

Our branch of the family had forever abandoned farming, ending a tradition that dated back to our seventeenth-century ancestor from France. Our patriarch, Pierre Blanchet, had immigrated to New France some three hundred years ear-lier.

Although he'd never resume farming, Papa did eventually rejoin the land of his roots. At the age of seventy-seven, he and my mother moved back to Québec, living in a town some eight miles from the old paternal farm. Having secured a future for their children, they returned to spend their remaining years in the land of their youth.

The old farm still exists. The barn was taken down long ago, the relics of our childhood escapades obliterated. The old chicken coop that once housed Lucette's precious chicken was demolished, and the apple orchard next to the house that had served up bountiful snacks was ripped up to clear the field for crops, but the old farmhouse still stands, worn by long years of faithful service and recent neglect.

When we left the farm, Ketchup, the buggy my siblings and cousins built, had been parked in an abandoned barn a half-mile from our farm. On a visit to the uninhabited place, we went to check on the buggy. We were dismayed to find that the roof of the old barn had collapsed on its contents, forever closing that chapter on our playful era.

Last family photo taken in front of our farmhouse. 1962.

I can still see the old farm in delightful detail. It's a warm Sunday afternoon, the breeze is rustling my hair, and light dust is swirling above the dirt road in front of the house. I can hear adult laughter coming from the house. The kids are playing outside, alternating between the barn, stable, chicken coop, and verdant pastures with whimsical pleasure. The cows are grazing peacefully, disturbed only by the momentary clucking sounds that emanate from the yard adjacent to the chicken coop.

Surrounded by cousins and siblings, with Puppé at my side, I'm oblivious to the past and future, aware only of this blissful moment. Our old farmhouse stands proud above this childhood scene, an enduring witness to a century of family milestones.

To a stranger, the frail old house looks ugly with age and disrepair—but not to me. It may not look like much, but in my heart, it retains a charm that can never die.

15

City Capers

I was thrilled with the invitation. It was a Friday in the winter of 1962 when my schoolmates invited me to join them in a casual game of ice hockey.

"Meet us behind Notre Dame at six o'clock," Donald said.

I was never good at sports, but that didn't matter. I looked upon our game as an opportunity to socialize with boys from my new school.

Lacking an ice skating rink, we were to slide around the icy road surface in our rubber boots. I'd retrieved my damaged hockey stick from the discard pile at the arena in Rock Island, and my sole hockey puck came from under the bleachers.

It was dark by the time I arrived at Notre Dame, but the moon and streetlights were enough to illuminate the glossy driveway that served as our improvised hockey rink. Donald, the intellectual boy from Stanstead, was also a good athlete and our designated referee. The team captains chose their players; I was the last one picked.

Despite my unimpressive contribution to the game, I relished the social interaction, counting myself lucky to be among the circle of elite schoolmates.

I was standing in the center preparing to face off with Denis, a peer on the opposing team. While waiting for Donald to drop the puck on the ice, I decided to impress my teammates with a memorable slap shot that was sure to earn me accolades.

I hit the puck with all my strength the instant it touched the surface. I heard a loud cracking noise just before my world began to collapse. Having recovered from the impressive swing, I was befuddled to see that nobody was rushing after the puck. Something more important had caught their attention: there was blood on the ice.

A chill shot up my spine. Denis was bent over the ice, holding his face and moaning. The other hockey players had assembled around him to assess his plight, forming an impenetrable circle.

"What happened?" I asked, knowing damn well that I'd just caused an accident.

"My eye, my eye!" Denis cried out in a shrill voice. My vigorous swing had struck him in the face, something I never factored into my brilliant strategy.

I tried in vain to enter the tight circle, watching his blood pooling in a foreboding puddle on the ice. But a teammate shoved me back with a nudge of his shoulder.

"Denis, are you hurt?" I said in panic. There was no answer.

Donald finally convinced Denis to lift his hand away from his eye so he could inspect the damage. A collective gasp arose from the crowd. Forever a Boy Scout, Donald pulled a clean handkerchief from his trouser pocket and pressed it to the wound.

"It hurts!" Denis cried. My self-esteem shattered into a million pieces.

"He may lose an eye," somebody remarked above the slow-motion confusion. Another boy nodded in vehement agreement. This can't be happening, I thought.

In a desperate attempt to correct my tragic mistake, I approached the tight circle once more, addressing Denis with useless words of sympathy.

"Denis, I didn't do it on purpose."

"Leave him alone," Donald said, pushing me back with his forearm. "This is not the time to apologize. We have to get him to a doctor right away."

Distressed over the accident and ostracized by my classmates, I quickly evaluated my options. Running seemed like a damn good alternative at that moment, so I dropped my hockey stick on the ice and made a beeline for the snowy woods behind Notre Dame.

I ran with the passion of a prison escapee, sobbing under the moonlit sky. The dark shadows would have normally frightened my superstitious brain, but I no longer cared. The trees shielded me from the guilt and remorse that assaulted my brain.

The chilling winter air ceased to matter as I ran through the deep snow and woods, heading for the safety of home. Having distanced myself from the scene, I slowed my pace to a pensive walk, trying to make sense of it all.

But I could think of no good ending. I was guilty of negligence and would soon have to face the consequences of that slap shot. I worried about the extent of his injury, my heart palpitating over the possibility that Denis might lose an eye. *Could he die?*

By the time I reached the threshold of our front door, I was a frightened and anguished boy. My mother immediately noticed the distressed look on her son's face.

"What's the matter?"

I decided to come clean. "I hit a boy in the eye with my hockey stick. I think he's hurt bad," I blurted out. I confessed the affair like a dying man talking to a priest.

"I'm sure he'll be fine. He'll probably be back at school on Monday," she comforted. My mother's reassurances managed to abate the emotions, but I remained skeptical about her conclusion. My imagination was too busy fueling the paranoia.

"But he was bleeding a lot."

"That doesn't mean anything. Small cuts can look worse than they are."

I slept poorly that night, waking up often to relive the bloody accident, my mind still reeling from the scorn of my classmates. When I heard the wailing of a distant siren, I bolted out of bed, convinced that it was the sound of a police car approaching our apartment to fetch my little sorry ass. Perhaps his parents had filed a police report—or, far worse, maybe Denis had died.

The siren noise faded, yet I continued alternating between sleep and waking dreams for the rest of the night. In the morning I felt better, but the butterflies would return every time I recalled the vivid incident from the prior evening.

The weekend was miserable. I constantly fretted over the condition of my victim. Monday finally rolled around, and I nervously stepped off the bus at school.

Denis was nowhere to be found, causing my fear to rise like a huge helium balloon. And there was a certain chill in the air, the kind attributed to cold shoulders rather than temperature. My hockey teammates ignored me all day, deliberately avoiding the subject.

"Forget about them. It was just a dumb accident," Mario said after hearing my story. I admired the monkey boy more than ever for his display of loyalty.

Although the anticipation was killing me, I didn't dare inquire about Denis, worrying that it might open up the floodgates to condemnation. Half of me wanted to know what had happened to Denis, but the other half dreaded learning the truth.

Denis missed school on Tuesday too. I was getting desperate for news, imagining the worst possible outcome. *Is he in the hospital? Will he flunk the year?* I finally worked up the courage to confront Donald.

"What happened to Denis? Why isn't he back at school?"

Donald eyed me with disdain. "You know *very well* what happened to Denis," he said, avoiding my question. At that moment, I would have eagerly jumped into the fiery caldron of hell just to end the penetrating guilt and self-castigation.

Denis finally showed up at school on Wednesday. Even before the first bell had tolled its deafening noise, the entire class seemed to know about his injury.

"Did you see Denis?" I overheard one classmate say to another. "He looks terrible! He could have busted an eye too," he added. At least my name hadn't been mentioned.

I finally did see Denis, and his appearance was rather troubling. His eye was swollen shut, the socket the color purple. The visible part of his eyeball was no longer white; it was red from the broken blood vessels. The repulsive eyeball seemed to swim in a vibrant pool of blood. And I could see fresh stitches on his eyebrow.

Denis pretended I didn't exist. That was just fine with me, as I was worried the alternative might involve an angry eruption. So, I avoided him as well. But after several days, the tension weakened my resolve. I worked up the nerve to speak.

"How are you feeling? Does it still hurt?" I asked Denis in the schoolyard.

"It doesn't hurt anymore. But you hit me pretty good," he said with a slight grin. That hint of a smile had the impact of a needle pricking an over-inflated balloon; the anxiety I'd accumulated over the prior week suddenly evaporated into thin air.

"You know, I'm not too good at hockey. That was a stupid shot."

"Yeah, but it was just an accident."

I turned away from Denis with moist eyes.

His injury turned from purple to green and then yellow before returning to its normal flesh color. My guilt would diminish in a similar succession of steps.

Robby, the boy who'd taught me my first English words, turned out to be a little turd. He was an aggressive kid with a bad temper that made it impossible to predict his next angry explosion. Every time he got mad, his inherited hatred for the French took center stage. He'd be nice to me one minute and threaten to beat me up the next, yelling offensive epithets in my face. He was also bigger and stronger than me.

"You fucken frog!" he shouted. We'd been playing with a group of boys in front of the house when he suddenly turned on me. *Was it something I said?*

"Wat is frugg?" I asked in the face of anger. But my question only prompted roaring laughter from my persecutor and his English friends. This was the first time I'd heard the expression, and I wondered what the hell it meant.

"*You* are a fucken frog," he repeated with emphasis. "A French sissy," he added. Well, I knew the word sissy and didn't like that one bit. Anger was beginning to override my natural aversion to danger, delaying my flight to safety.

"Goddamned little Canuck!" he yelled, trying to provoke a physical response. But I just stood there, staring at his hateful face, my pride refusing to acknowledge the taunts.

"You no call me bad name," I said to defend myself. He continued mocking.

Seeming disappointed that the provocation had failed to evoke the desired aggression, Robby walked up to my face, cleared his throat with a horking sound, and proceeded to spit a disgusting glob in my eye.

He'd just crossed the line. The little dink had called me names, insulted my ancestry, and disgraced me with a gooey expectoration that resembled tapioca pudding. I raised my right fist and swung with all my might. But the valiant attempt missed his face by inches, my inexperienced brain misjudging the length of my arms and the distance to his noggin.

It was exactly what Robby wanted. He spread his feet like a professional boxer, hunched his shoulders forward, raised his fists, and began swinging at my head. My next visual memory involves a black sky raining stars of all colors; he'd knocked me flat on my back with one punch. It happened so fast that I was left in a daze.

I should have known better than to swing. An earlier experience in St-Gérard had yielded similar results, teaching me the painful lesson: *Anger is not enough to win fights*. But Robby had pushed me into the red zone, short-circuiting my brain in the process.

Looking up from my unflattering position on the sidewalk, I saw Robby poised above my supine body like a lion over his injured prey, eager to give his English audience an encore performance. He beamed a victorious smile at my sore face.

"Stand up! You want another punch, you fucken sissy?" he barked. His punch had landed on my jaw, and I wondered if my mouth would ever work again.

"Robby, leave him alone!" somebody yelled. The unexpected warning was coming from the nice English girl next door, who lived with her family in a first-floor extension of our apartment building. Her name was Janice Wilson. I already had a crush on the thirteen-year-old. She also had a red-headed sister named Joyce.

Janice had heard the commotion, arriving on the scene just in time to save my little butt from further harm. I stood up in spite of the dizziness and embarrassment.

Janice quickly applied her incredible charm to diffuse Robby's offensive. He finally relaxed his boxer stance and stepped away.

"Are you hurt?" Janice asked as she reached my side. I was now indebted to this wonderful girl, who possessed a delightful personality that I already admired.

This wouldn't be the last time I battled with the English kids in the neighborhood. The name-calling and threats became commonplace. The older boys sometimes picked on me for no good reason other than the fact that they hated French kids and my pitiful size made me easy prey.

Two English boys had cornered me in the street, intent on playing a little game at my expense. One boy was slapping me on alternating cheeks, while his co-conspirator snickered as he waited for his joyful turn. Every time I made an attempt to outflank my aggressors, they'd tackle me to the ground and kick me like a disobedient dog.

"Let me go," I pleaded.

"Oh no, you're too much fun."

"But I didn't do anything."

"Yes you did. You're a Canuck, aren't you?"

Seeming pleased with their lynching experiment, the two boys threatened to repeat their sadistic pleasure every time we passed each other in the street, persuading me to remain secluded in the safety of our lonely apartment for whole days at a time.

These experiences left me distrustful of English boys. But as soon as they'd make a friendly gesture, I'd join in their games, happy to forget the aggressions of the past.

It would be unfair to say that all English kids partook in the assaults. There were many who were friendly despite our language differences. But from my perspective, it seemed like a disproportionate number carried around a historic grudge.

Of all the English kids I knew, nobody was sweeter than Janice. Our young neighbor oozed charm within a radius of ten miles. Janice had introduced me to the delightful game of spin the bottle. It was a perfect excuse to steal kisses from the girls.

There were six of us sitting cross-legged on the sidewalk in front of her apartment, spinning a Coke bottle on a warm summer afternoon. The only kissing partner I wanted was Janice. I rejoiced whenever my bottle pointed at Janice and her endearing blush.

At thirteen, Janice was already a woman with a bosom. I found her positive tone, sense of humor, and outgoing personality captivating. She'd engage me in fun activities, pushing me beyond my comfort zone. But then again, Janice did that with everybody.

She once stood barefoot at the entrance to their apartment, beckoning me to approach the screen door. I could hear loud music coming from inside.

"You have to listen to this song," she said. "It's called 'The Monster Mash.'"

She turned up the volume on the stereo as we stood around the living room listening to the weird noise; it sounded like a musical rendition of a Frankenstein movie.

"There's a dance that goes along with the song. You want to try it?" she teased.

"I don't know how to dance," I said.

"Come on, it's easy."

Before I knew it, her hips were gyrating to the music. My face felt hot as my limbs moved to the music in unnatural and spasmodic waves. I was dancing…sort of.

After she played the song over and over again, I slowly recovered from the rigor mortis, my muscles gradually releasing their tension. She laughed out loud, but never mockingly, offering encouraging words on my progress. More importantly, I was alone with Janice.

These are moments I remember well, a French boy smitten by an English girl. But to her, I was the kid next door—one of several who fell under her spell.

I was first exposed to Halloween in November 1962. This strange holiday—a variant of the Catholic All Saints Day—dates back to the ancient Celts and Romans. But we never celebrated this holiday in the little farming community of St-Gérard.

Halloween remained mainly an American holiday, imported by the Irish Catholics who fled the Great Potato Famine in the mid-nineteenth century. But Rock Island abutted the United States, so the celebration had naturally spread to border towns.

"We dress up in scary clothes and go door to door to beg for candy," Serge told me. This sounded a little hard to believe, and much too good to be true.

"But what do you wear?" I said.

"Wear anything you want. It doesn't matter: a ghost, scarecrow, bum—anything."

"And they give you candy for that?"

"Yeah, they give us candy, popcorn, apples, and even pennies."

Having confirmed the silly tradition with Mimi, I made plans to accompany a boy who was an experienced Halloween veteran. On the assigned evening, I draped myself in an old sheet and completed the absurd ensemble with a paper bag over my head.

I had no idea what "*tickertreat*" meant, but I was told to utter the meaningless expression every time a gullible person answered my knock at the door. And as predicted, the ridiculous action yielded apples, popcorn, and candy. *Go figure.*

Rock Island had an ice-skating arena, an amazing invention I'd only seen on television. It was located at the edge of Stanstead, on the shore of the Tomifobia River. My friend Mario was lucky enough to live in close proximity to that arena. The arched roof of the building was covered with shiny aluminum panels, its downward curve forming a frown. But there were no frowns on the faces of children inside.

"You want to come skating with us?" Mimi asked me one Saturday.

"I don't have any skates," I said. We had left our old skates behind on the farm, one of the many compromises my parents made to fit us into an apartment.

The disappointment was affecting my mood. I longed to join Mimi and her siblings at the wondrous arena on the opposite side of town. I loved skating.

I first complained to my mother and later to my father, hoping that they'd somehow resolve my dilemma.

"We can't buy you skates," my mother said to shut me up.

"Try on a pair of girl skates," Papa suggested. He was referring to the white figure skates that had survived the move only because they were in better condition than the rest.

"I'll look like a dumb girl if I wear white skates."

"Just try them on for size," he said. I thought it was a ridiculous idea. Pierre and Lucette were already snickering when I sat down on the floor to size the girl skates. One pair fit me fine, but I could never risk looking like a sissy and being ridiculed by neighbors and friends. *I wouldn't be caught dead wearing those stupid skates.*

"People will laugh at me," I said. I might as well have skated with a bull's-eye painted on my back; they'd tear me to shreds. And it would give the English kids a well-justified license to bully me on the ice. I could never wear those girl skates.

"Professional men skaters wear them," Papa said. My eyebrows furled up in hope at the face-saving rationale.

"Really?"

"Yeah, just like those," he said with no hint of trickery.

"You mean they wear white skates?" His nod caused a tiny smile to form on my lips. It might actually be an honor to dress like a professional skater, I thought.

My father had stretched the truth a bit; they wore figure skates all right, but usually not white ones. Nevertheless, I'd been given a credible excuse to go skating.

By Saturday afternoon, I was on my way to the arena with Mimi, walking with my white skates proudly draped across my shoulder.

"Hey, those are girl skates!" a kid yelled.

"Yeah, these are professional skates," I replied. His smile changed into a squint, my confident words having stumped my antagonist.

I skated with glee all afternoon, captivated by the ambiance of the stupendous arena with its manicured ice and piped music. Kids looked at me and jeered, but I knew better: they were ignorant of the fact that I wore the attire of a professional skater.

I went back to the arena often on weekend afternoons. The kids grew accustomed to seeing a nitwit boy prancing around on white skates, and my appearance gradually lost its comic appeal. It's even possible that some kids believed my father's story about the apparel of professional male skaters. I certainly did.

Later that winter, I received a pair of used hockey skates. I don't know who donated them, but I suspect it was somebody who had taken pity on the idiot boy with girl skates.

I received my first pair of wheels in the spring of 1963. The old bikes with the balloon tires had stayed behind on the farm, too worn out to make the trip. And Jacques had kept the majestic three-speed bike that I'd secretly borrowed a year earlier.

Papa was working in St-Gérard at the wood slat factory, paying sentimental visits to the paternal farm. Since I was the only child in the neighborhood without wheels, he made me a promise that lit my imagination like sparklers on St. John the Baptist Day.

"I may be able to assemble a bike for you from old parts," he said. He'd reuse pieces of the dead bicycles stagnating in the garage on our abandoned farm.

"When can I have it?" I said, bloated with anticipation.

"I don't know, but I'll try to do it soon."

It seemed to take forever, although it probably took only a few weeks. Then, one Friday evening, my father arrived in Rock Island for the weekend with the freshly-painted bicycle sticking out from the trunk of his car.

The bike might have seemed ugly to bystanders, but to me it was a work of art. Not surprisingly, it had large balloon tires and a heavy metal frame. Its lack of fenders gave it the rugged look of a workhorse, much different from the delicate filly I'd used in training. Riding on wet roads sprayed a narrow streak up my backside, but I didn't care.

My father had painted the bike bright red, making it impossible not to notice the vivid blur as I swooped down the steep hills of Rock Island. It became my red horse, obedient and loyal like Trigger, Roy Roger's famous Palomino. That trusty bike would facilitate my speedy escape from threatening bullies on several occasions.

It took me little time to tame the bike, my intense desire quickly surmounting all riding challenges. That bicycle gave me a newfound sense of freedom.

For the first time in my life, I rode over paved streets, the thrill exceeding my expectation. I'd roam around Rock Island and Stanstead lost in abandon, invigorated by the mechanized motion and engrossed in the dreamy vision of passing scenery.

The bike also dissolved national borders. I soon learned that United States Customs allowed children to ride across the border without constraint. We'd travel past the border station, waving at the friendly officers like kids without a country.

Derby Line was a lovely town directly across the border. The white houses contrasted sharply with the colorful flags that adorned their meticulous lawns. I admired that place. My bicycle had made it possible to visit the public library in Derby Line, the only place that stocked both French and English books. It became a summer retreat.

Rock Island was surrounded by tall hills. We became accustomed to the sharp contour of the land, flying down the asphalt mounds like brave bush pilots over the Serengeti. The only drawback to the hills was the constant threat of bicycle accidents. My riding confidence would soon be shaken by one such painful incident.

I was riding around the neighborhood with Mimi one warm August day. We were enjoying the breeze from the rapid pace, which was helping to cool down our bodies. I was leading the charge, with Mimi on my tail and slightly to my right.

While speeding down a long hill past our apartment building, I made hand gestures to signal my intention of turning right at the base of the hill. The whirling sound of the balloon tires against the pavement and the rush of the wind made it difficult to hear our voices. Mimi nodded, and I assumed that she'd understood my sign language.

When we reached the base of the hill, I initiated the right turn as planned while still traveling at high speed. But Mimi had apparently misinterpreted my message and was unprepared for my sudden dart across her direct path.

The noise was deafening. I heard a loud boom, followed by the eerie sound of metal scraping on pavement. I heard the noise but saw nothing of the accident.

I woke up on my back in the middle of the street, with the heavy metal bike weighing down on my face and one leg resting on a tire. My brain seemed to have been temporarily deactivated, because I had no idea what had just happened.

Baffled by my odd position, I quickly scanned the surface of the road for Mimi. She was lying about twenty feet away. She was also screaming like a banshee, her limbs still intertwined in the wheels of the damaged blue bike.

Although enfeebled by the crash, I managed to extricate my limbs from the red bike and raise myself on wobbly legs. I ached everywhere, and there were bloody gashes on my elbows and knees. But at least I could limp, so there were no broken bones.

But Mimi didn't look too good. By the time I reached her side, my heart was beating fast and the adrenalin was pumping hard through my veins.

"Where does it hurt?" I asked, kneeling at her feet.

"Stupid jerk!" she yelled amidst tears. Her face was filthy. The bountiful tears were plowing in little rivulets down her cheeks. She was not a happy girl. The scene reminded me of the time our dog, Puppé, had been injured by the sickle mower, the friendly animal unexpectedly growling threats and baring its teeth in anger.

"Can you get up?" I continued. It seemed that she couldn't.

"Leave me alone, jerk!" she barked. "I hate you," she added just in case the former curse had failed to communicate her emotional condition.

Our bikes were still blocking the street when I began worrying about traffic. Somehow, I had to get Mimi off the pavement.

"Go get my mother," she ordered after crying and sobbing for long minutes. These were the first reasonable words she'd spoken since the crash.

But I couldn't just leave her lying in the street, so I decided to seek help from neighbors. An elderly woman was already peering through her window when I reached the house and climbed the steps onto her porch. She quickly opened the door.

"We had a bicycle accident. Mimi is in the road. Can you help me?"

"Yeah, I saw you coming down the hill."

Mimi was still supine on the street. "It's all your fault!" she cried. It felt like the hockey accident all over again. Fear kept my emotions at bay, but I was still hurt. Once more, my negligent actions had nearly resulted in manslaughter.

"You were going much too fast," the elderly woman chided. "You should know better than to race down these hills," she added with furrowed eyebrows.

We managed to lift Mimi and drag her into the old woman's house. I went to fetch her mother while the old woman cleaned the bleeding sores.

Neither bicycle could be ridden home. I first returned with Mimi's bike, recounting the accident with remorse to Mrs. Caron and directing her to the appropriate house. After that, I came back to the scene of the accident to retrieve my own bicycle.

Our bikes were a mess, but Mimi's was in even worse shape than mine. Without the fenders, my bike was not much more than metal tubing with handlebars. But hers was more fragile; it looked like it had fought and lost a fierce battle with Big Red.

"She hates me," I told Maman when she came home from work.

"She was probably scared. She'll be back."

Mimi's inflaming words and the reproach of the old woman had planted emotional seeds that soon blossomed to the surface. I went off to cry in the privacy of my room.

Aside from the numerous cuts and bruises, Mimi suffered a severe sprain to her ankle—but there were no broken bones. She walked on crutches for a week, and her life soon returned to normal.

She hated me for about a week, avoiding eye contact whenever our paths crossed. But after I offered an apology, we were friends again. The painful lesson was over.

Over the summer of 1963, my favorite cousins paid weeklong visits to Rock Island. Danielle, the subject of my earlier physical exams, spent a glorious week. And Christian, the outgoing kid who'd spearheaded many audacious farm adventures, stayed two weeks. These were fun times, reminiscent of the carefree summers back in St-Gérard.

Forever in search of adventure, Christian, Pierre, and I had spent long hours excavating an unused sandpit in the hillside facing our apartment. We dug with pick and shovel in the heat of summer, on a futile mission to reshape the sandy landscape.

One day, I nagged Pierre and Christian into playing a game of cowboys and Indians. The childish game might have been enticing to a ten-year-old boy, but it sure didn't seem to stir much interest in the minds of my teenage partners.

"That's a boring game," Pierre declared.

"But I'll be the Indian. You can be the cowboys," I urged. The two older boys looked at each other with mischievous grins enlightening their faces.

"Okay, but just for a little while."

The chase began, and soon after I found myself tied to a telephone pole outside our apartment. Christian and Pierre had disappeared from sight to seek pleasures more suitable for their age.

"That's not fair! You can't just leave me like this," I screamed. But the two cowboys couldn't hear my complaint; they'd already galloped down the street and out of sight.

I stood there with my arms wrapped around the stupid telephone pole until it became obvious that they weren't coming back. Disgruntled with their half-hearted participation, I loosened the rope from my wrists and headed out in search of justice. I found the teenagers talking with other boys down the street.

"Hey, you promised to play with *me*," I said.

"Look, we don't want to play anymore," Christian said.

"But the game just started. You could at least play a little longer."

The insidious look on their faces should have been sufficient warning, but I was too naïve to decipher the body language. The boys strolled back toward our house to resume our childish game—or so I thought. But Christian and Pierre apparently had other ideas.

Helpless to do battle against two fifteen-year-old cowboys, I was quickly carried into our apartment and tied to a straight-backed chair in the parlor near the front entrance. My hands were tied around the back of the chair, and my feet were firmly bound to the legs. My escape would be a near-impossible one.

"There, that should keep you busy for a while," Christian said.

"It's not fair! We only played five minutes," I complained.

"We'll be back later," Pierre said when they left the apartment.

They'd finally gotten rid of the annoying kid. Happy to have removed the little pest from their teenage lives, they'd gone outdoors to once again pursue more mature games.

Dissatisfied with my unjust treatment at the hands of the two cowboys, this little Indian resolved to escape captivity on his own. Otherwise, I could have been confined to that chair until my mother returned home from work. *I can free myself*, I thought.

But no matter what I tried, I couldn't budge the noose around my wrists and ankles; the ropes seemed intent on keeping me idle in the vacant apartment.

A brilliant idea suddenly flashed in my brain: I'd pivot the chair forward by shifting my weight and then tiptoe over to the bed in the adjacent room. The tiptoeing maneuver had been inspired by Wile E. Coyote, one of my favorite cartoon characters. Once in the bedroom, I was sure to find a tool to end my incarceration.

I slowly rocked the chair back and forth to build up momentum, mentally preparing my toes to bear the brunt of my weight. The motion took more strength than I'd expected, causing me to bite my tongue gently as if to increase my fortitude.

The floor was quickly rising to meet my face when I realized that my feet had failed in their duty; there would be no tiptoeing to the bed. My toes never even touched the floor.

I struck the linoleum flooring headfirst, the awkward position of my arms shifting my center of gravity from torso to noggin. My head struck with a whomping sound, and I became dizzy on impact.

I found myself lying on my face with the chair still firmly attached to my ass. It was the least intelligent predicament I'd ever faced, and there was nobody to save me.

There was something in my mouth—I could taste blood. In fact, there was lots of blood accumulating in a little pool on the floor next to my head. And this blood wasn't the light red color I associated with minor cuts; it was a maroon color.

I nearly messed my pants. It only took a few seconds to realize that my incisors had dug a hole in my tongue. I rubbed my tongue against my palate to confirm the fact.

There was nothing I could do except stare at the blood puddle expanding at my cheek. I broke out in pathetic sobs that expressed a primal fear for my life and took a few moments to worry about my mother's reaction when she found me dead by the door.

"Help me, I'm hurt!" I yelled at the screen door.

About fifteen minutes later, the two cowboys finally heard my frantic calls and came to the rescue. They quickly untied my hands and feet, smiling at my ludicrous pose.

"Are you all right?" Christian asked.

"No, I hurt my tongue," I said with distress in my voice.

"Let me see," Pierre said. I opened my mouth wide to give him a glimpse. "You bit your tongue. Go put a cold compress on it right away."

Getting up from the floor, I fumbled my way to the bathroom to check on the condition of my tongue. I was appalled by what I saw in the mirror. There was a bleeding hole in the center. I slid down onto the toilet seat to avoid fainting.

After an hour, my tongue had swelled to twice its normal size, making it difficult to talk and to be understood. This became a source of entertainment for my siblings, who likened the muffled sounds to those of somebody talking with a potato in their mouth.

The hole in my tongue needed sutures, but we never went to the doctor. The last time I'd seen a doctor was at the age of six, when I'd had a bad case of chickenpox. So this injury would have to heal itself, leaving a permanent crater in my tongue.

The incident happened on a Friday. My tongue resembled a rare sirloin steak for the weekend, impairing my appetite and ability to communicate. The hole is still there, now healed into a sizable flap of skin that stands in testimony of my childhood idiocy.

16

Chasing the Russians

I was a devoted altar boy. We'd been in Rock Island just a few months when a pleasant nun stopped me after Mass to dispense an invitation to join up.

"We're always looking for new altar boys. Would you be interested?" she said.

I accepted the offer without hesitation; it would give me a chance to make friends. And I would also get to wear an angelic uniform that resembled the priest's clothing. There was only one problem with my decision: I'd have to cope with my panic attacks. Since I was in denial, I never factored my phobia into my decision.

A few days later, I was at the old Notre Dame School being sized for the altar boy uniform. The same nun who'd extended the kind invitation took my measurements, selecting used garments off the rack that she thought would fit my puny frame. It would still need length adjustments.

"It should be ready tomorrow," she said.

When I returned, the nice nun helped me try on the red cassock, white surplice, and red sash, standing me in front of a full-length mirror to inspect the finished product. She had sewn a narrow red ribbon around the neck of the angel-white surplice.

The cassock covered me from neck to ankles, and the pleated surplice that extended down to my thighs contrasted nicely with the red garment underneath. The waistband over the cassock had an embroidered sash that hung below the knee with dignity.

"So, what do you think?" the nun asked.

The transformation was amazing. I stared at the stranger in the mirror. That sure didn't look like the boy who'd enjoyed playing doctor with little girls. Nor did it look like the nitwit kid who'd flirted with manslaughter.

Dressed for the part, I would now begin my training. This involved memorizing Latin prayers, studying the ritual of Mass, and learning my place in the sanctuary. The training was administered by an older boy who looked to be about twenty.

"I'm Roger. I'll be instructing you and scheduling your duties."

Roger still lived with his parents on a long hill down the street from our apartment. Exactly how Roger had become director of the altar boys remained a mystery, although there was a rumor that he'd once been a seminarian.

I enjoyed the theatrical flair that accompanied the role. The choreographed bowing motions, the candles, the holy water, the frankincense, and the bells were all part of an elaborate stage performance. I relished the spotlight of the sanctuary.

After the training period, I began serving Mass, struggling to fend off my fear of fainting while performing my holy duties. The typical heart palpitations, sweating, and momentary loss of vision threatened to disgrace me at most religious services.

Feeling like a privileged member of some holy order, I once attempted to proselytize a neighborhood boy. He was English and Protestant. I nagged him to join me at Mass for days; he finally relented, walking to the church with Maman and me.

I wasn't serving Mass that day, so we were able to sit together. I'd glance at him with a patronizing smile, but he looked bored, understanding neither French nor Latin. Apparently not impressed with our Catholic rituals, he never came back.

In May 1963, Roger made an exciting announcement after the Sunday service. He'd made arrangements for the altar boys to join the Boy Scouts on a camping trip to Lake Massawippi. The one-week excursion would take place the last week in June.

"It's only fifteen dollars per person," he said. Although the idea of camping with the Boy Scouts had instantly roused my interest, this last bit of information shattered all hope of participating. My father had been unemployed since spring, letting his beard grow and snapping at us without provocation. He was grumpy and depressed.

I never considered asking my parents to pay for the camping trip. My mother was earning twenty-two dollars a week, so the trip would have cost a whole week's pay. Given our financial status, asking for the money seemed selfish and frivolous.

I discarded the signature paper that Roger had handed out. I stopped thinking about the camping trip altogether, but Roger didn't forget. Two weeks after passing out the applications, he reminded the laggards to return their signed forms. I ignored the reminder without offering an explanation.

It was now June, and for a month I'd succeeded in avoiding face-to-face contact with Roger, worried that he'd press me to justify my lack of cooperation. I'd still attend the mandatory altar boy meetings, but I rushed out of the building the minute they ended. Roger finally caught up with me at church one evening after practice. *Merde.*

"Why haven't you turned in your signed paper?" he asked.

"I'm not going," I replied bashfully, staring at my shoes.

"Don't you want to go?"

"I can't." I squirmed with discomfort, aware that he'd continue to needle me with pointed questions until the root of my embarrassment had been exposed. But I had no intention of dishonoring my family. I'd never permit myself to admit that my father was unemployed and that Maman was forced to support the family on a small income.

"Is it about the money?"

"I'm just not sure I want to go," I lied.

"I bet you haven't even asked your parents."

"I don't think they'd let me go."

"Let's go ask them right now," he said, walking out the door.

I was stunned; the unexpected twist caused a surge of adrenalin to explode in my head with a flash. It was the worst possible scenario I could imagine. I didn't want Roger to meet my moody father, with his awful beard, and I didn't want him to know about our money problems. I also might be accused of having planned the self-serving scheme, shaming my family into giving up the money.

"That's not necessary."

"Don't worry, I won't get you in trouble," he said. But I wasn't convinced.

Roger started walking a purposeful stride down the long, winding hill toward our apartment building, with me behind him. He was moving like a man on a mission, his gait exuding confidence in the outcome of his objective. I rushed to keep up with his determined pace while my mind churned with the bad consequences. There was no telling what Papa would do, given his current emotional state.

My heart was pounding like a jackhammer by the time we reached the house and climbed the forged iron staircase to our second-floor apartment. I opened the door slowly, quietly stepping inside the small entrance parlor with Roger on my heels.

"Stay here. I'll go find my mother." I headed down the long and narrow corridor toward the other end; Maman was ironing clothes in the kitchen.

"The altar boy leader is here to talk to you about a camping trip," I said almost in a whisper, not wanting Roger to overhear our private exchange. My voice seemed awkward and unsettled—I despised asking my parents for favors.

"He'll have to talk to your father," she said, pointing down the hall toward the living room. With these few words, Maman had washed her hands of the decision, giving me no choice but to introduce Roger to my depressed father. This was not going well at all.

I entered the living room feeling like a condemned man heading for the scaffold. I stepped inside the small room, finding Papa sitting alone in the rocking chair. He looked up when I approached, his face wearing a neutral expression.

"My altar boy leader wants to talk to you," I said in a low voice.

"Oh? What does he want?" he asked with a discernible hint of impatience.

"They're going camping near Magog."

My father continued to stare straight ahead at the wall while I fidgeted like a nervous chipmunk. Silence pervaded the room for long seconds until he finally let out a dissatisfied sigh.

"Well, bring him in," he said. I quickly stepped into the hall and signaled Roger to join the little conference in the living room.

"Papa, this is Roger, our altar boy leader," I said with considerable difficulty. Roger stepped into the room with confidence, extending his hand for a friendly shake. My father remained seated in his rocker with an indifferent look on his face. He shook Roger's hand unenthusiastically, as if annoyed by the imposing visit.

I was afraid of being mortally wounded by the verbal shrapnel that might fly any minute, so I retreated to the entrance parlor. I wanted no part of this dangerous exchange.

"I want to talk to you about an upcoming camping trip," I overheard Roger say. "I'd like Michel to come with us." My chest tightened with nervous anticipation.

"How much?" my father asked bluntly. He'd always been a man of few words.

"It's only fifteen dollars," Roger replied.

"That's a lot of money."

"Well, if you give me ten dollars, I'll pay the rest," Roger said.

I couldn't believe my ears: Roger was offering to pay for a share of my camping trip out of his pocket. The room was steeped in silence for a few seconds while my father pondered the offer. I felt like a criminal waiting for the jury to decide on a verdict.

Papa reached for the wallet in the back pocket of his trousers and handed over the ten dollars without a word. He then reinserted the wallet without budging from his chair.

"Thank you, Mister Blanchette. I'm certain Michel will enjoy it." Roger shook my father's hand one last time and turned away to rejoin the corridor.

After hearing the finality in Roger's voice, I crawled out of my hiding place and met up with Roger halfway down the bowling alley. His face was beaming with success.

"You're going," he whispered with a wink. I didn't know whether I should be laughing for joy or crying from shame. I felt like a rat for placing my father in such an awkward position, and like a beggar for accepting charity from Roger. I knew that Papa was wasting precious family money to finance my vacation.

I thanked Roger and left him on the porch before returning to the living room. I'd have to face the music sooner or later; it might as well be now. I could see no point in delaying the inevitable, given that unresolved feelings tend to fester with time.

"Thank you for the camping trip," I said in a timid voice. But I wasn't there only to voice my appreciation; I'd also returned to cover my guilty ass. "You know, this wasn't my idea. Roger insisted on coming to see you," I said.

"Oh, yeah?" he said with a touch of cynicism. And that was all—he said nothing else. There would be no reprimand or accusation. The case was closed.

I turned around and ran outside to inhale fresh air, feeling blessed and relieved. In an instant, my dread had been replaced by a sense of adventure. I'd be going on the camping trip after all, a weeklong game of cowboys and Indians in the woods of Magog.

The parade was already in progress. I was sitting on a grassy knoll with my parents, watching the noisy display on the street below. The loud fanfare was in honor of St. John the Baptist, an important religious figure whose holiday we celebrated every June 24.

Farm tractors were pulling makeshift floats, the occupants waving at the passing crowd like celebrities. There was a marching band playing off key, its majorettes leading the way with fancy baton tosses and twirls. And there were clowns pulling pranks and handing out balloons to the children lining the parade route.

But my mind was not on the small parade; it was on the upcoming camping trip. Our bus would leave in just a few hours to take us to beautiful Lake Massawippi. My brain was titillating with glorious images of tents, beaches, and camp-fires.

It was an idyllic day. The warm weather, festive atmosphere, and anticipation of group fun enveloped me in a pleasant shroud. We sat on the old blanket while I kneaded my mother's tender arms like a baby sucking on a pacifier. Her skin felt soft, cool, and reassuring; fondling her arms satisfied my need for intimacy.

My daydreams were suddenly disrupted when I saw my mother wiping her eye. It had been quick and subtle but still noticeable.

"What's the matter, Maman?" I asked.

"It's nothing," she replied. My mother had never been good at concealing her emotions. It was her nature to be tearful—a trait she'd unfortunately passed down to her youngest son. Several minutes passed before she confirmed my sus-picion.

"You'll be gone a long time," she said while looking down at the street.

"It's only a week," I replied.

I was touched by her sentimental reaction to my departure, but it troubled me that my amusement had to come at her expense. I'd never been away from home for a week before. Maman was losing her baby, the boy who still sat on her lap to fondle her arms.

Once the parade ended, I kissed my mother goodbye and hopped excitedly to Notre Dame School, where the bus would pick us up in the early afternoon. In one hand, I carried the little green suitcase that contained my pants, shirts, and underwear. In the other hand, I held the simple brown paper bag that held my camping gear.

In addition to our clothes, they told us to bring four necessities: a canteen for drinking water, a small bowl with eating utensils, a flashlight with fresh batteries for nighttime, and a small shovel to dig little cesspools in the great outdoors.

I didn't have a canteen, so I had to borrow one. I took the plastic cereal bowl and utensils from the kitchen, the flashlight from the junk drawer, and the improvised shovel was an old gardening tool. My improvised camping kit would have to suffice.

We waited for the bus at Notre Dame while little waves of paranoia aggra-vated my nerves. *What if the bus doesn't come?* I fretted over that disheartening possibility until the yellow school bus finally pulled up to the curb, with Roger onboard.

The bus did leave on time, rolling toward our destination as we sang Boy Scout songs. I was going somewhere alone; this was the most independence I'd ever had. Glancing around, the boys seemed to range from eight to thirteen years of age.

Our drive to Lake Massawippi seemed to last forever, but it took less than an hour. The school bus finally pulled up in front of a red-brick monastery in the lakeside town of Ayer's Cliff, leaving its young occupants in the parking lot. The rolling green hills and deep blue water were just like I'd pictured in my daydreams.

From there, we walked the rest of the way to our campsite, which was in the forest behind the impressive monastery. Up the hill we went with our little suitcases and paper bags, Roger leading the way to our resort. Most boys were giddy with excitement.

The camp contained an assortment of tents and rustic log cabins with dirt floors. The little cabins housed four kids each, with two pairs of vertical bunks separated by a narrow passageway. These rough buildings and their homemade bunks were the culmination of a recent Boy Scout construction project.

Our sleeping quarters were assigned upon arrival. I'd be sharing a small log cabin with three other boys. I was hoping to sleep under the stars in a real tent, but this was only a minor setback; my camping expectations remained unblemished.

I settled in a lower bunk while the other kids scrambled for the upper berths, apparently the more prestigious properties. Even before we'd unzipped our suitcases, a whistle sounded in the clearing outside the tents and cabins.

"Everybody out! Out, out, out!" the harried voice yelled. *What the hell is that? Why a stupid whistle?* As the kids stumbled out into the clearing, we were ordered to stand in formation, in straight lines like an army platoon.

"Keep your chins up and your backs straight," the Boy Scout leader ordered. He sounded a lot like a drill sergeant; his voice was loud and strict. He told us to stand with our legs apart and our hands folded behind our backs in a casual military pose.

Next, we were each issued a multicolor handkerchief, along with a stupid ring to hold the distinctive cloth tightly under our chins. The neck ornament was mandatory—we were required to wear the silly scarf every morning at roll call and at Mass. *Roll call?*

Soon, the Boy Scout leader—Alain—was shouting the list of rules. We were expected to awaken at five-thirty each morning to the stupid whistle, and we had three minutes to get our butts outdoors. The kids who were late in closing ranks would receive the tougher work assignments. *Work assignments?*

Once assembled, we'd walk down to bathe in the lake before attending early Mass in the monastery chapel. Breakfast was around seven-thirty, cooked outside over an open fire. After breakfast, work teams would be assigned illustrious chores such as cutting down small trees and clearing brushwood. Ill-behaved kids would be sent home on public transportation, and their unhappy parents would be billed for the full bus fare.

Nothing of what Alain said was consistent with my blissful visions. This sounded more like a military camp than a fun game of cowboys and Indians. And it seemed like the entire week had been organized in detail, leaving no time for innocent games. My heart slid down to my ankles even before Alain had finished outlining the rules. I'd be enduring a week with some twenty army recruits.

I hadn't anticipated the rigor of the Boy Scout camp. I had expected carefree days of swimming in the gorgeous lake, climbing the mountains, and cooking yummy marshmallows over bonfires while belting out French folk songs.

As promised, we were awakened at five-thirty every morning and escorted down to the lake in our bathing suits like little sheep. The twenty of us would stand around, shivering, meekly dunking ourselves up to our necks, our arms wrapped around our chests, our genitals shrunken from the cold water, and jumbo goose bumps covering our bodies.

I then had to cope with the panic attacks while attending Mass in the little chapel inside the monastery. The unfamiliar place and the godforsaken hour seemed to aggravate my fainting phobia. This was about as much fun as the bath in the cold lake. Even worse, I was asked to serve Mass. Once, in the midst of a debilitating attack, I had to abandon my altar boy duties in the middle of Mass, collapsing on a sanctuary chair.

Despite the rigors of the camp, the afternoons turned out to be more loosely organized than I'd expected, and we managed to fit in playful activities that I found enjoyable. We went on long hikes, a pleasant relief from the boring work assignments.

I enjoyed the food too. Our three meals were cooked over a large open fire. Breakfast was generous, lunch was simple but tasty, and dinner was always interesting. The food was great going in, but at the other end it was a different story: I was hopelessly constipated.

With my lofty expectations beaten down to approximate the harsher reality, I was finally beginning to enjoy my life at camp. And then the Russians landed.

It started on Monday afternoon. We'd barely finished our lunch around the campfire when the annoying whistle shrieked unexpectedly—again. Puzzled by the urgent call, we made our way to the usual gathering place, hurried along by our leaders.

"I want to tell you about an important development," Alain said with Roger at his side. We were standing at ease in the clearing outside our sleeping quarters. "We've just received a report of a crashed Russian airplane. The Royal Canadian Air Force believes it may have come down in this area."

The story sounded preposterous, but the announcement managed to captivate my imagination. *Is this guy serious? What was a Russian airplane doing over Magog?* A chill shot up my spine and my brain became sensitive to his every word.

"We've been asked to keep our eyes open for anything suspicious. We plan to hike the hills to the north this afternoon to assist the search," he added. While he spoke these words, I scrutinized his face for any evidence of deception; I could find none. He looked serious, as did Roger, both leaders straight faced at the head of our stunned group.

Once dismissed, the kids spoke of nothing but the Russian plane. The forest was soon overrun by our excited babbling. We spouted loud opinions and theories, the vivid imaginations of preadolescent boys hard at work.

"I think this is baloney. None of it is true," one kid said.

"I'm not so sure. Why would they lie to us?" another boy said.

"They want to scare us so that we stay obedient."

"But you can't trust communists. It's all possible."

"Just wait and see; this'll blow over by tomorrow."

"Do you think they would really bomb us?"

"No, that's stupid!"

The group of boys soon became split into three camps: the believers, the nonbelievers, and the skeptics. I was an avid nonbeliever, convinced that our leaders were toying with our brains to keep us out of mischief. But some kids were already scared and shaken by the threat of real communists stalking the woods nearby.

We were too naïve to ask the most obvious questions. How in the world could a Russian jet fighter contain enough fuel to reach Magog? And how could enemy aircraft possibly fly across the free world undetected by radar?

Despite its implausibility, the Russian story became the focus of our camping trip, hovering over our heads for most of the week like a bad monsoon. Although I was a nonbeliever, I kept up nervous vigilance, eager to confirm the truth.

We set out on our hike in the hills to the north that afternoon. The incessant chatter along the way was all about the Russians. The rumors were exaggerating with every mile. Later, we stumbled onto the remains of an abandoned campfire.

Our leaders knelt down to poke and scratch the charred wood like forensic anthropologists.

"I think this was left by the Russians," Alain announced after completing a careful examination, as though the burned wood had somehow exposed a devious pattern that could only be attributed to the hateful communists.

Several gasps were heard above the quiet hush.

"Oh my God, they were here," a kid said. The jabbering rose to a fevered pitch.

"Hush up or you'll give us away," Alain said.

The boys continued whispering among themselves, some nonbelievers becoming skeptics and some skeptics turning into believers. But I remained a nonbeliever.

We returned without further incident, filling the rest of the day with normal camping activities. But the campfire incident had seeded doubt in my brain.

Tuesday morning, Alain informed us that the authorities now believed the Russian pilots had ditched their plane deliberately to enter Canada. One of the two parachutes had been found in a tree in the wooded hills. Alain raised an indistinct satin cloth as tangible evidence, allegedly a remnant torn from the parachute.

Oh shit.

"These are Russian spies, armed and dangerous," he said. An audible gasp arose up from the gullible crowd; the story had just turned a new page. It was at that moment that I became a skeptic, increasingly agitated with every new turn in the story.

Later in the afternoon, we hiked up another hill in search of the dangerous spies but found nothing new. At least the long walks were pleasant, taking us on meandering paths through the serene woods and momentarily lifting our thoughts from the communists.

Wednesday morning, the leaders informed us that the Russian spies had broken into a nearby farm the night before and stolen food from the elderly owners at gunpoint. The old couple had been fastened to chairs using farm ropes. The spies had also stolen clothes from the old man, switching their airmen uniforms for civilian clothing.

"Dressed as civilians, the flyers will be harder to find," Alain said.

As we'd done on prior days, we spent most of the afternoon in hot pursuit of the spies, scouring the countryside to no avail. The unfolding developments kept us on a high state of alert, with the worrisome thought of communists never far away.

Although I was professing to be a skeptic, the daily updates were beginning to weaken my resolve. My nerves were wreaking havoc on my head and stomach. But I tried not to show it, feigning bravado among my peers. I suspect that many boys did the same thing, concealing their growing concern with blustery comments.

The plan for Thursday included a ten-mile hike on a narrow road that ran along the shores of Lake Massawippi. Roger would be our only guide on this journey. Unlike the previous missions, this one had nothing to do with the Russians. Our destination was the lakefront chalet owned by the family of a boy in our group.

It was a hot day. We strolled in our shorts, bare-chested, with our shirts tied around our waists. The long walk on the steamy pavement was relaxing, though the lake emitted a blinding glare that caused us to squint. The birds chirped happy calls from nearby trees.

Our escape from the forest furnished a much-appreciated respite. Roger did little to restrict our behavior, except to give us the occasional reminder to keep up a brisk pace. We sang songs, laughed ourselves silly, and admired the nature around us.

Bathing in sunshine, we drifted from one topic to another like frogs jumping among lily pads. However, all of our conversations inevitably turned back to the Russian spies. Despite my brave face, I was dying to correlate my opinion with those of my peers; the uncertainty surrounding that stupid story was really troubling me.

"Do you think it's true?" I asked my walking partner.

"I don't know," he replied. "I suppose it's possible." Most kids were in the same rut, skeptical yet fearful at the same time. Nobody dared exclude any option.

"Let's go talk to Roger," I said. Roger collaborated with Alain in delivering the daily updates on the Russians; it was clear he knew everything. I was hoping the blissful atmosphere of our march might act as a truth serum, seducing him to make a discreet admission that would end the troubling uncertainty.

We accelerated our pace to catch up with Roger. He seemed in a pleasant mood when we pulled up by his side, as he smiled down at our sweaty faces.

"Is this Russian story really true?" I asked him.

"Well, what do *you* think?"

"I'm not sure."

"Is this just a game we're playing?" my walking partner asked him.

"No, it's not a game. We'd never do that. It's true," he said with a serious face.

Merde. Our curiosity had only succeeded in raising the bar, leaving me more troubled than ever. *Can Roger be telling us the truth?*

We returned from the long hike tired from exertion and beaten by the blazing sun. The evening was lazy. We retreated to our bunks at nine o'clock as usual, unaware that the Russian saga was about to reach its climatic ending.

Around ten o'clock, I woke up with severe abdominal pains, the result of my weeklong fight with constipation. My little cesspool shovel had remained unused since our arrival at boot camp, my innards now holding five days of digested food. The condition had haunted me throughout the week. I couldn't explain why my bowels had ceased to function, but I suspected nerves. This had never happened before.

The idea of digging a hole in the woods, squatting over the trench without falling in, and wiping my ass with green leaves didn't sound at all appealing. I was embarrassed to go in the daylight and scared to go at night when the wildlife chased its prey. And the unnerving business about the Russians had done nothing to move things along either.

But I could no longer ignore the pain; it felt like my abdomen was about to rip open. I jumped out of my bed, grabbed my shovel and flashlight, and headed out to the woods.

Having distanced myself from the tents and log cabins, I dug my hole and squatted while listening to the denizens of the night. An owl was hooting here, frogs were croaking there, and crickets chirped everywhere. But I was in too much pain to succumb to the fear.

I wondered if there were bears in the woods, pitying the poor animal that dared sink its teeth into my bloated abdomen. He'd be in for a big surprise, I thought. With my gut in distress, I no longer felt intimidated by the threat of ravenous animals.

I pushed like a squaw in labor, feeling the sharp knife travel down my spine while my butt was hovering over the hole. The pain was excruciating, and my eyes were blurry from tears. I thought I'd faint from the pain.

Then, I finally rid myself of the festering poison. I felt like a new boy, proud of a momentous achievement I could never admit. I walked back to the log cabin with a sore butt and hopped in my bed to resume a fitful sleep.

I woke up to the shrill of the damn whistle. It was still dark. A shock immediately traveled the length of my spine—something was wrong. It was one o'clock in the morning. We all rushed outside with our flashlights, gathering in the clearing on wobbly legs. The boys stood around yawning like bear cubs startled out of hibernation.

"We think the spies are nearby. We heard gunshots," Roger said. The reaction to the announcement was mixed. Some kids were giddy with excitement—perhaps at the prospect of ending the dubious saga once and for all—while others were on the verge of tears. A sizable lump was lodged in my throat. "The police and the army are on their way, but they may be here too late," he said.

I'd suddenly turned from skeptic to believer. In my tired and dumbfounded state, I had no energy to resist this last affront on my nerves. With panic all around me, I became convinced that the craziness was real. Alain and Roger wouldn't drag twenty kids out of bed in the middle of the night just to play mean tricks, I reasoned.

"It's dangerous to wait here. We have to go out looking for them," he said. I couldn't believe it. So, we'd search the woods for Russian spies in total darkness? *Have these guys completely lost their marbles?* There was no time for debate.

"Are they crazy?" I said to the next kid.

"I don't know, but I'm really scared."

Armed with our flashlights, we started running through the woods in search of armed Russian pilots. Roger was leading the charge, with the rest of us on his heels. We were terrified of being left behind, so we ran in close formation, bumping into each other every time Roger slowed his pace, like the bumbling Keystone Cops in those old movies.

The sound of a single gunshot suddenly rang out. Some kids gasped while others cried. I prayed.

"Be quiet," Roger said, "and keep your heads low, or they'll find us."

I crouched in the darkness, surrounded by kids who were wheezing with fear. One of the younger boys was crying, asking to go home to his mother—I couldn't agree more. I turned around to comfort him and shut him up, thinking he might reveal our location.

"Don't worry, you'll be all right," I whispered, not believing a word of what I'd said. My flashlight revealed that the kid had peed in his pants.

For the first time in my life, I seriously questioned whether I'd survive the night. It was now apparent that we were in grave danger; some of us might even perish. I thought about my mother, hoping that she could forgive me for joining the ill-fated camping trip. I'd just resigned myself to the possibility of injury or death.

Roger's voice aborted my daydream. "I see one of the spies crossing the field up ahead," he said. "On my signal, we'll have to run and jump him before he reacts."

My head was in a fog, and I found it difficult to discern fantasy from reality. *Is all this really happening?* I made the Sign of the Cross, thinking this might be my last time.

Roger gave the signal, and we rushed to our feet, screaming at the top of our lungs like a band of Iroquois warriors attacking colonists. The adrenalin made me run faster than I thought possible, yelling with primal fear like the rest of my compatriots. The final lurch toward our human target felt exhilarating. My fate was in the hands of the gods.

I could see the man dressed in dark clothing; he was brandishing a pistol that closely resembled a plastic cap gun. When we approached, he tried to run in the opposite direction, but a couple of the older kids tackled him to the ground. The spy with the ski mask was now on his back, his body covered with several screaming kids.

"Don't hit, don't hit!" the communist yelled in perfect French.

Huh?

One of the kids reached for the ski mask and yanked it off. It was Alain.

With adrenalin still rushing through my veins, my fear instantly turned to anger. I felt a vengeful urge to kick Alain in the most sensitive places just to hear him yelp like an injured puppy. My vision of the little boy with wet pants was too fresh.

I disdained Alain and Roger. They'd deliberately played with our minds and emotions, causing us to fret over nonsense for most of the week. As I watched them beam their celebratory smiles, spiteful thoughts rattled around in my furious brain.

Laughter penetrated the dark night, as the boys voiced their relief. Unlike me, most of the boys reacted to the innocuous outcome with humor. Our leaders recounted their prouder moments, expressing surprise at their raving success.

The excitement was over, so we strolled back to camp at leisure. I used the time to complain about our lousy treatment to other kids, grumbling incessantly.

"I can't believe what they did!" I said.

"The whole thing was stupid," the kid replied.

"They took advantage of us to play *Russians versus altar boys*."

"Yeah, they seem to think it was pretty funny."

"Well, I think it was terrible. I hate those guys."

Having returned to camp, the leaders stoked a bonfire and served hot dogs and Kool-Aid to celebrate the demise of the Russian spies. I hesitantly accepted a glass of Kool-Aid but refused to partake of any food. I was too upset and tired to eat.

At one point, Roger glanced my way with a pacifying look that seemed to say, "This was just an innocent game." But I stared back with disdainful eyes that clearly said, "You lying bastard."

A boy invited me to join him in his tent to escape the cool night. We sat on the canvas floor sipping our drinks while I launched into another diatribe about our nitwit leaders. Disgusted, I soon retreated to my bunk as happy sounds faded into the night.

On Friday, we received our reward for the successful four-day prank. We were allowed to sleep late, and the itinerary for the rest of the day was left nice and easy. Sleep had done wonders to calm my anger too; the hoax now struck me as pretty clever. After all, I'd turned from non-believer to skeptic, and finally petrified believer.

It seemed amazing to me that so many boys had fallen for the ludicrous story. It was full of gaping holes, yet the frequent updates had succeeded in eroding our resolve a little at a time.

The experience made me realize that it's possible to brainwash people into believing just about anything. If twenty boys could be fooled by a few teenagers, then the world wasn't safe from social, political, and religious leaders with devious intentions. *Anybody can be brainwashed* was the lesson I learned that week.

We spent Friday afternoon on a public beach at the lake, enjoying the warm sand and refreshing water. It was a fun-filled day, yet the week was drawing to a close.

"Hey, I saw a nude family on the beach," a boy reported.

This news captured the interest of every boy in our group despite our religious status as altar boys. We all wanted to see naked people, although we'd never admit it.

"Where are they?" several voices inquired.

Several boys soon ran off in the direction of the pointing finger at the same time. They returned a few minutes later, laughing at the sighting of naked flesh.

Inspired by this latest reconnaissance, I resolved to see the nude family with my own eyes. I too was soon scanning the beach for flesh, with another boy on my heels.

It didn't us take long to find them. Their bottoms were covered with a blanket, but I could still make out four butt cracks: two big ones and two little ones. The man, bare-breasted woman, young girl, and little boy were casually munching on snacks.

"How can they undress like that?" I thought. I wasn't as baffled by the breach in morality as I was amazed by their courage to strip amidst strangers.

"I think they're pigs," the other boy said.

But I wasn't so quick to judge, especially given my past experience with girls.

On Saturday, we packed up our measly belongings and cleaned up the camp for the next group of unlucky recruits. By mid-morning, we were back on the bus for the trip home. It seemed silly, but I felt a bit sad leaving Lake Massawippi. The experience had aged me; I'd even adapted to the strict regimen of the camp.

We entered Rock Island and were dropped off at Notre Dame once again. I excitedly rushed up the hill to our apartment with my little suitcase and battle-worn bag. My mother greeted me cheerfully, but nobody else seemed impressed that I'd just survived a life-threatening scavenger hunt looking for Russian spies.

I never saw Lake Massawippi again, and this would be my only time camping with the altar boys. I figured that the memory would be enough to last me a lifetime.

17

Ghost Tales

School was distressing Lucette. Her tearful reports were beginning to erode my parents' opinion of the Ursuline school for girls. My sister's independent spirit placed her at odds with the strict regimen of the sisters, with predictable results: she endured insults from the nuns, who were obliged to adjust her defective attitude. It was for her own good, apparently.

"I hate that school," she told Maman.

"But you must be doing something to upset the nuns."

"No, they're all frustrated old maids."

One cold winter evening, Lucette had to walk home from school alone in the dark, a distance of two miles. That's when my parents decided that the harassment had gone too far. The Ursulines were compromising Lucette's safety as a form of punishment.

"We have to pull her out of that school," my mother told Papa.

They knew it would be futile to confront the cloistered Ursuline order. Their teaching methods dated back to the seventeenth century, and they weren't about to change. So, they instead decided to send her back to St-Gérard. She'd complete the school year and then abort her stressful affiliation with the Ursuline nuns forever.

Lucette was overjoyed with their decision. She'd rejoin old friends and resume her studies under the tutelage of the gentler St-Gérard nuns, whom she now appreciated more than ever. My parents made arrangements for Lucette to board with Uncle Roland and Aunt Yolande. She'd be sharing a bedroom with Jacqueline, a favorite cousin her age.

In September 1963, Lucette left Rock Island to return to Mater Domini. Her departure would compound the loneliness that already afflicted our spirits.

We knew Uncle Roland's house well. I'd been roaming this place since I was little, inspecting every nook and cranny with delight. My uncle's house had been built at the turn of the century, like most others in St-Gérard.

The place looked like a traditional Québec home, its square dimensions disturbed only by the large summer kitchen that stuck out from its right side like an extra appendage. The main house itself looked like a plain white box with a slanted roof.

There was an old unpainted garage attached to the back, its rickety doors accessible from the dirt road on the right side of the house. I learned to respect and fear this garage. Its dark and dusty chamber held a frightful reminder of my grandfather's death.

Grandpapa Blanchette had died in 1954 at the age of sixty-eight. I was only two years old at the time, so I'd never known the man. But everyone spoke fondly of him, describing him as a lanky man with a good-natured disposition.

Grandparents, Napoléon and Dérilda Blanchette.

"Your grandfather was always smiling," my mother used to say.

He died at home from an undiagnosed ailment accompanied by a deadly fever. Nobody ever determined the exact cause of death. While the tall man languished in bed, his feverish feet left indelible imprints in the varnish of the footboard. Years after his death, that footboard remained in my uncle's garage, like a revered artifact.

"Can I see Grandpapa's bed again?" I'd ask. My cousin Ghyslain would oblige my requests, making a path in the clutter to the old footboard. I never tired of those appalling imprints, the only tangible reminder of Grandpapa. The outline of his long feet always sent tiny shockwaves up and down my spine.

My Uncle Roland's place was a dairy farm. The old barn, stable, and silo stood around a hundred feet from the house, at the far end of the gravel driveway. Despite the tough times, my uncle had managed to hold onto his farm while working full-time at the granite quarry where my father had also toiled for twenty years.

The inside of the farmhouse was typical for its age. The large kitchen dominated the first floor, leaving just enough space for a small living room, bedroom, and bathroom. The large summer kitchen could be reached from outside or through the main kitchen.

The second floor included three small bedrooms, accessible from a narrow hallway. An additional bed had been squeezed into the opening at the top of the stairs. This is where my cousin Ghyslain slept; I shared his bed on our many return visits to St-Gérard. My uncle and aunt occupied the downstairs bedroom while their four children slept upstairs. One of the upstairs bedrooms was also reserved for my grandmother.

Grandmaman Blanchette was a tough old bird when I was young. Her rules were harsh and her verbal reprimands stung. She was intolerant of little children, barking threats and reproaches in response to provocations that only *she* seemed to detect. In her presence, the prudent policy was to do nothing and say even less.

"Get out of the garden—you'll trample the vegetables!" she'd say.

"You little pig—you've already had a chocolate!"

"Stop making that noise—don't make me come over there!"

"Give me that apple—you shouldn't eat between meals!"

We were never safe from my grandmother. Her body stood only four feet off the ground, yet we reacted to her advance as though being chased by a rabid coyote.

Despite repeated warnings to stay out of my grandmother's bedroom, Ghyslain and I periodically sneaked in to inspect the ancient remains. The room seemed a throwback to the prior century, with old memorabilia sitting atop austere furniture. The quietude of her room was eerie, the large crucifix from Grandpapa's coffin still adorning the wall.

"Do you want to try the bed?" Ghyslain would ask.

Her tall bed contained a chicken-feather mattress with a thick and fluffy surface. We'd throw ourselves up on the bed, the sudden decompression causing dozens of little feathers to flutter up in the air and tickle our noses. After sinking down in the deep recesses of the feather mattress, we'd climb out giggling with naughty satisfaction, the tiny feathers still clinging tenaciously to our hair and clothing.

This was the perfect house for a haunting.

Grandmaman Blanchette
giving one of her stern looks.

Lucette and Jacqueline were startled awake at precisely the same instant. It was around one o'clock in the morning on a school night in October 1963. Both girls bolted upright in bed. They sat in the darkness like two fence posts, frozen with fear, while listening to the horrifying clamor that had woken them from their sleep.

"Did you hear that?" Lucette whispered.

"Yes, I heard it," Jacqueline replied, her voice barely a whimper.

"What *is* that?"

"I don't know, but I'm afraid."

The terrifying noise was coming from the hallway. It was the distinct sound of metal clinking against the floorboards, a steel chain slithering across the linoleum flooring. And the dreadful noise was growing louder, traveling in the direction of their bedroom situated at the far end of the upstairs hallway, at the front of the house.

"Turn on the light!" Lucette barked.

"I can't...I'm too scared!" Jacqueline said through her tears.

The only light fixture in the room was affixed to the center of the ceiling, its chain dangling some six feet above the bedroom floor. They'd need to stand and walk in order to reach it. Neither girl could imagine taking that risk amidst the benumbing sound.

The clinking noise was slowly crawling toward the bedroom of the two frightened sixteen-year-old girls. It reached the threshold of their bedroom just as Lucette and Jacqueline implored God to spare them from the invisible horror. They were holding hands, expecting to face a supernatural terror of untold proportions.

Suddenly, Lucette discerned a feeble green glow reflecting off the wall ahead. She instinctively turned her head back to trace the source of the unnatural reflection. Two vivid green shapes were floating on the wall above the headboard, just a few feet from their paralyzed bodies. The projections resembled theatrical masks, one face happy with a diabolical smile and the other angry with a maniacal frown.

Desperate to escape the horrific masks, they quickly turned to face the back of the room, only to be accosted by a pair of red eyes illuminating the rear wall with the color of blood. The fiery glare emanated from a children's doll that had been propped up on the bureau, the bloody eyes staring at them threateningly, as if to say, *I'm watching you.*

Frozen by the horrific sight of the green masks and glowing eyes, and by the continuing rattling of chains across the linoleum floor, the girls sat motionless in bed for long minutes, with primal fear gnawing at their teenage sanity.

Hoping to end the ghastly affair, Lucette suddenly stood up on the bed in a burst of courage. This craziness had to stop. Leaning toward the center of the room, she frantically fanned the air in wide, sweeping motions, trying desperately to find the light cord.

After a few insufferable moments, she touched the chain, but it quickly evaded her clutch as if to deliberately prolong the frightful taunt. But her frantic grasping was eventually rewarded; she found the swinging chain and gave it a yank. The room was instantly flooded with bright light, and the frightful display evaporated.

A few seconds later, Lucette and Jacqueline were barreling down the staircase screaming at the top of their lungs; my Aunt Yolande bolted out of bed, her sleepy head trying to make sense of all the commotion. My Uncle Roland was working the night shift at the granite quarry, so he wouldn't be home until three o'clock in the morning.

Out of breath and barely coherent, the girls recounted the frightening episode to my bleary-eyed aunt, their overlapping voices stirring up significant confusion.

"We heard a chain dragging on the floor—"

"And we could see two green faces on the wall—"

"The doll was flashing red eyes—"

Unable to calm the girls down with her words, my aunt gave them each a pill to tranquilize their nerves and allowed them to spend the rest of the night on the living room couch. My uncle would soon investigate the strange occurrence, she promised.

By the time Uncle Roland arrived from work, the girls hadn't slept a wink in spite of the pill. They repeated the entire story once more with vivacious animation, their emotions unabated by the medication my aunt had dispensed a few hours earlier.

"Come upstairs with me," my uncle said after they'd finished the spirited tale.

They relented to his request, but only after putting up some resistance. They slowly climbed the stairs behind my uncle, holding onto his belt for security. The girls cowered behind their protector even after they'd reached the illuminated bedroom.

"I'll turn off the light now to show you that there's nothing here," he said.

Their hearts were palpitating and their eyes were glazed over with fear when the light was extinguished. Looking around, they saw and heard nothing. The cord was pulled a second time, and the soothing brightness was restored in the room.

"See—nothing," my uncle affirmed. "You must have been dreaming." Lucette and Jacqueline vehemently denied the allegation but were unable to persuade him otherwise. Like my father, Uncle Roland was a practical man who was leery of hocus-pocus.

The girls slept in the living room for a week after their strange encounter. When my aunt ordered them to return to their own bedroom, they kept the light turned on throughout the night, enduring long bouts of insomnia. And that doll was summarily removed from its nesting place on the bureau, shoved into the depths of a drawer.

Yearning to find a plausible explanation for their life-changing incident, Lucette and Jacqueline decided to approach trusted clergy members for saintly enlightenment. Within days, news of their haunting encircled St-Gérard like buzzards over fresh road kill. Not surprisingly, the reports were greatly embellished.

One rumor claimed that the girls had foisted thieves who'd climbed up on the roof with the intention of robbing the family while they slept. The frightening sounds hadn't been produced by ghostly chains but rather by the creaking of old wood planks on the roof. And the green faces imprinted on the wall were the moonlit shadows of the thieves standing on the edge of the roof. The rumor also alleged that Lucette and Jacqueline had deterred the thieves with their bloodcurdling screams, sparing the family countless loss.

Another rumor had a supernatural origin. It alleged that a forged-iron worker who had once owned my uncle's house had murdered his nagging wife and buried her body in the gravel basement. Her body had never been recovered, yet someone in town claimed that the murder had appeared in the regional newspaper (date unknown). It was her unsettled spirit that roamed this house, clanking chains forged by her own husband.

Lucette and Jacqueline first paid a visit to the rectory to see Father Berger, the stoic parish priest. He listened attentively as they repeated their story one more time. He seemed to find the incident entirely plausible from a spiritual point of view.

"Do you pray for the souls in purgatory?" he asked them. Both Lucette and Jacqueline replied that yes, they certainly had, just like their Catholic teachings prescribed. "Then, that's probably the reason," he said. He felt that their generous prayers must have prompted the visitation from lost souls who sought their good intentions; they should continue praying for the souls in purgatory. Apparently, the frightening episode had been a masked request from yonder to double-up their prayers for them.

Next, they confided in a few nuns who were teaching at Mater Domini. Like the priest, the good sisters attributed the incident to the desperate actions of unhappy souls who'd failed to pass into the afterlife. Once again, they were asked to pray for the souls of the deceased; their prayers would accelerate the voyage of lost souls to eternal life.

Then, Lucette approached Grandpapa Côté, anxious to share the strange happening with a close relative. Consistent with the opinion of the local priest and nuns, my grandfather also leaned toward a more supernatural interpretation.

In the absence of a better explanation, opinions rapidly coalesced on the ghost theory. The spirits who'd accosted Lucette and Jacqueline were more naughty than dangerous. The frightening display was meant to send a message rather than to harm, they were told. It seemed the girls had been gullible targets of a ghostly prank.

I was there when Lucette told my parents. It was Friday evening, and we'd just arrived in St-Gérard for another weekend visit with relatives. My mother instinctively knew something was wrong the minute she laid eyes on her daughter. Lucette's face had lost its normal hue, reflecting back a dull gray color. Her eyes were glazed over, as though she'd been heavily medicated, and her usual smile had completely vanished.

My parents, Lucette, and I were in the car near town when she made the announcement. I was sitting in the back seat with Lucette. The news had not yet traveled to Rock Island, probably so that my overstressed mother would not be alarmed.

"I have something to tell you," she said in a low voice.

"What's the matter?" my mother replied with wide eyes, already sensing bad news.

"We had a visit from spirits."

"Come on now, what do you mean?" Maman said in an agitated tone.

Lucette proceeded to relay the whole story in detail. I'll always remember her serious tone, the distressed look on her face, and the raccoon bags under her eyes. She told us about the conversations with the clergy members and their opinion that this had been the naughty work of unsettled spirits. By the time she'd finished, I had goose bumps all over my body and my hair was standing up on end. *Holy shit!*

My calm father didn't seem to believe the story, suggesting that the stress from their studies and the resulting fatigue might have made them emotionally susceptible. In other words, he thought they'd worked themselves into a state of delirium. But Lucette insisted that the experience had been real, not merely a figment of their teenage imaginations.

My mother and I were baffled by the story but gave her the benefit of the doubt. Our Catholic teachings had prepared us for such encounters. It was obvious from her dismal appearance that she'd suffered a life-changing experience, so the story was already credible as far as I was concerned. My sister had witnessed a real haunting after all. That could only lead to one important lesson: *Ghosts really do exist.*

I started dreading my Uncle Roland's house the moment I heard the ghost story. The problem was that we always slept there on our weekend visits.

I'd sleep at the top of the stairs with my cousin, the location of his bed posing some perils of its own. The eerie door into the walk-in attic was barely two feet from our bed, which made me about as fidgety as a calf in a meat processing plant.

Both the door and frame had been stained a dark mahogany color, which conjured up the image of a wood coffin. That door was a constant source of fear. To make things worse, a large window adorned the upper portion of the door. I worried that this might be an ideal place for a ghost prank, with burning eyes and green faces peering through the window at my hapless form on the adjacent bed. The thought kept me up for hours.

Ghyslain was a nonbeliever. Always a pragmatic boy, he seemed convinced that the girls had dreamt most of the ghost story and invented the rest. In a way, I found his skepticism comforting; at least he'd given me no further reason to panic. But I took no chances, caution being one of my genetic propensities.

We were lying in bed one day talking nonsense when he admitted to a strange happening. The story instantly increased my nervousness.

"I was in bed one night when I felt something cold touch my feet," he said. "It was as if two cold hands had gripped my toes. I tried to pull away, but I couldn't. My feet were paralyzed; I couldn't budge them. But it went away after a few minutes."

"Did it hurt you?" I asked.

"No, but it felt cold like ice."

"What do you think it was?"

"I have no idea, but it didn't upset me much."

I didn't know if Ghyslain had made up this foot-grabbing anecdote to scare me or if he was telling the truth. Naturally, I took the more cautious route and assumed the story to be true. The tale seemed more credible because it had been told by a skeptical boy.

Intimidated by the ghost stories, I took to sleeping with the blankets pulled over my head even in the heat of summer. Only my nose was exposed to the air in the room. And to protect against supernatural tickles and grabs, I'd crouch into a fetal position just to be on the safe side. Needless to say, these were not restful nights.

Wrapped in the blankets like an Egyptian mummy, I became rather susceptible to the air quality in our bed. Ghyslain would make light of my self-imposed exile by spewing noxious gasses under the blankets. I don't know what kind of food that boy ate for supper, but his farts could have enlarged the hole in the ozone layer. And the stench naturally ascended toward the only opening in the covers, near my nose. Undeterred by the odor of bodily decay, I remained in my hideout, believing that fresh air was less important than the preservation of sound mind.

Lucette and Jacqueline never rescinded their original story, remaining steadfast about the haunting. Forty years later, they still get goose bumps recounting the event that rattled their teenage lives one weeknight in 1963. The ghosts never made another appearance, seemingly pleased with the raving success of their naughty prank.

18

The Diary

My father hadn't worked since spring, after losing three jobs in the span of six months. He believed that age discrimination was hindering his efforts to find work but hated to see his nervous wife working a low-paying job at the jeans factory.

My Uncle Gérard, one of my father's younger brothers, stopped in Rock Island for a quick visit in July. He and his family were on vacation, heading north to spend two weeks with relatives. My uncle noticed my father's depressed state.

"Why don't you come to Manchester?" my uncle said. "You can stay with us until you find steady work. There are plenty of jobs in New Hampshire."

My father was born in the United States and had lived part of his youth in New Hampshire. Despite years of disuse, his English was still passable, the dialect a bit rusty but not entirely forgotten. He was twelve years old when his parents returned to Québec for good. Since Papa was a naturalized citizen of the United States, no time-consuming paperwork would be required to rejoin the land of his birth. It was a low risk.

"I don't think so," my father said. The long months of unemployment had decimated his self-confidence, leaving him skeptical about finding any work.

"Why not? There doesn't seem to be much here."

"Yeah, but I don't want to leave the family behind again."

"You could come for a few weeks just to try it out."

"I don't think so," my father repeated. He was worried about relocating us once more, merely to lose his job in a country hundreds of miles away from his roots.

"Think about it while we're gone," my uncle said. They'd return in two weeks; my father would have some time to consider the possibility.

My mother reacted more positively to my uncle's offer. The idea of living in the United States had always intrigued her. The few relatives we had living there seemed to be happy, their families enjoying an enviable lifestyle and financial status.

My father's uncle, Émile, and his kindhearted wife, Arzelie, came up to the farm to visit us every few years. They owned a three-story apartment house in Manchester, drove a late-model car, and brought us hand-me-down clothes that looked brand new. We took them to be the stereotypical Americans: affluent and contented.

As soon as my uncle and his family left, my mother began a subtle campaign to encourage Papa to extend his job search across the border. Her approach involved gentle support rather than overt pressure. My father's dismal mood made him stubborn, so she knew that a frontal attack would only worsen the emotional turmoil.

"I can support the family if you go to Manchester," she said.

When my uncle returned in mid-July, my father had decided to give it a try, having obtained my mother's blessing for his temporary exile from family. He'd travel to Manchester and look for a job after all. But he was still pessimistic about the outcome.

His luck changed almost immediately. Within a week, Papa was employed as a maintenance man at a Catholic hospital in Manchester. Notre Dame Hospital would remain his loyal employer for years. His self-confidence quickly recovered.

News of my father's job restored hope, and we were elated beyond words. I began daydreaming about the United States, a country with large white houses and colorful flags like those I'd seen in Derby Line. My brain was already embroiled in adventure.

Several relatives had previously made the daring move to Manchester. My brother Jacques had abandoned his job at the wood slat factory in January, boarding with Uncle Gérard and working at Waumbec Mills—a large textile manufacturer.

My Uncle Léopold, my mother's youngest brother, was also there with his family. And New Hampshire harbored close cousins, such as Sylvie, Christian, and Guy, with whom we'd bonded since early childhood. So, this glorious city promised to furnish work as well as reunite us with lost members of our family.

"So, are we moving?" I asked Maman.

"Not yet," she said. "We have to save up the money and apply for visas."

"But when can we move?"

"That depends on immigration. Not everybody gets approved."

"You mean we could be stuck here in Rock Island?"

"I don't know. We'll just have to see."

By September, only five of us were left in Rock Island: Réal, Denise, Pierre, Maman, and I. With Papa working two hundred miles away and Lucette attending high school back in St-Gérard, loneliness descended on us.

The void left by my father and Lucette, the sudden end of our summer freedom, the changing color of the leaves, and the disheartening return to Sacré-Coeur made it all worse—this was the loneliest period I'd experienced in my young life.

Although I had avoided close contact with my father during his unemployed months, I now missed him terribly. He hadn't been much of a father figure over the prior six months, but I had still sensed his reassuring presence. And now he was gone.

Papa would return for weekend visits about once a month, spoiling me with little inexpensive toys as if to make up for lost time.

"I brought you a little something," he'd say as he handed me an unwrapped present.

I was always impressed with the gift. One of my favorites was a little plastic rocket with a parachute. It was launched from a rubber slingshot pointed at the sky, the fragile parachute deploying as soon as the rocket began its sharp descent back to earth. The tiny American flag affixed to the rocket made the toy even more precious.

He'd also given me a cap pistol modeled after a German Luger. The plastic replica was perfect. That toy would furnish endless hours of play, while I chased enemies in the nearby woods.

But his Sunday departures left an empty feeling, with bothersome physical symptoms. From September to December of 1963, I vomited at school every Monday morning. The disorder was predictable, affecting me at around nine o'clock.

I knew from the start that the loneliness was inducing my nausea. Monday morning was always gloomy, filled with painful reminders of our isolation. I woke up from the weekend without a father and rode the bus to school without my sister Lucette.

It was my first week in sixth grade, and I had a new teacher. She wore a stern look on her face to assert her authority over the boys. It was always like that at the beginning of the school year, as teachers adjusted to their new charges.

"I don't feel well. May I please go to the bathroom?" I said, standing at her desk. The woman looked a little like Aunt Bee on the *Andy Griffith Show*.

"No, you'll have to wait till recess," she said, watchful for any vagrant tendencies. I returned to my seat suppressing the urge to vomit.

A few minutes later, I was back at her desk. "I think I'm going to throw up."

"Sit down right now, Mister Blanchette. I told you to wait until recess," she barked. I spent the next excruciating hour swallowing hard to avoid puking on my desk.

That same teacher would eventually grant my Monday bathroom requests, her confidence in my character seemingly raised by my proven performance in class. There, I'd often encounter the hooligans who launched credible threats against my body.

Once I reached the bathroom, my routine was always the same. I'd enter a stall and wait until the room was empty before heaving into the toilet. I didn't want the retching sound to provoke relentless teasing and callous humor.

"Are you sick?" the boy asked. I hadn't heard him enter the bathroom.

"No, I'm okay."

"Do you want me to call the teacher?"

"No, I was just clearing my throat," I lied.

As I was often lonely, I decided to write a journal. I don't recall when or where I got the idea of jotting down my thoughts on paper, but it turned out to be a blessing. I could freely express my feelings without fretting over the consequences of my words.

My mother lived on an emotional roller-coaster, crying frequently under the pressure of raising a family alone. I never told her about my chronic loneliness and vomiting episodes, fearing that my ailments would compound her stress.

I kept my diary in an old three-hole punch binder with a black vinyl cover. I don't remember where I got the binder, but it was probably a school remnant abandoned by one of my sisters. I stowed it under my clothes in the bottom drawer of my bureau, away from the roving eyes of siblings who might make fun of my secrets.

But I do recall the origin of the paper. Mimi had taken me to visit a bookbinder who only spoke English. The nice man ran a small business on the second floor of a dingy building in Derby Line. From time to time, we'd stop by to pick up free paper.

"Do you have paper we can take?" Mimi yelled above the noise of presses.

"Take what you want," he shouted, pointing at the discard pile on the floor.

I can still smell the ink and hear the deafening din of those printing presses.

My diary became a close, personal friend, and I added an entry every evening without exception. Free to spill my guts, I'd recount the events of the day, recording the joys, disappointments, anger, and loneliness. Every visit from my father was meticulously described, along with any gift he'd left behind.

Here, I could call the bullies bad names without endangering my safety. I could praise the merits of our charming neighbor, Janice, without embarrassment. And I could boast of my school accomplishments without sounding pompous in front of others.

"I walked to Mass with Maman tonight in a big snowstorm. Old Man Haskel saw us walking and stopped to pick us up in his old Hilman. Maman tried to say some English words, but mister Haskel couldn't understand a thing she said…"

"We had an arithmetic quiz today, and I got a 92. I'm getting pretty good…"

"I served Mass this morning. I felt like fainting again. I hate that…"

From time to time, the journal entry sounded like a letter to my father.

"Papa, I miss you and am eager to see you again," I wrote in the Sunday evening entry that recorded his departure.

Even before penciling in my first entry, the fate of my diary was fixed: I'd destroy it on the same day we were to leave Rock Island. In spite of its therapeutic value, the diary was capturing details of unhappy months that I wanted to obliterate from memory. Its final destruction would wipe out the evidence of lonely times.

My father was happy again. Once his self-confidence had recovered, he resumed his previous habits with gusto. Unfortunately, that included spending money.

My father had been a teenager during the Great Depression, so he witnessed the hard years of deprivation. The experience spawned an entire generation of misers, people who worked their whole lives to save for a rainy day, afraid to part with a dollar.

But when it came to money, my father stood apart from his generation. In fact, his curious attitude toward spending placed him at odds with his contemporaries. His peers honored the prudent adage *save now for the bad times*, whereas my father practiced the motto *spend it now while you can*. And he did so with a big smile on his face.

Papa believed that a dollar saved was a dollar wasted. From his point of view, it was the equivalent of squandering a God-given talent with inaction. Savings accounts were useless, he thought, the lousy interest a mere sham to fool people into stagnation.

Money was made to spend, he thought. And the blessed invention of credit extended its reach even beyond the limits of his modest earnings. Debt had never disrupted my father's sleep, but it drove my mother crazy. It was the wart on my father's character.

Papa didn't spend his money on gambling or booze; he had no such vices. His weakness was reserved for gadgets. He loved all mechanical things. He'd always shown an ardent interest in bicycles, motorcycles, airplanes, trains, and automobiles. The man would gaze at cars with the eyes of a man swooning over a voluptuous woman.

Two months after getting the job in Manchester, my father drove up to Rock Island in a magnificent white and gray Oldsmobile 98. This was a true luxury automobile. The huge 1958 model had amazing power windows and seats, and plush fabric.

"This is the best car we've had. The seat is like a couch," I wrote in my journal.

Months before going to Manchester, Papa had traded in the Hilman, replacing it with a 1957 Dodge that could more comfortably accommodate our family. So, the grand Oldsmobile was his second car trade in a year gravely affected by unemployment.

"What are you doing with that big car?" my mother asked him.

She was furious. Maman was still supporting the family on twenty-two dollars a week with no contribution from Papa. He was supposed to be saving his money to pay the moving expenses while Maman continued to feed us. We couldn't afford doctors, dentists, or clothing, and our drawers were filled with hand-me-down clothes.

"I couldn't trust the old Dodge for long runs. It was starting to go," he said.

"At least you could have told me. We don't need an expensive car."

"Well, I got a good price. It was on sale. I had to buy it fast."

As always, he gradually won over my mother with a heavy application of charm. And he promised to start sending money in the mail to support the family.

When my mother failed to receive the promised cash in the mail, she drafted a seething letter critiquing his monetary habits and mailed it to Manchester. The letter resulted in one token payment, but she received no ongoing contributions.

My father's fascination with automobiles was relentless throughout his long life, causing my mother's hackles to be raised once a year for more than half a century.

My mother filed the immigration papers in September; this too would come out of her measly paycheck. With no transportation, we'd walk the two miles to Stanstead to meet with Mrs. Veilleux, the woman who sent our applications to the American embassy.

"How long will it take before we know?" I asked Maman.

"Mrs. Veilleux says she doesn't know."

"Why does it take so long?"

"There are quotas—only a certain number are accepted each year."

I admired Maman more than ever. This strong woman was raising the family alone, and she had pulled us through a difficult year. Our troubles had brought us even closer.

"We went to Stanstead to see Mrs. Veilleux tonight. She says our papers were sent, but she doesn't know how long it will take," I wrote in my diary.

The applications required medical evaluations, so we were soon off to a Sherbrooke hospital. Réal, Pierre, and I were assembled in the same room, standing in our underwear as the doctor checked our heart, lungs, and glands.

I'll always remember the afternoon of Friday November 22, 1963, like most people who lived through that infamous day. We were sitting at our desks when the principal interrupted class, his harried voice bringing terrible news.

"The President of the United States has been assassinated," he said. This caused the entire class to gasp in surprise. I stared at the wall-hung speaker in shock. "They've already arrested a communist suspect," he added.

So, the communists have murdered President Kennedy. Visions of atomic explosions and brutal torture passed over my frightened brain. This was the worst news I'd ever heard. *Will Russia now invade the United States?* I wondered about the future of our free world, worried that this terrible deed would launch a nuclear war.

I also suspected that the United States would now close its borders, forever blocking our passage to greener pastures. For all I knew, my family could be stuck in Rock Island for eternity. A black veil fell over my mood.

The rest of the day was a big blur, the lectures falling on deaf ears. My brain was too busy fighting a nuclear war with the Russians to pay attention. *Will we ever see my father again now that he lives in the United States?*

I climbed aboard the school bus with my head still enveloped in a thick fog, my body trembling from the consequences of Oswald's rampage. I took a seat next to a window, gazing at the passing landscape without noticing the people or details.

That's when I felt the oncoming panic attack. With no hope of escaping from the moving bus, I leaned my head against the window pane and resigned myself to letting the symptoms take their harrowing course. Sweat beads formed on my forehead, African drums beat inside my chest, and dark blots obliterated the passing landscape.

My forehead rattled against the window pane every time the bus rode over a bump, but I didn't care. At one point, I thought I could hear soft moaning. *Is that coming from me?* Yes, it was. After leaving my backpack at home, I raced up the long hill to meet my mother at the factory, desperate for the soothing comfort of a loving face.

"President Kennedy was killed by a communist today. I can't believe this happened. I don't know if we can move to Manchester anymore," I wrote in my diary.

My journal entries reflected a bleak outlook on life for several days.

There was good news in December. Mrs. Veilleux informed Maman that our immigration papers were in the evaluation stage. The entire family would have to travel to the consulate in Montréal to meet with officials. It seemed that were one step closer.

"Does it mean we have the visas?" I asked.

"No, it just means they're looking at the applications," Maman said.

My mother hired Mister Veilleux, the retired husband of our scribe, to transport us to Montréal in his private automobile. We'd leave in the early morning and return late in the evening. I was eager to go to Montréal, a place I'd never seen.

By the time we reached Montréal, which is situated about a hundred miles from Rock Island, our faces were green from nausea. The problem was the driver. Mister Veilleux had the uncanny habit of applying pressure to the accelerator in short bursts. He'd press down on the gas pedal, causing us to lean back in our seats. Then, moments later, he'd abandon the accelerator, shifting his foot onto the brake pedal as if to undo the damage to the speedometer. This sudden deceleration caused us to shift again, rocking back and forth like navigational buoys in a stormy harbor.

When we finally reached the city, I was most impressed by the sight of skyscrapers. I'd never seen such tall buildings in my life, and I wondered who had climbed their scary heights to build them in the first place. Leaning my head back against the seat, I looked out the rear window at the amazing towers that ascended a mile above my head.

Our visit to the consulate was a day of bureaucracy. First, we spent hours in the lobby waiting for an official to see us. Then, there seemed to be a problem with Réal's papers. In a deliberate attempt to bypass the legal requirement for a work permit, Mrs. Veilleux had claimed Réal as a dependent child. But Réal was twenty-one years old now, which meant that he'd need employer sponsorship before he could immigrate.

After haggling over the issue with Maman, the official finally conceded, allowing the exception with a displeased look upon his face. Our visas were finally approved. We were elated with the news, our spirits suddenly exalted in the hope of a better life.

"We have our visas! We'll be moving soon. We don't have a date yet, but at least it's for sure now. I can't wait to leave…"

Tragedy struck Janice in December. Janice and her sister were walking up a steep hill in a blinding snowstorm when they were hit by a car. The driver lost control of his automobile on the hill, sliding onto the sidewalk and mowing down the girls like candlepins. Janice was thrown down a deep embankment, suffering severe injuries.

The nicest girl in the world had nearly lost her life to a shopping trip. While she lay unconscious in the ditch waiting for an ambulance, the Christmas gifts that she'd bought for her family were stolen. I felt sad and sick to my stomach.

"Janice and Joyce were hit by a car Saturday. Janice is hurt badly. They don't know if she'll be normal again. I'll pray for her every night. I hope she's okay…"

Janice survived the ordeal despite the broken bones, concussion, and crushed pelvis. Her recovery was long, but her cheerful spirit eventually prevailed.

My parents decided to leave on December 27, 1963. There were no Christmas presents that year, as all our money had been used on visas, debt, and relocation expenses. That was perfectly fine with us kids—our departure would be the best present of all.

The departure date was fast approaching, and I was finding it increasingly difficult to concentrate in class, especially during the lectures. My attendance at Sacré-Coeur was coming to an end. I was staring outside the classroom window one day when I saw the upperclassmen installing Christmas decorations on the front lawn of the school. The commotion had drawn my attention away from the lecture.

One by one, the three life-size magi were mounted on the metal wire that spanned the roof of our one-story school building, and a wooden post that was pounded into the front yard. The wise men were looking up at the sky, holding coffers of gold, frankincense, and myrrh. The Star of Bethlehem shone brightly over their heads.

"Pay attention, Mister Blanchette!" the teacher warned. But I couldn't help thinking that we too had been guided to a more promising place by an illusive star.

Pierre and I climbed onboard the bus for our last day at Sacré-Coeur on the eve of Christmas 1963. Five minutes before the parting bell was scheduled to ring, our teacher stood up to announce the latest student rankings for our sixth-grade class.

"Michel is the winner with the highest grade this term," she said.

The applause had barely subsided when she interrupted the class for another announcement. "Michel will not be with us in January. His family is moving to the United States." A courteous applause was given, followed by friendly hand-shakes.

The day before our departure, my friend Mario spent the afternoon at our house. His silly antics made me laugh even more than usual. We'd hardly spoken about the move. When it was time for him to leave, I accompanied him to the sidewalk. He'd ridden his old bicycle to our house; it was cold, but the streets were clear of snow.

"Well, good luck," I said.

"Yeah, thanks. I'll send you news from time to time," he said.

"Maybe I'll stop by sometime, if we come back to visit."

We shook hands. I'd never seen Mario cry before, but he seemed on the verge, his eyes shiny and red rimmed. He jumped on his old bike, waved goodbye, and accelerated down the hill pretending to be a scared kid on a runaway go-cart.

"I played with Mario for the last time today. I thought he was going to cry before he left on his bike. I'll miss that nut…"

On the eve of our departure, I packed up my meager possessions in cardboard boxes—mostly my clothes and the few gifts I'd received from my father. But my diary faithfully remained in the bottom drawer of the empty bureau, awaiting its fate.

The movers arrived early on Friday. For the second time in two years, my father had hired Albert Houde to transport our belongings. The same cattle truck that had earlier transported our possessions to Rock Island would now take them to Manchester.

A few hours before we were supposed to leave, I entered a final entry in my journal. In a way, it seemed futile to write anything in the doomed diary, but this entry was emotionally significant: it documented the happy ending to my story.

"This is the last time I write in this diary. It's a dream to be leaving. There were some good things here, but I felt lonely a lot of the time…"

When the movers started carrying our furniture down the long corridor toward the front door, it was time to destroy the evidence. I sat on the floor of my barren bedroom with my legs crossed, the faithful vinyl binder at my feet and a trashcan at my side.

I kept the binder open while removing one page at a time and rereading each entry in chronological sequence. The private journal spoke about my father's departure, the gifts he'd brought, vomiting at school, the murder of President Kennedy, our trip to Montreal, and the fun times with Mimi, Janice, and Mario.

Once I had reread each page, I shredded it into tiny pieces and threw the resulting confetti in the trashcan. It took me about an hour to finish the ritual, reliving the prior six months of my life in vivid detail along the way.

Then it was over. I was at peace now, Rock Island already a vague memory.

"It's funny, but I don't hate this place anymore," my last entry had read.

We were finally on our way. We'd just descended the semi-circular staircase to the sidewalk when Mimi ran up to my mother with a big smile.

"My mother would like you to stay for lunch," Mimi said.

"That's very generous, but we don't want to trouble her," Maman replied.

"She's already made the beans and soup; it's no trouble."

"Say no! Say no!" I whispered to my father while tugging at his pant leg.

My mother looked at me with eyes that said, "Stop that right now."

"Well, tell your mother we'll be right there," Maman said.

Damn neighbors! Now our departure would be delayed. With my diary destroyed and the apartment empty, I had no interest whatsoever in prolonging our stay. I wanted to erase Rock Island from my young life as soon as possible.

Lunch lasted more than an hour; it would have been rude to eat and run without taking the time to socialize with our good neighbors. When my father stood up to leave, I ran to the front door like a boy engaged in a footrace. My mother hugged Mrs. Caron while the kids exchanged good wishes—all except for the five-year-old son, who was too busy blowing spit bubbles.

We'd been good friends for fifteen months, but I had no idea how to say goodbye to Mimi. It seemed dumb to shake a girl's hand, and I was too shy to attempt a hug. So, we just smiled at each other and said goodbye without any fanfare.

"Good luck at your new school," Mimi said.

We drove up the long hill toward the center of town, passing by the clothing factory where my mother had worked hard for the past fifteen months. In a few minutes, we'd reached the United States border, where our cattle truck was stopped at customs.

There seemed to be a problem of some kind. The rear doors of the small truck were propped open, and several border officials began a lively discussion with the movers. My father calmly stepped outside the car and started walking in the direction of the truck.

"I hope there's nothing wrong," my mother said, expressing my exact sentiments. We both sat there biting our nails in a fury. My mother had a worried look on her face.

Long minutes passed without news from my father, who'd since joined the little conference behind the truck. I began to panic. *What if they refuse to take us?* I'd much prefer to be arrested by the border police than have returned to our lonely apartment.

A few minutes later, my father walked back to the car at a slow pace. He opened the passenger door and leaned down to address my mother. We were desperate for news.

"There's a problem with the refrigerator," he said. "They need some paperwork." But we had no such paperwork. The fridge was our newest appliance, and the border officials apparently wanted proof that it hadn't been purchased for resale. "They want to see the tag in back of the fridge," Papa said before heading back to the melee. Inspecting the tag would involve moving everything out of the crammed space, since the heavy appliances had been the first items loaded on the truck.

My mother was becoming even more nervous now, which did nothing to assuage my own anxiety. *How will I face my classmates at Sacré-Coeur?* The mere thought of aborting our relocation, even if only temporarily, was downright disheartening.

After a few more minutes, my father reappeared. This time, he headed for the driver side. That was an enormous relief; it suggested a resolution of some kind.

"I paid the fine," he said. When the movers had balked at the prospect of emptying the contents of the cattle truck, the officials offered the option of paying a fine to import the new appliance into the country. My father had accepted immediately.

We breathed sighs of relief as Papa fired up the engine on the big Oldsmobile 98 and started crossing the familiar town of Derby Line. Time seemed to pass slowly as I glanced left and right at the pretty white houses adorned with American flags. I'd own one of those big houses someday, I promised myself.

I was sitting on the front seat between my parents, feeling happier than I'd been in nearly two years. I'd regained a father—one without a bad temper or a beard. And we'd soon reunite with Jacques, uncles, aunts, and cousins.

In the warmth of the car, our winter coats were soon shed along with our lonely past. Like a child in need of his security blanket, I instinctively reached up to fondle my mother's arm through the thin fabric of her sleeve. The little Canuck was home.

Epilogue

We returned to Rock Island for a brief visit one year later, arriving two days after Christmas 1964. It would be our last time. My father dropped me off in the center of town, and I walked the short distance to Mario's house for an unannounced visit.

Mario and I had exchanged occasional letters, his silliness persisting on paper. I chose not to tell him about my visit; this would be a surprise.

I climbed the steep staircase to the old apartment building filled with anticipation, eager to see my friend once again. I knocked at the door wearing a proud smile. A few seconds later, I heard feet galloping across the kitchen floor. A barefoot little boy in pajamas appeared at the door, with Mario not far behind him.

"Hello, Mario," I said from the threshold. He stared at my face as if I'd just landed from Mars. His face had turned pale, his eyes looked startled, and his mouth was agape. "My parents went to visit the Caron family. I wanted to see you."

He continued to look at me as though he'd seen a ghost. His mother arrived in the kitchen to locate the source of the frigid air, finding me still standing in the open doorway, with Mario stupefied. This wasn't like Mario; he'd never been the shy type.

"Come on, Mario. Invite your friend inside," his mother encouraged. I stepped into the warm kitchen and dropped my coat on a nearby chair. But Mario looked as though he was in a daze, his face bearing a bewildered expression.

"Show him your Christmas gifts," his mother pressed. She'd seen the awkward greeting I'd received and was trying to rectify it. But Mario appeared to be robbed of all sensibility; he was even struggling for words.

He went to get his Christmas gifts from the bedroom, but he did so without enthusiasm. In contrast, his little brother was dying for attention, showing me his own presents with great animation. Having suffered through fifteen minutes of awkward silence, I decided that it was time to end my surprise visit; it was a complete bust.

"I have to go meet my parents," I said, lifting my coat from the chair.

"Okay," he said. We exchanged goodbyes without a handshake, and I headed out into the crisp air to rejoin my parents at the Caron house. I felt disappointed. I'd expected a heartfelt reception but instead had been greeted like a total stranger.

After that, we ceased writing letters. It was as though my unexpected visit had broken the sacred trust between us. I later wondered if Mario's goofiness had concealed problems at home and if my fateful stop had threatened to expose his sham. Regardless, my visit had been the catalyst that made us realize that we now shared nothing in common—so we quietly parted ways to escape the pretense. The silly boy who'd lifted my doleful spirits through 1963 was gone from my life.

From the center of town, I walked down the curved hill toward our old apartment building. Light snow was falling, blanketing the street with a fine powder that created the perfect ambiance for reflection. I slowed my pace to ponder my dismal visit with Mario, absorbing the familiar sights I passed along the way. I took notice of the movie theatre, hardware store, bank, barbershop, iron factory, Notre Dame School, corner store, and miles of pavement I'd roamed on my red bike.

I'd been elated to leave this town a year ago, but I now felt a bit of nostalgia strolling past my old haunts on this dreamy evening. The place took on a completely different aura without pangs of loneliness weighing down my heart. I knew it wasn't the town itself that I'd sought to escape, but rather the emptiness begot by family separation.

When I reached the Caron apartment, I was greeted with another surprise: Mimi was no longer the little tomboy I'd known. She smiled at me shyly, saying little while standing at the kitchen counter washing the dishes with her younger sisters.

I couldn't stop looking at her; she'd blossomed into a beautiful girl. She was wearing light mascara and eye shadow that emphasized her pretty eyes. And she even had boobs! She was working at the kitchen counter when I observed her new curves. Her shapely hips and pointed butt were well accentuated by the teenage clothes.

I was a twelve-year-old boy in the body of a nine-year-old, whereas she wore makeup and a bra. I felt a tinge of embarrassment, sensing that this friendship too had reached the end. Mimi had transformed into a woman, but I was still a boy.

This was the last time we saw the Caron family. I never found out what became of Micheline. My fondest memories are not of the pretty young woman I once saw in 1964, but of the spirited little girl with the dirty face, a ready smile on her lips, and an audacious look in her eyes that beckoned me to play one more game.

I also never saw Janice again.

My father died on the morning of July 25, 1998. His departure was like the rest of his life: mellow and without fanfare. He took one breath and held it for eternity. The view from his hospital window looked down on the spot where Pierre Blanchet, his immigrant ancestor, had disembarked the boat from France around 1667.

Every time I visit my father's grave in the small cemetery in St-Gérard, I make a point of stopping by Mario Roy's gravestone. I'll never forget little Mario.

Jean Moreau, the teenage bully who lived near our farm, turned into a good family man with several children of his own. He died at the premature age of thirty-one from the same terrible disease that had afflicted his father two decades earlier.

My mother and siblings are still around, and we've remained a close family. That includes my cousins Christian and Sylvie, who we enjoy seeing several times a year. My sisters Denise and Lucette have returned to the land of their birth. They both reside near Disraeli, not far from my mother's apartment. After my father's death, my sister Doris resumed a religious life with her congregation. She has since accepted a leadership role at the Motherhouse of the Sisters of the Cross, and is now living in the little village of La Puye, in the western part of France. Réal, Jacques, Pierre, and I have permanently settled in our adopted land, some forty years after crossing its seductive border. And by the way, Lucette can still deliver a stunning chicken imitation.

St-Gérard and Rock Island still look much the same as they did. Our old Mater Domini school in St-Gérard was converted into a clothing factory, but the original brick building remains intact. The Ursuline School in Stanstead permanently closed its doors at the end of the 2003–2004 school year. Needless to say, none of Lucette's children attended that school. And Sacré-Coeur is now a public school under a different name.

I hold many pleasant memories from my childhood years. But there is one in particular that captures the essence of my early years on the farm. It's a warm summer afternoon, and I'm bathing in the old metal tub, admiring nature through the opened garage door. Everything is quiet. I can hear the soft breeze playing with the leaves on the maple trees. The birds are chirping their happy calls, and I hear faint moos coming from the green pasture past our monochrome barn. Enraptured by the quietude and breathtaking panorama, I sway my hips and sing a familiar refrain.

> *Maman, tu es la plus belle du monde.*
> *Aucune autre à la ronde n'est plus jolie.*
> *Tu as pour moi, avoue que c'est étrange,*
> *Le visage d'un ange du paradis.*

> Mother, you are the loveliest in the world.
> No one else around is prettier.
> To me you have, strange though it may seem,
> The face of an angel from paradise.

> —Marina Marini, Fernand Banifay,
> "Maman, la Plus Belle du Monde," 1957

978-0-595-34820-6
0-595-34820-3

www.ingramcontent.com/pod-product-compliance
Lightning Source LLC
Chambersburg PA
CBHW061340280526
45784CB00001B/78